Booktalking
the
Award Winners

1993–1994

Edited by
Joni Richards Bodart

H.W. Wilson
New York   Cambridge   Dublin
1995

International Standard Book Number 0-8242-0876-5
International Standard Serial Number 1083-608X

Printed in the United States of America

TABLE OF CONTENTS

DEDICATION

This one's for Lisa,

with love and hugs,

because without your help

and your support

I *never* would have made that

deadline!

ACKNOWLEDGMENTS

As always, I have many people to thank, for many people contributed to this book in large and small, but always essential, ways. First, the booktalkers themselves, who signed up enthusiastically for titles and responded promptly with terrific talks. Their names are listed in a separate section. Most are librarians or teachers, but one—Lisa Heiser—is a senior theatre major at the Denver School of the Arts, and to her I'm especially grateful. She learned how to write talks and then took over the stack of titles that no one else had volunteered to tackle, freeing me for the more lengthy and tedious business of editing. Lisa is an addicted reader, a talented writer and booktalker, my almost-stepdaughter, and a very special person indeed. Thanks, Lisa—you're great!

Family and friends are still supportive and essential to my mental health and work schedule (as in, keeping me sane, and keeping my nose to the grindstone). To all of you who helped along the way, and especially during the final two frantic weeks with their multiple crises, many thanks. Without you, deadlines might have come and gone unmet.

Thanks, Jim, for everything, from beginning to end. You said it would all work out and it has—but it would've been a lot harder without your help. Maybe one of these days you'll even convince me that the sky won't fall if I quit worrying about it!

Norris Smith, Bruce Carrick, Judy O'Malley, and others at Wilson also provided encouragement and support in generous quantities.

And finally, thanks are due to you, the people who use this series and who continue to encourage kids and adults to read the books we write the talks on. After all, you—and they—are the reason this series exists in the first place!

—Joni Richards Bodart
August 1995

INTRODUCTION

Welcome to the second annual volume of the Booktalking the Award Winners series! This new series will help you promote the best of children's and young adult literature to your clients, students, and patrons by providing you with booktalks on titles that have won awards during the previous school year. Each volume will include over two hundred booktalks on fiction and popular nonfiction, a description of the awards, and a variety of indexes to help you locate titles by award as well as by title, author, subject, and age level.

But not all award-winning titles are suitable for booktalking, so you won't find *every* title that has won a prize in this series. We've omitted strictly informational books, since they are rarely read for pleasure, and picture books, unless they fit into the "picture books for all ages" category. And a few titles had to be dropped when the booktalkers who had hoped to do them were frustrated in all their attempts to obtain copies from publishers' representatives and local libraries—it's really impossible to create a booktalk without the book.

Among the awards themselves, we decided to concentrate on those at the national level, omitting all state and regional awards. This decision reflects the practical constraints of publishing an annual volume at an affordable price: print space and preparation time are necessarily limited, and national awards tend to have the broadest appeal. (If you have a particular need for booktalks on titles honored in your state, check the title index at the back of this volume—many books that win state or regional awards have won national prizes as well.)

Now that I've told you what's *not* in this series, what *is* in it? Most of the titles that appear on broad-based lists of the best books published for children and young adults during the 1993–1994 season are included here—in fact, the various lists issued by the American Library Association and *School Library Journal* account for more than half the titles in this book. (Although titles chosen by *Booklist* are important in collection-building, so many of them are purely informational that we felt it wiser to focus on material more naturally suited to booktalking.) The rest of the talks represent annual awards by smaller organizations and awards in specialized areas: illustrated books, books for reluctant readers, mysteries, science fiction, promising first novels, and literature dealing with minority groups. Since English-language titles that win awards usually become available in the the United States no matter where they were originally published, we have also included a sampling of British, Canadian, and Australian prize-winners. So, although you won't find every single award-winning title from 1993–1994 in this volume, I hope you'll find more than enough to make your booktalking life easier.

The talks themselves were written by a cadre of experienced booktalkers, many of them longtime contributors to the *Booktalk!* series. Some are librarians, others are teachers, but all are enthusiastic pushers of books and reading. If you would like to become a member of this group, please don't hesitate to write to me care of the Wilson Company or at the address below. I'd like to see a couple of your talks and will get back to you within a few weeks with information on procedures.

If you know of awards fitting our guidelines that you'd like to see made a part of this series, please let me know. We have done our best, but that's never a guarantee of perfection!

In addition to the annual volumes, we are also planning two retrospective volumes, one on children's titles and one on YA titles. The former will include talks on almost every Newbery book still in print and every Caldecott that qualifies as a "picture book for all ages." The latter will feature in-print titles from the Best Books for Young Adults and the Recommended Books for Reluctant Readers lists. But once again, we will be limited by the space available, in these two volumes, to about five hundred talks each. We will therefore try to select the titles that will be most useful to you and most interesting to your clientele. Out-of-print books will not be included, but those that have been reissued in paperback will be. These two retrospective volumes should be ready in 1995 and 1996.

But now it's time to get on to the booktalks. I think this is a great collection of titles, and our contributors would seem to agree: the "feeding frenzy" when the list of titles came out was immediate and enthusiastic, and very few books ended up on the "orphans list." I can't speak for the other people who worked on this volume, but the titles in it and the talks about them were my source of recreational reading for several months!

We hope you and your clients, students, or patrons will enjoy using this book as much as we enjoyed putting it together!

—Joni Richards Bodart
P.O. Box 370688
Denver CO 80237-0688

CONTRIBUTORS OF BOOKTALKS

Bette DeBruyne Ammon
  Missoula Public Library
  Missoula, MT

Mark Anderson
  Fairfax County Public Library
  Fairfax, VA

Barbara Bahm
  Tonganoxie Junior High School
  Tonganoxie, KS

Jo Berkman
  Dodd Junior High School
  Freeport, NY

Jeff Blair
  Olathe South High School
  Olathe, KS

Suzanne Bruney
  Fairfield County
    District Library (ret.)
  Lancaster, OH

Monica Carollo
  Cumberland School
  Whitfish Bay, WI

Lisa M. Costich
  Allen County Public Library
  Fort Wayne, IN

Bernice D. Crouse
  Fulton County Library
  McConnellsburg, PA

Marijo Duncan
  Phoenix Public Library
  Phoenix, AZ

Susan Dunn
  Salem Public Library
  Salem, OR

Jennifer A. Fakolt
  Boulder Public Library
  Boulder, CO

Sister M. Anna Falbo, CSSF
  Villa Maria College Library
  Buffalo, NY

Susan R. Farber
  Chappaqua Public Library
  Ossining, NY

Mary Fellows
  Weston Public Library
  Weston, OH

Dara Finkelstein
  Naperville, IL

Barbara Flottmeier
  La Crosse Public Library / North
    Community Library
  La Crosse, WI

Mary Hedge
  La Porte County Public Library
  La Porte, IN

Lisa Heiser
  Theatre major
  Denver School of the Arts
  Denver, CO

Bob Johnson
  San Jose Public Library
  San Jose, CA

Carol Kappelman
  Dover Grade and Junior High
  Dover, KS

Deb Kelly
  Park County Library, Meeteetse
    Branch
  Meeteetse, WY

Abbie V. Landry
  Watson Library
  Northwestern State University
  Natchitoches, LA

May Harn Liu
  Thomas Cooper Library
  University of South Carolina
  Columbia, SC

Cynthia Lopuszynski
  Crystal Lake, IL

Diantha McCauley
  Augusta County Library
  Fishersville, VA

Kathy Ann Miller
Ottawa Public Library
Ottawa, KS

Rosemary Moran
Tulsa City-County Public Library
Tulsa, OK

Linda Olson
Superior Public Library
Superior, WI

Sue Padilla
Ida Long Goodman Memorial
Library
St. John, KS

Evette Pearson
Northwestern State University
Natchitoches, LA

Kristina Peters
North Carroll Branch
Carroll County Public Library
Greenmount, MD

Marianne Tait Pridemore
San Jose Public Library
San Jose, CA

Karol Rockwin
Longwood School District
Middle Island, NY

Donna L. Scanlon
Lancaster County Library
Lancaster, PA

Helen Schlichting
Sac Community School
Sac City, IA

Colleen Stinson
Town of Haldimand Public Libraries
Caledonia, Ontario, Canada

Julia Wright Thomas
Koelbel Public Library
Littleton, CO

Pamela A. Todd
Carbondale Public Library
Carbondale, IL

Susan Trimby
Fossil Ridge Public Library
Braidwood, IL

Diane Tuccillo
Mesa Public Library
Mesa, AZ

Cara A. Waits
Tempe Public Library
Tempe, AZ

Maureen Whalen
Rochester Public Library
Rochester, NY

Melanie L. Witulski
Sanger Branch
Toledo-Lucas County Public
Library
Toledo, OH

BOOKTALKS

Across America on an Emigrant Train
By Jim Murphy
(Notables, SLJ/C)

Robert Louis Stevenson is still a struggling, unknown writer in 1879, when he receives word that the woman he loves is gravely ill. He immediately decides to travel from Scotland to San Francisco as quickly as possible, hoping to reach her in time, hoping somehow to save her life. Since Stevenson has little money to spare, he buys a second-class ticket on an immigrant ship, joining other frantic travelers on what turns out to be a difficult and stormy crossing. Once in America, Stevenson, already weakened by his sea voyage, boards a special immigrant train for the journey to the West. It's an experience he's totally unprepared for. The train is jammed with hundreds of passengers lugging boxes and bundles, chattering in different languages, all desperate to reach their destinations. Schedules are unpredictable and sleeping arrangements uncomfortable, for little if anything is done to make the trip easier for these new Americans. Before he knows it, Stevenson is trying out his language skills on his fellow passengers and collecting impressions for a new book. Travel across the American frontier with Robert Louis Stevenson, and discover the hardships, danger, and romance of an epic journey.

—Helen Schlichting

Aestival Tide
By Elizabeth Hand
(VOYA/SF)

"'The Wave is come,' Nasrani breathed. He traced the air above the image, leaned forward until his cheek pressed against the moist wall, and closed his eyes. Teeth had been drawn jaggedly in the mouth of the wave, teeth and a tongue that unfurled until it reached the smooth base of the hillside.

"Behind him the whistling grew louder, was swallowed into a gurgling roar. Too late he turned and tried to run. But it was already there, it had found him as it would find his sisters and all the others who waited for it, arrogant or fearful or unknowing. Just as they had always said, as had been predicted for a hundred years, as it had come centuries before and would come again to claim the city they had been proud and foolish enough to build within its path. He tripped in darkness and fell, and as he slumped to the ground he heard it, a million feet pounding up the twisted passageway, its voice a roar that deafened him, winding and turning until it found him crouched beneath its image and crushed him there, while all about the stones shrieked and tumbled into sand.

"'Ucalegon,' he whispered. The wave devoured him."

And so the Orsinas' absolute rule over the city of Araboth came to an end—a city long protected and fearful of the outside world, which must now face its own decadence if it is to survive the Aestival Tide.

—*Cara A. Waits*

Note: The passage in quotes is adapted from page 374 of the paperback edition.

Alice in April
By Phyllis Reynolds Naylor
(QP)

Was April *ever* going to be over? Alice didn't think so. It had started out fine, with a wonderful April Fool's joke on her brother, but the whole rest of the month was turning into a joke on *her*. First her aunt had announced that Alice was now "the woman of the house," whatever that meant. It sounded like a lot of responsibility for a thirteen-year-old—practically a full-time job. It certainly had its drawbacks: after insisting that her father and brother get medical checkups, Alice had to have one too. Yech!—imagine letting some doctor see you naked! And at school it was even worse, with the boys looking at all the girls and sizing up their figures. Alice was about to get a nickname—one that everyone in school would know. Depending on what these boys thought of her figure, she'd either be called something like "Montana" or "Colorado" or something like "Kansas" or "Nebraska." Or (horror of horrors), she might not get a nickname at all!

Alice couldn't wait for April to be over. But if she could just keep from dying of embarrassment, she'd eventually make it to May, and then things would *have* to get better, wouldn't they?

—*Barbara Bahm*

Alien Secrets
By Annette Curtis Klause
(Notables, SLJ/C, VOYA/SF)

Puck was heading home in disgrace, expelled from school and expecting the worst possible reception from her parents, who were doing scientific research on the planet Shoon. In fact, she couldn't imagine anyone being in more trouble—that is, until she met Hushwa'sshoonyashanyaha, an alien traveling on the same spaceship. Her problems were nothing compared to his!

He'd had the most valuable relic his people possessed stolen from his care—a relic dating back to their days of slavery under the horrible Grakks. Hush had traced the stolen object (called the Soo) to the very ship they were traveling on, but he wasn't sure who had brought it aboard or where it was hidden. The more Puck heard of his story, the more sympathy she felt, and the more determined she became to help him recover the Soo.

It was ironic that the Soo should be hidden on this particular ship, for this had been a Grakki slave transport in the bad old days before the war. Hundreds of Hush's people had suffered and died here. Now their ghosts haunted the ship, mingling unseen with the living passengers (who included some very suspicious-looking characters).

Who had the Soo? Where was it hidden? Who was killing off crew members with Grakki assassination techniques? Alien secrets—can Puck and her new friend Hush find out the truth?

—*Jeff Blair*

Anne Frank: Beyond the Diary
By Ruud van der Rol and Rian Verhoeven
(Batchelder Honor, BBYA, Notables, QP)

When the Secret Annex was betrayed, and the police broke through the hidden door and arrested the family that had been living like mice between the walls for more than two years, Anne Frank was taken away—but her diary was left behind. She never knew what became of it. She never knew that she would, ironically, achieve her childhood dream of becoming a famous author—her words would touch the lives of people all over the world.

The diary she kept during the two years she and her family spent in the Secret Annex, hiding from the Nazi regime, has been translated into more than thirty languages and read by millions of people. But there is more to Anne's story than her life in hiding. This book takes you back to the years before the Secret Annex, when Anne was a lively young girl growing up in Amsterdam—birthdays, schoolwork, friends, snapshots—and when Amsterdam was one of the safest, most tolerant cities in Europe. It also takes you forward to her last months in the camps where she died.

For the whole story of Anne and her family, and the horror they struggled to escape, look at *Anne Frank: Beyond the Diary*.

—Helen Schlichting, Marijo Duncan, and J. R. B.

America Then & Now
Selected by David Cohen, Text by Susan Wels
(BBYA, SLJ/YA)

"There is nothing permanent except for
change"—*Heraclitus*
"The more things change, the
more they stay the same"—*Alphonse Karr*

And here's the proof—pictures from America's past, placed side by side with ones from America's present. Sometimes the new pictures show radical change, but other times they're hauntingly familiar. Is America so different now from the way it was a hundred years ago? Maybe yes, but look again—maybe no.

—Jeff Blair

American Dragons: Twenty-five Asian American Voices
Selected by Laurence Yep
(BBYA)

"A dragon appears in many guises and is always adaptable, the survivor par excellence. Asian Americans display the same versatility as they move back and forth between their Asian culture and their American one." Here you'll meet twenty-five varieties of dragons, Asian-Americans who have experienced the emotions and problems of growing up in two cultures. "Who am I? What am I?" How *do* you mesh two cultures? There may never be one easy, simple answer.

Lensey Namioka says that sometimes a tough math problem can be like a game of pick-up sticks: "You look at the jumble of sticks and it's a complete mess. But after a while you notice how one stick is supported by a second one, which in turn is supported by a third and a fourth. You begin to see how the various sticks depend on one another. Then it becomes a matter of deciding which stick to take first. . . . I looked at the exam problem from several different angles. I considered various equations and saw how they depended on other equations. . . . And now for the next move. Yes, that was it. And then another deft move. And suddenly there was nothing left of the problem but a few isolated sticks to be picked up—easy pickings." Perhaps learning how to be Asian American is also like playing pick-up sticks.

Dragons are ancient symbols of strength and survival; perhaps it is time to bring forth new traditions, time to create American dragons.

—*Cara A. Waits*

The Apprentice
By Pilar Molina Llorente
(Batchelder, Notables)

Some kids know exactly what they want to be when they grow up. Do you? Arduino did. He lived in Florence long ago, during the Renaissance. His family were tailors, but Arduino wanted to hold a paintbrush, not a needle and thread.

With much reluctance, his father gave in to his pleading and apprenticed him to live and work for three years with a master artist. But the artist was a jealous old grouch, in no hurry to teach Arduino anything; instead he made him sweep floors, haul water, and run errands all day long. At night Arduino slept in a cold corner under a staircase, with only a dirty blanket for warmth. Meals were pretty bad too, but the housekeeper told the apprentices scary stories while they ate to keep their minds off the food. From the other apprentices, Arduino learned of something even scarier, something horrible kept in the attic. What could be up there, making the terrible cries and groans they sometimes heard?

One dark night, Arduino decided to find out. He climbed the stairs silently and found a locked door with a curtained window. Holding his breath, he pushed the curtain aside and looked into the attic room. What he saw there, and what he decided to do about it, were to change his life forever!

—*Suzanne Bruney*

Arena Beach
By Donna Staples
(QP)

My name's Terra Bliss, but call me Tee—everyone does. I've lived here in Arena Beach all my life, and I can't imagine living anywhere else. I have everything I could ever want: the Pacific Ocean practically in my backyard, a boyfriend, a car, a job. Okay, so my mom's kind of spacy, but what else can you expect from someone who calls herself Celestial Bliss and channels a spirit named Astraeus?

I'm supposed to graduate from high school this spring, but really, what's the point? Skeg, my boyfriend, doesn't have a high school diploma, and he does just fine. And Turbo, my boss at the garage? He has a doctorate in astrophysics, and look what *he's* doing. Even if I do finish high school, I don't see how anything's really going to change.

Except . . . except for that guy in the brown Cadillac. He's been asking around about my mother, and I know why. His name is Walter Spray—and he's my father.

He wasn't around when I was born, so what's he doing here now, seventeen years later? What does he want? I get the feeling that by the time I find out, Arena Beach may never be the same for me.

—Donna L. Scanlon

Baby
By Patricia MacLachlan
(BBYA, Notables)

The end of the summer was always an occasion for Larkin. After she and her friend Lalo helped the final ferryload of tourists get all their belongings onboard, after all the seashells, horseshoe crabs, and driftwood had been carefully packed for the trip home, after all the teary good-byes had been said, the island was finally theirs. Each year her family greeted this time of solitude with a special candlelight dinner.

The seasons of the island rose and fell in a rhythm as predictable as the tides. Quick-changing colors ushered in autumn, leaves flying until they were gone and the shape of the island could once again be seen. Soon winter would dominate, the wind shaking the windows and churning the sea black. Herring gulls would take refuge from the wind on the porch, waiting for spring, a spring that would come so fast and cold you hardly knew it was there. Then summer, visitors spilling off the ferry again, flooding the island, the air buzzing with their voices. But at summer's end they would flow away like the tide, leaving behind small signs of themselves: a child's pail with a broken handle, a white sock at the water's edge.

This year, that wasn't all that was left behind, but Larkin and her family didn't discover the baby until the next morning.

[Stop here for a short talk.]

There she lay in their driveway, with a note pinned to her clothes. "This is Sophie. She is almost a year old and she is good . . . I cannot take care of her now, but I know that she will be safe with you. . . . I have watched you. You are a good family. I will lose her forever if you don't do this, so please help her. I will send money for her when I can. I will come back for her one day. I love her." One of Larkin's teachers had once told her, "Life is not a straight line, and sometimes we circle back to a past time. But we are not the same. We are changed forever." Because of Sophie, Larkin and her family—Lily, John, and Byrd—are about to be changed forever.

—*Kristina Peters and Deb Kelly*

Beardance
By Will Hobbs
(BBYA)

Cloyd Atcitty's mind is on grizzly bears as he and his old friend Walter ride up into the San Juan Mountains of Colorado, prospecting for gold.

Maybe it's because of what his Ute grandmother told him when he was a little boy:"In the earliest of times, a person could become an animal if he wanted to, and an animal could become a person." As Cloyd grew older, he realized it was only a story . . . but it was a story he'd always wanted to be true.

Maybe it's because he found a turquoise bearstone in the burial cave of the Ancient Ones, above Walter's farm, and named himself Long Bear. Or because he danced the Bear Dance for two days and two nights, until his spirit left his body and looked down on himself and saw . . . not a Ute Indian boy dancing, but a bear.

Or maybe it's because Cloyd knows that something he said led Rusty, the bounty hunter, to find and kill the only grizzly left in Colorado. Or so he thought.

For whatever reasons, Cloyd is ecstatic when he learns that there may be four grizzlies left in Colorado, a mother and her cubs. His only thought is to find them. Not in his wildest of bear dreams does he guess that to save them he will have to become one of them, and den up with bears.

—*Julia Wright Thomas*

Behind the Secret Window:
A Memoir of a Hidden Childhood During World War II
By Nelly J. Toll
(IRA)

Quiet! Don't make a sound! Calm your frightened breath, try to still your thudding heart. It's hard, being squeezed into the tiny, dark cubicle behind the trap door. You want to move, to breathe freely, but if they find you . . . God, if they find you, you'll be shot in the street, or herded into a truck and never seen again, like your brothers, like your aunt—because you're Jewish too.

Behind the Secret Window is Nelly Toll's story of her own "hidden childhood" during the Nazi occupation of Lwow, Poland, during World War II. When she was only six years old, Nelly saw the terror begin for her people: first, all Jews were marked with yellow armbands; next, their homes were seized and they were forced to move to a tiny ghetto section of the city; then the German "cleansing actions" started, and people began to disappear, herded onto trains destined for labor camps or death camps.

For thirteen months, the eight-year-old Nelly and her mother hid from the Germans with a Gentile couple, ducking into the secret space behind a bricked-up bay window whenever a patrol or a spying neighbor came by. They spent over a year speaking in whispers, walking on tiptoe, and living always with the sick dread of discovery. Nelly survived by painting pictures of the childhood she wished she had, and by keeping a journal. *Behind the Secret Window* is Nelly's journal: a haunting, true story of one girl's survival in a world turned upside-down with horror.

—*Jennifer A. Fakolt*

Bel-Air Bambi and the Mall Rats
By Richard Peck
(BBYA, SLJ/C)

Ladies and gentlemen! In this corner, the champions, the Mall Rats, terrors of Hickory Fork and its surroundings. The Mall Rats, who control the town after dark, who've turned the mall into their private hangout, who run the high school and the grade school as well, who make up the football and cheerleader squads. The Mall Rats . . . you *don't* want to mess with them.

And in *this* corner, the Babcock Kids—Brick, Buffie, and Bambi, late of Bel-Air and now reluctant Hickory Forkites. Their father, a TV producer, went bankrupt and whisked them away overnight to his childhood home to sort out their lives. Hickory Fork is a *major* change of pace for them all. But it's Bambi who decides that if they're going to be staying awhile, then they'd better get the place shaped up—starting with the Mall Rats.

Bel-Air Bambi versus the Mall Rats. Those Rats never had a chance.
—*Jeff Blair*

Best Destiny
By Diane Carey
(VOYA/SF)

Heroes weren't always heroes, you know; once they were just kids growing up like everyone else. But they quit being like everyone else when they did something extraordinary, something that made them part of the evening news and the morning headlines. Many people think that's when they became heroes. But that's not true. Long, long before, things had happened to make them into the men and women who could someday do the right thing and become heroes. Heroes are made from the tiny experiences that shape them as individuals, that change the way they understand the world. They begin to see that one person can sometimes prevail against many, that even a small action can make a big difference in the long run. To understand why someone is able to do courageous things that the rest of us only think about, you have to look at who that person was as a child, as an adolescent, learning the lessons that would later enable a hero to emerge and do the right thing—save the child in the burning building, rescue someone from certain death, do the difficult, the impossible, and make it look easy.

Captain James Tiberius Kirk is a hero. To learn why, we must get to know the young Jimmy Kirk, growing up in Starfleet and struggling with life problems that sometimes seem too much for him. It's Jimmy who will be able to show us why he became Captain Kirk, not chief Surveyor Kirk, or Sixth-Level Accountant Kirk, or even plain Mr. J. T. Kirk from 101 No Particular Avenue. It has been said that it was Jimmy's destiny to become a starship captain. Let him show you how that destiny was formed.

—*J. R. B.*

Beyond the North Wind
By Gillian Bradshaw
(VOYA/SF)

Aristeas had been warned about the Arimaspians, who were rumored to lurk in these parts. According to legend, they were big, one-eyed monsters—they sounded too horrible to be real. But, as Aristeas would soon find out, they were very real indeed, and even worse than their reputation.

He was sitting by his campfire that night, playing his lyre, when two hideous creatures loomed up out of the darkness—Arimaspians! They were big, all right; they were *huge*. They had bristly red hair and long yellow fangs, and they wore the skins of a number of unfortunate animals. And in the middle of each monster forehead was one flaming eye, glaring down at Aristeas. That was all he had time to notice before he was knocked out cold.

When he came to, he was tied up and lying in a heap on the ground while the two Arimaspians argued—over him. One of them wanted to eat him right there, but the other thought it best to take him back to their queen, Colaxis, so *she* could eat him: " . . . you *know* Colaxis wants any human we catch. It's been a month since she had a bite of human flesh, and that's her favorite dish."

Finally the monsters agreed to take their prisoner to Colaxis, who might want to question him before converting him into an entree. Aristeas knew he was in big trouble, for more reasons than you might think . . . because Aristeas was on a secret mission. To complete this mission, he needed to get into the stronghold of the Arimaspians, which he was now going to do. He needed to meet this Colaxis, which he was also going to do. But most of all he needed to stay alive and healthy, and that was looking less likely every minute. Aristeas had only one hope: maybe the monsters were stupid—stupid enough to be tricked, after they took him beyond the north wind.

—Lisa M. Costich

Black Ships Before Troy: The Story of the Iliad
By Rosemary Sutcliff
(BBYA)

It started with such a little thing: a golden apple tossed into a crowd of wedding guests by a spiteful, slighted goddess. The apple was labeled "To the fairest," and that was the spiteful part, for there were three beautiful goddesses among the guests and each thought that she alone should have it. But who would dare choose between Hera, Athene, and Aphrodite?

The decision is referred to Paris, a handsome young shepherd who lives on Mount Ida, remote from civilization. Although he was born a prince, the son of King Priam of Troy, Paris was abandoned as a baby because of a prophecy that called him the firebrand that would burn down the city. Found and raised by a herdsman, he has grown up so innocent of the world that he does not even recognize the three goddesses when they approach. Hera offers him power, and Athene, great wisdom, but he rejects both to give the apple to Aphrodite, who promises him a wife as fair as herself.

That can only be Helen, the fairest of mortal women. She is already married to King Menelaus of Sparta, but that detail means nothing to Aphrodite—or to Paris. While a guest at Menelaus's palace, Paris courts Helen, who falls in love with him and returns with him to Troy, leaving her husband and daughter behind.

Then from every corner of Greece are kings and heroes assembled: Agamemnon, Ajax, Odysseus, Achilles, and all their followers, ready to burn Troy to the ground to recover Helen. The prophecy has come true—Troy is about to be burned, and all because of Paris. But Troy is a great city, strong and well-defended. What will happen when the black ships of the avengers arrive?

—Donna L. Scanlon

The Boggart
By Susan Cooper
(Notables, SLJ/C)

The Boggart has always been. For more centuries than he can count, the Boggart has haunted the owners of Castle Keep in the Scottish Highlands. Being one of the Old Things in the World, the Boggart lives by his own set of rules. He revels in practical jokes, setting people against each other, and other tricks of a Boggart's trade.

But now the last of MacDevon line, the only occupant of Castle Keep besides the Boggart, is dead. Distant relations in Canada inherit the castle, and during their preparations for its sale, the Boggart is accidentally trapped inside a desk that's shipped back to Toronto.

When the desk opens, the Boggart sees a whole new world, a world very different from anything he's ever encountered in all his many centuries—a world of electricity, computers, automobiles, and pizza. It's a world that the Boggart finds extremely interesting, but is it a world he can make his own? Will he be able to stir up as much mischief here as he did in Castle Keep?   —*Jeff Blair*

A Bone from a Dry Sea
By Peter Dickinson
(BBYA, Notables, SLJ/C, VOYA/SF)

Once, millions of years ago, it had been covered by ocean, but now it was dry earth—very dry and very hot. The Badlands they called it now, the African Badlands, situated in the middle of a country long torn by civil war. But peace had finally prevailed, and the Badlands were at last accessible to Vinny's father and the other paleontologists searching for fossils, for proof that human ancestors had walked this land in prehistoric times.

Vinny had come to the dig to get to know her father, a man who had become almost a stranger to her since her mother's remarriage. And at first it had seemed to be working—Vinny felt as though she'd found the missing piece of her life. So why did her dad have to get so angry about a book? After all, Vinny had worked hard to prepare for the dig, reading all the books her father had suggested and even adding a few extras, like the one he got so mad about. She was very excited by what it had to say, but he wouldn't even listen to her, wouldn't give the book a chance. Sure, the sea-ape theory was controversial, but out here in the Badlands it didn't seem so far-fetched to Vinny. After all, this site used to be a sea! Why couldn't the apes have used the water to escape from this terrible heat? And why wouldn't her father even *consider* that possibility?

Well, Vinny was willing to back off if that was the price of keeping peace with her father, but she wasn't about to give up on the sea-ape theory, not when she had a gut feeling it was true. And then they found that bone, that very unusual scapula with the inexplicable markings. A bone from a dry sea: was it just another fossil, or a fragment from a nearly unimaginable world?

—*Sister M. Anna Falbo, CSSF*

The Books of the Keepers
By Ann Downer
(VOYA/SF)

In this sequel to *The Spellkey* and *The Glass Salamander*, we find ourselves traveling through the Thirteen Kingdoms again, meeting elves, goblins, a wolf-girl, a former Leopard-woman, and a changeling child along the way. Once again, we find ourselves in league with Caitlin and Badger, as they search Above, Below, and Elsewhere, delving into the secrets of past ages on a dangerous quest for the hidden Books of the Keepers, the lost books of magic.

—*Barbara Bahm*

The Broken Land
By Ian McDonald
(VOYA/SF)

By choice Mathembe Fileli does not speak. Her language is one of gestures and movements that blend into a graceful dance. She understands the Old Speech with which she grew up in Chepsenyt, as well as the tenets of her Confessor faith, but she has no use for the New Speech of the Emperor Across the Water. She is content with the way things are in Chepsenyt.

Most of her neighbors are satisfied too. In Chepsenyt the Confessors coexist peacefully with members of the other major religious sect, the Proclaimers, as they go about their daily routines. An advanced bio-technology is at the heart of village life. Even the houses are living organisms, and Mathembe's father raises organic transport creatures called "trux." Light is provided by "gloglobes," and sewage and garbage are devoured and digested by genetically-engineered beetles. Thanks to biotechnology, life in Chepsenyt is clean and pleasant and happy.

All that changes the day the soldiers of the Emperor Across the Water descend upon the village and discover two rebels hiding there. As punishment, Chepsenyt is burnt to the ground; all its people—Proclaimers and Confessors alike—are driven out into the world as refugees. In the months of turmoil that follows, Mathembe is separated from her parents and her brother. She begins a long journey across the country, searching for her scattered family, never guessing that she is destined to reunite and heal her broken land.

—*Donna L. Scanlon*

Brown Angels: An Album of Pictures and Verse
By Walter Dean Myers
(Notables)

Brown angels: scrubbed shiny and dressed up in their Sunday best. Brown angels: barefooted, barlegged, playing in the summer sun. Brown angels: smiling shyly, beaming proudly, standing tall for the photographer who makes their images live on long after their own lifetimes.

Brown angels: images from dusty antique shops, flea markets, trunks dragged out from dim attic corners, or from picture albums long forgotten on a dusty shelf. Brown angels: someone's children, someone's grandchildren, perhaps now with children of their own.

Take a trip back in time and meet a young man determined to have his pet rooster with him at this very important moment. Another boy proudly holds the reins to a matching team of billy goats and shares his wagon seat with his dog. A little girl in a starched white pinafore holds her doll carefully—a doll as blonde as she is black. Two teen-aged brothers stare proudly at the camera, their long legs looking even longer in short pants and dark stockings. Babies, just barely able to sit up, smile wide-eyed or stare stolidly at the camera—what did they do when the photographer's flash went off?

Where are they now, these little ones from long ago? These little ones who were their parents' pride and joy? All that's left are the captured moments of their childhoods—brown angels, caught for all time in mid-flight.

—*J. R. B*

Note: Show appropriate pictures as you describe them in the talk.

Brown Honey in Broomwheat Tea
By Joyce Carol Thomas
(King Honor, King Illustrator Honor)

Brown honey and broomwheat tea,
Sweetwater, Daddy calls me,
Liquid ambrosia with fire.
"Be careful what you
    ponder," Granny smiles,
"Over a cup of steaming leaves,
    for it will surely come to pass."

A girl ponders what it means to be black, growing up in a family that's warm, caring, and strong. But just the same, at times life is hard:

Sometimes the broomwheat is bitter
And the cupboards are bare.
No money, little food,
And the honey in the pot is hiding.

She shares her dreams, her hopes, her fears, her joys, her family, and her "broomwheat tea: good for what ails you, especially when poured by loving hands."

—Monica Carollo

A Brush With Magic
By William J. Brooke
(VOYA/SF)

When Li, a poor rice farmer, pulls a basket from the river, he hardly expects to find a baby inside, much less a baby clutching a paintbrush. Li can't believe his luck—his *bad* luck! How is he supposed to feed a child when he can scarcely feed himself? But too late now—he can't exactly throw the baby back in the river. So he names the boy "Liang" and takes him home to raise.

As Liang grows up, he discovers that his brush is magic. Anything he draws with it will come to life. Somehow the neighbors do not appreciate this blessing. Liang saves the village from a flood, but all they can see is how badly he's messed up the rice-planting. Oh, if only he could leave this pokey village and journey to the Court of the Emperor, make his fortune, and win the hand of the Emperor's beautiful daughter! Then one day it seems that his wish will be granted.

But you have to be careful what you wish for. Emperor's daughters are not always what they seem, and magic isn't always the way to your heart's desire. Join Liang, his half-monkey half-man friend Monk-Li, and the brave handmaiden Lotus for *A Brush with Magic*

—*Donna L. Scanlon*

Bull Run
By Paul Fleischman
(BBYA, Notables, SLJ/C)

July 21, 1861. The North and the South meet for their first major battle of the Civil War at Bull Run, a creek near Manassas, Virginia. The Union soldiers are confident of victory and a swift conclusion to the war, but by the end of this bloody battle they will be in headlong retreat, with nearly four more years of savage fighting ahead of them.

Listen to witnesses from both sides tell the story of the battle of Bull Run and the effect the war had on their lives. From the North meet Lily Malloy, a Minnesota farm girl whose beloved brother has run away to join the Union army; Dietrich Herz, a German immigrant eager to fight for his new country; and Edmund Upwing, a coachman hired to drive spectators to a picnic view of the fight. Among the Southerners you'll hear Flora Wheelworth, a Virginia gentlewoman who finds herself caring for the wounded from both sides; Toby Boyce, an eleven-year-old determined to kill a Yankee "before the supply runs out"; and Carlotta King, a laundry woman and slave.

These American meet and mingle at the First Battle of Bull Run, and through their stories you will know what it was like on that hot morning in July 1861 as the country tipped over the brink of war.

—*Donna L. Scanlon*

The Burning Baby and Other Ghosts
By John Gordon
(QP)

The day after Barbara Pargeter disappeared, Bernard Friend called the police. (Bernie ran the old car garage—or dump, as most people called it.) He let the police know how concerned he was about Barbara and how eager he was to do anything he could to help them find the girl. But he also wanted to be sure that the search of his property would be completed quickly, so he could start tearing down the old shack out back. Bernie had plans for that shack, plans he had to get started on as soon as possible. He'd already announced that he was going to use the lumber from the shack to build a huge bonfire for the Guy Fawkes celebration—an event that would take everyone's minds off what he called "the ghastly business with Barbara." But there was something ghastly about Bernie's bonfire too, something that meant that he alone must build it, something that made the tunnel of tires under the bonfire very important, something so secret that you'll find out about it only when you read *The Burning Baby.*

—Helen Schlichting

The Bus People
By Rachel Anderson
(BBYA)

Most of us have noticed the special, smaller buses driving to and from school each day, buses that carry special students—those who are not able, physically, mentally, or even perhaps emotionally, to ride on the regular bus with "normal" students. But have you ever wondered about these kids—what they're like as people, and how they handle their difficult lives?

Bertram knows. He drives one of the special buses, beginning work most days before dawn. It takes time for him to go to each individual home and pick up each individual passenger—and to him the kids *are* individuals. Mrs. Lovegrove feels the same way. She rides along to help the kids on and off the bus, and to cope with unexpected problems.

Who are the passengers? Well, there's Andy, who keeps getting ambushed by seizures; sweet Rebecca, who's mentally retarded; Marilyn, who drip, drip, drips like a melting Sno-cone; and Fleur, who was kept in a dark cupboard when she was little and now doesn't speak—a beautiful child who seems to live in another world.

Enter the lives of these and other children as Bertram drives them to and from their special classes. For some of these kids, the trip on the bus is a high point in the day. Listen to their stories and share their dreams; life is life, no matter how hard.

—Carol Kappelmann

Calling on Dragons
By Patricia C. Wrede
(VOYA/SF)

There's trouble brewing in the Enchanted Forest. It all starts out innocently enough when Witch Morwen's cats discover a rabbit in her garden. This rabbit doesn't have fangs or webbed toes like the last one they found, but it stands seven feet, eleven inches tall (counting its fuzzy ears) and answers to the name of Killer. And according to Killer, it's been a *very* bad day. This morning, when he woke up, he was a normal-sized rabbit, but now . . . a bunny behemoth, and all because of that clover he ate for breakfast.

It's obvious that the dastardly wizards have returned to the Enchanted Forest and are once again plotting evil deeds. And there's no doubt that the worst is yet to come. It will be up to Queen Cimorene, Kazul the Dragon King (who just happens to be female), Telemain the Magician, Morwen the Witch and her nontraditional cats (none of them black), and now Killer the Rabbit to rescue the King's magic sword and thwart the evil wizards.

It is going to be an extraordinary adventure, even though, as Killer says, "Rabbits aren't *supposed* to have adventures." (But they're not supposed to be named Killer, either.)

—Bob Johnson

The Cat Came Back
By Hilary Mullins
(QP)

Stevie Roughgarten lives at a boarding school, is captain of the women's ice-hockey team, and is having an affair with Rik Wood, one of her teachers. She's trying to figure out who she is and what her future may hold. But what Stevie doesn't realize is that she's falling in love . . . with Andrea, one of her classmates and teammates. Because of that love, her life will be very different from anything she's imagining now.

Stevie is about to discover just how special and wonderful life can be when you're in love for the first time, in love with someone who loves you too.

—J. R. B.

The Champion
By Maurice Gee
(BBYA)

Rex was very excited when his mother announced that an American soldier was coming to stay with them. The soldier had been wounded and was coming to recuperate in their own town of Kettle Creek, New Zealand. The very thought of an American soldier in their home set Rex to daydreaming. He was fascinated by the war, especially now that the Japanese threat to New Zealand was past. Rex was sure "his soldier" would be a real hero—of high rank, with lots of decorations, and eager to brag about the number of enemies he'd killed. Rex knew that Jackson Coop would be just as brave as the heroes in the magazines he read so faithfully. But when Jack got off the train, Rex was crushed— the soldier had no medals on his chest, his bag showed that he was only a private, and worst of all, Jackson Coop was black. Rex was not only disappointed, he was ashamed. He wanted his soldier to be the perfect hero. Now he was afraid that people would tease him because of Jack— there were a lot of prejudiced people in Kettle Creek. Rex decided not to like Jack at all, but as it turned out, he was almost the only one in town who felt that way. Most everyone else saw that Jack was fun and caring, and that he knew a lot about dealing with injustice and prejudice. And when faced with incredible danger, he showed Rex what being a friend was all about, and what it really meant to be a champion.
—*Helen Schlichting*

Champions: Stories of Ten Remarkable Athletes
By Bill Littlefield
(BBYA)

What makes a champion? It is something that only a gifted few possess, like good luck or natural talent or single-minded purpose? Undoubtedly all these qualities play a role in the making of a champion, but for the ten athletes you'll meet here, earning the title of champion means much more. From their lives we discover that champions can come from anywhere, and often from some very ordinary place, and that being a champion is not just about success— it's also about learning from failure. Some of the people you'll meet here have familiar names and well-known achievements, and have gone far beyond success in a particular sport. These are individuals who, in their own ways, have shown perseverance and grace under pressure. Such athletes understand the value of finding a passion and working hard and believing in yourself. Life for them is most meaningful when they have goals beyond winning the next contest, goals that can involve making the world better for those who will follow. Take a look at how achievement, determination, struggle, and idealism made ten athletes into champions—champions you won't forget.

—*Helen Schlichting*

Changeweaver
By Margaret Ball
(VOYA/SF)

In the land of Hindu Kish, only women know the true magic. In the town of Gandhara, only women have the birthright to rule. With their magic, these women can light a fire, discipline a child or husband, and take care of everyday matters. But sometimes a girl is born with special magic—wild magic—and that can be dangerous. Such a woman is Tamai. She possess a magic so powerful that she's considered a hazard by her own people. What's worse, she can't seem to develop the kind of control necessary to direct this devastating power.

That's why she's the one selected to accompany Charles Francis Carrington on a seemingly hopeless expedition. Carrington, a fearless explorer, is determined to go where no Englishman has ever gone before—to the fabled empire of Chin. Veiled in mystery and magic, Chin is guarded by evil spirits and ruled by a profoundly wicked emperor.

Carrington, of course, doesn't believe in magic, or in love. But by the end of their journey, he just may believe in both.

—*Bette DeBruyne Ammon*

Charms for the Easy Life
By Kaye Gibbons
(BBYA, SLJ/YA)

My mother was a very smart woman, but I was afraid to trust her. After all, hadn't she married my father—a man who made a mockery of his wedding day and a joke of his entire marriage? So when it came to making really important decisions, I turned to my grandmother. Now *there* was a woman who had her act together. Charlie Kate they called her, and although she wasn't a licensed doctor, she treated absolutely everything from malaria to leprosy, and usually with success. She hadn't let her husband make a fool of her. When he became unbearable, she simply withdrew from him and gave more of herself to my mother and her patients. And later, when he left her, she yelled, "To hell with him!" and went on with her life, making it better instead of worse. She was a confident, strong-willed woman, and I wanted so much to be like her. So I turned to *her*, not to my mother, in 1940, when I got that really bad feeling that something terrible was about to happen. Oh, it happened all right—World War II. And I had to grow up real fast and make some major decisions: should I go to college, or find work, join the war effort, or marry . . . marry! Why, I'd never even had a boyfriend! No wonder I needed answers, advice, maybe even a lucky charm or two to get me through it all.

Charms for the easy life: sometimes they work, and sometimes they don't.

—*Sister M. Anna Falbo, CSSF*

Child of an Ancient City
By Tad Williams and Nina Kiriki Hoffman
(VOYA/SF)

Vampyres haunted the mountains, Kurken said, horrible creatures, neither alive nor dead, that slept by day and fed on men's blood by night. He had lived in the mountains all his life, and knew well the dangers of the journey their small caravan had begun. He had begged them to avoid this route, but the Under Vizier would not hear of it and the group headed due south, into the mountains. And now the worst had come to pass: they were being stalked by a vampyre. The bloodthirsty creature had killed several of them already. It seemed that nothing could stop it. They'd tried doubling the guard at night, sharpening their swords, even building a bonfire. Kurken's people would have barred their doors and windows against it, but here in the forest there was no such protection. A special herb could be used, but it didn't grow anywhere near their camp. There was only one other trick to keep a vampyre at bay, and Kurken wasn't at all sure that it would work, but with weeks of travel ahead and their number steadily dwindling as the vampyre satisfied his nightly hunger, they were desperate enough to try.

It was said that the vampyre might stop to listen to a story if it caught his interest. If they could keep the vampyre's attention until the break of day, they had a chance. The next night Masrur told the tale of the

Four Clever Brothers, and followed it with the story of the carpet merchant Salim and his unfaithful wife. Later, while relating the story of a clever orphan who found a cave of jewels and outwitted a gang of forty thieves, Masrur saw a strange and menacing figure lurking just outside firelight—a black shadow shaped like a man, its face in darkness, except for two red eyes that burned like coals. Kurken had been right—the vampyre could be distracted from his hunt by a good story. But would they have enough stories to last until their journey's end? And would the vampyre continue to listen despite his increasing hunger?

It was a perilous situation, with no guarantee of safety. Sit down around the campfire now and listen as the stories are told, but watch out of the corner of your eye for the shadow beyond the ring of firelight. Darkness has fallen, and the meager meal is over. Tonight Masrur begins with the story of the Little Man with No Name.

—J. R. B.

City of Light, City of Dark: A Comic-Book Novel
By Avi
(VOYA/SF)

When Carlos found the token, he thought it was just a regular token, good for one ride on the bus or the subway. How much could it be worth? A dollar and a quarter, right? Then why are so many people after it?

Like Sarah, a nice girl from his school, who just plain asks for it outright. He tells her to buy her own, but she only wants his, and she won't tell him why. Then there's Mr. Underton, a very sinister man who sics a flock of trained pigeons on Carlos when he won't give up the token, and the strange behavior of the bag lady—she breaks into Carlos' apartment when nobody's home and rummages through his things. To top it off, old man Theo's been looking all crazy and distracted whenever he runs into Carlos or Sarah.

It's a mystery, that's for sure. Carlos can't begin to imagine what makes this token so special. Not, that is, until he holds it tightly and feels its magical powers running right through him—powers that can ultimately cause the entire city to become a City of Light or a City of Dark.

—Barbara Flottmeier

Crazy Lady
By Jane Leslie Conly
(BBYA, Newbery Honor, Notables)

I bet you know somebody like my neighbor Maxine. Somebody who wears strange, mismatched clothes from the thrift store. Somebody who'd just as soon cuss you out as look at you, even when you haven't done anything. Some old guy or old lady kids love to torment just to see them lose it and get red-in-the-face mad. Somebody that everybody says to stay away from, cause they're *crazy*. Yeah, you know what I'm talking about.

It's not like I wanted to get involved with Maxine and her goofy son Ronald. But Miss Annie . . . well, I'd better start at the beginning. Name's Vernon Dibbs. There's five of us kids and my dad. When all this started we were still trying to deal with my mom's death a year before. I'm fifteen, the middle kid, too old to be "watched" and too young for a real job. Slippin' between the cracks in more ways than one. A big crack I was slippin' through was school. I needed help. Funny, but it was a chance meeting with Maxine that put me on to Miss Annie, a neighbor who turned out to be a retired teacher. Miss Annie said she'd work with me, but I'd have to pay for it—something about not appreciating what's free. Well, the only payments she'd accept were chores done for Crazy Lady Maxine. That's how it started.

Sometimes Maxine's ok, and I guess Ronald thinks I'm some kind of hero. But Maxine can go off on binges and turn on you like a snake. You never know what's coming next. Ronald is everything to her, but the social workers don't think that's enough to keep her sober. I'm worried. One more time and they'll take Ronald away, for sure. And I'm "involved" up to my eyeballs. One kid can't do much, but maybe a neighborhood can. Somehow I've gotta get them to help Maxine, and then—get Maxine to let them do it.

—Pamela A. Todd

The Crocodile Bird
By Ruth Rendell
(BBYA)

Liza wasn't at all prepared for the outside world. How could she have been? Although she was nearly seventeen and had been carefully educated, she'd lived her entire life at Shrove Manor, cut off, by her mother's decision, from the rest of the world. Her mother had never allowed a telephone, television, or even a newspaper to invade their privacy. Since Liza didn't go to school, she had no friends in the village, and her mother had never mentioned any relatives. No one but the milkman came by the house, and he had the mind of a child. Had her mother really believed she could protect her little girl forever? Hadn't she realized that sooner or later Liza would have to face the world?

Well, it had finally happened, so quickly that Liza was nearly frozen with shock. The police were gone now, but soon they would return and take her mother away. They would take her to court, take her to prison, punish her for murder! And it wasn't her mother's first murder, no, not nearly. Except, the police didn't know that—not yet, anyway. Only Liza knew about those secret killings, and she'd never tell. No, she'd protect her mother, but first she would have to save herself.

The crocodile bird: it was safe in the mouth of the crocodile, but no place is safe forever.

—*Sister M. Anna Falbo, CSSF*

The Cuckoo Child
By Dick King-Smith
(SLJ/C)

The moment he saw it at Wildlife Park, Jack Daw knew he had to have one of his own. So what if it would probably grow to be nine feet tall and weight more than three hundred pounds? So what if he had no idea how he was going to hide such a creature from his mother and father? And so what if he had no clue about how to take care of it? All Jack knew was that he *had* to have one. After all, he'd always been fascinated by birds, and this was the biggest, most beautiful bird he'd ever seen. An *ostrich* . . . for his very own . . . yes, it was meant to be! The hardest part would be to slip one of those ostrich eggs into his backpack when the park ranger wasn't looking. After that it would be easy, right?

Wrong! Find out what happens when Jack's ostrich grows too big to hide!

—*Sister M. Anna Falbo, CSSF*

Daniel Boone: The Life and Legend of an American Pioneer
By John Mack Faragher
(SLJ/YA)

He was a woodsman, a man who loved nature and the wilderness and sought a place to hunt and live at ease, but as an explorer and pioneer, he opened the way for thousands to follow and crowd him out. He was a husband, a father devoted to his family, and a friend to many, but he also craved solitude. He was a religious man who loved the Indians and hated violence, and yet he rose to fame as the leader of a war of dispossession.

Daniel Boone's life was full of adventure, and also full of contradictions. Meet the complex human being behind the legends, and get to know one of our country's greatest frontier heroes.

—*Deb Kelly*

Daughter of Elysium
By Joan Slonczewski
(VOYA/SF)

"Trees rose before him, right up to the sky-ceiling, covered with shimmering butterflies. The scent of blossoms, where the insects sipped nectar, was compelling. The little black-lined tails of the nearer ones seemed to wink at him. Closer, one could see the fat orange-stalked caterpillars devouring the leaves; the trees must require special care, to keep up their food supply.

"Beneath the trees, the Elysians stood or sat upon crescent-shaped benches of nanoplast. A few conversed quietly, but most simply stared or meditated, seemingly lost in thought, as they viewed the butterflies. 'Butterfly viewing' was an Elysian custom, he recalled. They almost seemed to be praying. Did Elysians have any sense of worship? . . . Blackbear wondered uneasily. With a pang, he suddenly missed all his brothers and sisters again. It was more than he could bear; even the secret of immortality might not be worth a year of loneliness."

At the request of its rulers, Raincloud Windclan, her husband Blackbear, and their two children travel to the strange underwater planet Elysium. Relations between the Elysians and the Urulites were tense, and Raincloud's skills as a translator and diplomat were needed to avoid war. But it was Blackbear, with his scientific curiosity, who made the incredible discovery—the secret of immortality. Would there be a price to pay for such knowledge? Would it be his own daughter of Elysium?

—*Cara A. Waits*

Note: The passage in quotes is adapted from pages 22–23 of the hardcover edition.

Dawn Land
By Joseph Bruchac
(BBYA)

On cold winter nights, when the People of the Dawn Land, the Abenaki, gathered around the fires and told stories, they spoke about the Ancient Ones, creatures of the first world, cold-hearted giants who ate human flesh. Young Hunter remembers the stories well. Now those fearsome monsters have returned, and Young Hunter has been chosen to go out and meet the danger that threatens his people. Two seers of the Abenaki, Bear Talker and Medicine Plant, teach him the secret of the Long Thrower, the bow that shoots deadly arrows from afar. Armed with this weapon and accompanied by his three brave and loyal dogs, Young Hunter leaves all that he knows and loves to make the journey into the unknown, where he must fight the stone-hearted cannibals alone.

—*Maureen Whalen*

Days of Grace: A Memoir
By Arthur Ashe
(BBYA)

Arthur Ashe grew up learning that reputation counts—especially a reputation for honesty, principle, and courage. As a world-ranked tennis player, he demonstrated these qualities, both on and off the court. He won with grace and lost with dignity. He made it to the top in a sport where black players were a rarity, overcoming prejudice and obstacles that white players never encountered. When heart problems ended his career, Ashe took up other activities and causes he enjoyed and believed were important. He knew that a man's success wasn't measured just by his bank book, but by his actions as well—"We make a living with what we get and a life with what we give." Ashe never expected a blood transfusion would change his life, but in 1988 he learned that as a result of receiving contaminated blood during heart surgery in 1983, he was HIV positive. Suddenly he was faced with even more difficult challenges and fears.

This is the story of Arthur Ashe's climb to the top as a world-class tennis player, of his post-competition career, and of his struggle against AIDS. This is the story of a man who lived his whole life with honor, dignity, and grace.

—*Helen Schlichting*

Death Is Hard to Live With:
Teenagers Talk about How they Cope with Loss
By Janet Bode
(QP)

Sometimes life is terribly hard. You're haunted by events you cannot comprehend, plagued by circumstances that spin widly out of control, overwhelmed and made helpless by what life has brought you. Sometimes death is at the center of this confusion, and Janet Bode has talked to dozens of teenagers who've been through it, who've lost friends and relatives, often to random violence. Their stories may help you deal with it and even, perhaps, begin to make sense of it.

In "Neighborhood Spirits," Vince explains how he began spraypainting murals to honor the neighbors and friends who had died in his part of town. The murals are not only tributes to the dead; they also make the survivors feel better—they keep a memory alive. But now the neighborhood is changing, and the murals may be lost. While this makes Vince sad, he also realizes that perhaps it will mean a new beginning.

If you have lost a loved one, a family member, friend, or even a pet, you may find help in understanding what you are feeling from these teenagers' stories. If you want to help a relative or friend during a time of loss, you will find suggestions on how to do it. And if you want to make sense of the part that death plays in life, you may find some answers here, in *Death is Hard to Live With*.

—*Susan Trimby*

Deerskin
By Robin McKinley
(BBYA, SLJ/YA, VOYA/SF)

Before Ash came, Lissar was all alone. That's a strange thing to say about a princess, especially one who was the daughter of the most popular king and the most beautiful queen in seven kingdoms, but nevertheless it was true. The king and queen were so much in love that they spent all their time with each other; Lissar was brought up by servants. Then, when she was fifteen, her mother died, and her father almost went mad with grief. The other rulers of the seven kingdoms sent their condolences, along with gifts for the king, and one of the princes sent Lissar a beautiful fleethound puppy named Ash.

Ash was the first friend Lissar had ever had, and they were inseparable. The next two years were the happiest of the princess's life. She had her dog, and she'd made friends with one of her serving women. Her rooms had been moved to the first floor when Ash arrived, and now they opened out onto a small walled garden, where she and Ash could run and play. As Lissar grew into a young woman, no one really noticed how beautiful she was becoming—just as beautiful as her mother had been.

But all that happiness ended on the night of her seventeenth birthday. There was a grand ball, and Lissar's new gown had been created especially to enhance her growing beauty. Her hair was carefully arranged, and she looked very little like herself and very much like her mother. When the king gazed upon his daughter, she was terrified. She didn't see love or pride in his eyes, but a menacing blackness, a treachery that convinced her she was in mortal danger.

And so she was. The next day she and everyone in the palace learned what the king had in mind. It was a fate so horrifying, so unthinkable, that it seemed almost impossible, but Lissar knew her father meant every word he said. She also knew that somehow she had to escape, to get away, to save herself and Ash. Obeying her father would be madness, and disobeying him meant certain death.

• • • • •

They called her Deerskin, after the beautiful white leather dress she wore. Her eyes were black, with no hint of color, and her long hair was as white as her dress. She was accompanied by an elegant fawn-colored dog with long curly fur. She didn't remember anything of her past, not even her name, but she knew about edible plants and plants with healing powers, so she thought she might have once been apprenticed to a gardener or a healer.

What had happened to Lissar, that she left behind not only her former life but even her memory?

—J. R. B.

Definitely Cool
By Brenda S. Wilkinson
(QP)

Roxanne was about to start junior high—a new school, and everything that implied. She worried about looking cool, meeting people, making friends, saying the right thing—all of it. Would she have girlfriends? How about a boyfriend?

It was pretty awful at first. Everyone was trying too hard; people cared about where you lived and what you wore. And just as Roxanne was beginning to feel comfortable with her new friends, something happened.

When the word about the hooky party came out, Roxanne immediately knew she couldn't go. Her mother would never allow it. The kids were all going to cut classes Friday afternoon to get an early start on the party, which would go on most of the night. Marcus was getting the beer. He seemed to take it for granted that Roxanne would go with him.

It was time for Roxanne to make some important decisions about her life and the direction it was taking, time for her to decide—was she definitely cool or not?

—Carol Kappelmann

Detour for Emmy
By Marilyn Reynolds
(BBYA)

Fifteen-year-old Emmy is one of those inspiring examples everyone likes to read about—a teenager who has overcome a difficult childhood and is really going to make something of herself, despite the odds. Her father disappeared a long time ago, and her mother stays out late and comes home drunk, usually with a new boyfriend. When Emmy was little, she was always the one kid whose parents never showed— not at Back to School Night, not for teacher conferences, not even for the class play. Her brother David has given up on school altogether and hangs out with the drug crowd now (that is, when he's not running away), but Emmy has come through all right.

She's made friends who are there for her when her family isn't. An excellent student, she's also MVP on the soccer team, a member of student council, and a regular in the choir—she has built a life outside her home. And now she has Project Hope, a special program for talented students who are faced with financial problems or family situations that might keep them from going on to college. If Emmy attends the project meetings and keeps her grades up, she'll receive free college tuition after she graduates from high school. It's the chance of her life, and she can't believe her good luck.

But then something happens to change all that, something Emmy never thought could happen to her. She's pregnant. She and her boy-friend Art have always been careful: they've made plans for a future to-gether and the children are supposed to come later, after they've both got degrees and jobs, not while they're still in high school. Once, just once, they didn't use a condom, and now this! Art wants Emmy to have an abortion, and he means it—he says he'll leave her if she doesn't. Her friends think she's totally irresponsible for getting pregnant in the first place and crazy to even consider having a baby. Her mother is bitterly angry—she may not have been a great mom, but she had hoped that Emmy's life would be different. And finally, the Project Hope counsel-or advises Emmy to withdraw from the program. So the stakes are very high when Emmy makes her decision—to have the baby and raise it herself.

Getting pregnant was the easy part. Being a mom at sixteen is going to change Emmy's life forever.

—*Susan Dunn*

Dinosaur Fantastic
By Mike Resnick and Martin Greenberg
(VOYA/SF)

Dinosaurs—giant lizards who once ruled the earth. Endlessly fascinating, endlessly mysterious. Why did they vanish? What did they really look like? How intelligent were they? What if there were still dinosaurs alive today—how would we treat them? What if time travel were possible, and we could go back to the age of the dinosaurs and find out all the answers for ourselves?

In "Just Like Old Times," a convicted murderer does exactly that. As punishment for his crime, Cohen's brain is transferred back into the body of a T-Rex. Too bad the judge who sentenced him didn't have some foresight, because by the time Cohen is through, that judge may have sentenced *himself* to death!

Even dinosaurs have rights—they shouldn't be shut up in cages. They should allowed to run free—right? Today animal activists picket zoos and try to release animals they think are being unfairly or improp-erly treated. But what if those animals were dinosaurs? What then? Sometimes it pays to know just what you're trying to set free before you actually open the gates. The "Last Rites" could be yours!

People have wondered for years about the Loch Ness Monster, speculating that it might be a surviving dinosaur that was trapped when the loch was formed. Perhaps they're right—but unless there's someone who can communicate with the creature that lives in the dark waters of Loch Ness, how will we ever know? Curren once knew the song of the monster, but that was long ago, and he can no longer sing "Curren's Song."

Someday genetic manipulation might make it possible to us to have pet dinosaurs the size of dogs or cats. But what if shrinking a dinosaur didn't really change its personality, or its predilection for flesh? In "Rex," Jonathan finds out what just might happen then.

Or what if dinosaurs are still with us? Suppose they *didn't* become extinct, but just learned to hide really, really well. If they turned into enormous chameleons, able to imitate anything, how would we ever find them? Perhaps we could, if we were very careful, and had very good cameras that could catch even a dinosaur creeping away, "On Tiptoe."

All kinds of dinosaurs, all kinds of ideas, all kinds of conflicts in all kinds of lives—all for you to discover in *Dinosaur Fantastic!*

—*J. R. B.*

The Disaster of the "Hindenburg":
The Last Flight of the Greatest Airship Ever Built
By Shelley Tanaka
(QP)

Irene Docher was sixteen when she and her family boarded the airship *Hindenburg* on May 3, 1937, for what was supposed to be the experience of their lives—a luxury trip from Germany to America on the biggest, most advanced airship the world had ever seen.

The *Hindenburg* was no ordinary blimp. It was as large as a fifteen-story building, larger than any aircraft that exists today. Under its shiny skin, its rigid frame was lined with bags of hydrogen, a lighter-than-air gas that could lift the great ship into the sky. Once aloft, the *Hindenburg* could sail majestically through the air, driven forward by propellers. It was a marvel of engineering. Special care had been taken to isolate the hydrogen gas, to protect it from sparks or heat. Hydrogen is extremely flammable, but the engineers felt they had made it safe.

On board, Irene could sample all the luxuries of a posh hotel. She could take a steaming shower whenever she wanted, adjust the temperature of her cabin against the chill of the night, or enjoy a delicious meal prepared by a master chef, while a pianist played softly on the airship's baby grand. The *Hindenburg* didn't roll or pitch like an ocean liner; the pilot steered so carefully that hardly a drop of water spilled from the boiling pots in the kitchen.

As the *Hindenburg* approached its American terminal, Irene could see clusters of people far down below. They were waving hats and handkerchiefs, and she waved back. Then she stepped away from the window—and saw flames. The whole airship was exploding in fire! Her mother threw her little brother out the window and shouted at her to jump! All around her people leapt from the burning *Hindenburg*, but Irene couldn't move. Then she felt a hand gently push her from the window ledge, and she fell.

What caused the *Hindenburg* disaster? Was it an accident, or was it sabotage? Could it happen again? Relive the last flight of the greatest airship ever built, and find out.

—*Suzanne Bruney*

Dog Wizard
By Barbara Hambly
(VOYA/SF)

Antryg Windrose had made a new life for himself in Los Angeles, the "city of dreams." He missed his magic, but now he had Joanna. He was just getting used to ordinary life when Ruth, Joanna's best friend, called in near-hysteria, saying that Joanna had disappeared. Antryg knew that only a member of the Council of Wizards, rulers of his home world, could kidnap Joanna, so he returned there through the Void. He was met by three Council members who bound him so he could not work his magic to escape. But they denied having taken Joanna. They had summoned him back for his knowledge of the Void, the passageway to other worlds. Having placed him under a death sentence, they demanded he find out who was using the Void to bring hideous creatures from other worlds into theirs. Antryg had little choice but to cooperate, and hope his investigations would somehow lead him to Joanna. With Kitty the librarian, his sole ally on the Council, he began to search the vaults beneath the Citadel of Wizards. There he found his old friend, the Dead God, but no sign of Joanna. He also began to develop a theory: what if a renegade member of the Council itself was behind the evil? But where would that leave Antryg? Could he find Joanna, close the gates to the Void, and get back to L.A. before one of his fellow wizards had him executed?

—*Abbie V. Landry*

Dogzilla
By Dave Pilkey
(QP)

It's barbecue time in the city of Mousopolis, and as the resident mice unwittingly let loose lovely smells of barbecue sauce into the air, a disturbing rumble is heard from a nearby ancient volcano. "And, suddenly, up from the very depths of the earth came the most terrifying creature ever known to mousekind: the dreadful Dogzilla!" This mangy mutt is terrorizing the entire city of Mousopolis. Will the brave troops, led by the Big Cheese, be able to save their city? Or will it all depend on Professor Scarlet O'Hairy? Can this old Dogzilla be taught new tricks? Only a reader of *Dogzilla* will find out. Special Warning: this book is rated E.G. (Extremely Goofy).

—*Bette DeBruyne Ammon*

Don't Give Up the Ghost:
The Delacorte Book of Original Ghost Stories
Edited by David Gale
(VOYA/SF)

Grandma would never have come back from the dead if Tata hadn't taken it upon herself to move into Grandma's house and do some major redecorating. Central air, walk-in closets, and new walls were one thing, but gilded toilets, a wet bar, and an electric massage bed were definitely *not* Grandma's style. "Reclaiming her residence" was the way most of the family saw it, after the trouble started. For Grandma didn't really make her presence known at first—not until the night of the housewarming party, when the gate-crashers showed up. They learned the hard way that you don't mess with Grandma—ghost or no ghost.

You'll enjoy messing with the ghosts in this collection of stories. You'll meet a ball-playing ghost, one that haunts a fifth-grade classroom, time-traveling spirits, and more. And if you should ever inherit a house from *your* grandmother, just remember, *don't* mess with the toilets.

—*Jeff Blair*

Doomsday Book
By Connie Willis
(BBYA, Hugo, Nebula)

By the year 2054, traveling back in time is no longer a science-fiction fantasy. It can be done, but it can be very dangerous. Kivrin is about to find out how dangerous.

As a history student attending Oxford University in England, Kivrin is studying the Middle Ages, and that's where she wants to go—to the year 1320, to be exact. Her professor, Mr. Dunworthy, is against it. He says the Middle Ages are much too risky. After all, the life expectancy in 1300 was only thirty-eight years. And once Kivrin is back in the past, there's no way to protect her from getting trampled by a horse, raped by a drunken knight on his way home from the Crusades, or burned at the stake as a witch! Not to mention the Black Death—the plague that killed over half the people in medieval England.

Professor Dunworthy is overruled. The doctors have vaccinated Kivrin against medical catastrophes, and the school staff have prepared her to blend in as well as their knowledge of the period will allow. She has worked hard to ready herself in every possible way. So she goes. She arrives in Oxfordshire, England, on December 13th, 1320, and begins an adventure even more dangerous than anyone could have imagined.

Meanwhile, back at Oxford in 2054, Badri, the technician who controls the computerized console that sent Kivrin back in time, comes down with a mysterious virus. His last words to Professor Dunworthy before passing out are: "Kivrin . . . I need you to come. . . . There's something wrong . . . slippage!" Soon the mysterious virus has become an epidemic, killing thousands of people. Professor Dunworthy can only hope Kivrin isn't facing the same fate, and that someone will be alive on this end of time to bring her back to the 21st century.

—*Sue Padilla*

Dragon's Bait
By Vivian Vande Velde
(QP)

Alys can't believe it—with just a few short questions, questions she'd tried to answer truthfully, Inquisitor Atherton had proven her a witch and sentenced her to execution—by dragon! Alys is just lucky that the dragon who shows up for the occasion is just about as unpredictable as a dragon can get. Oh, there's the usual overwhelming size, the vast spread of the wings, and the dangerous breath of fire, but Selendrile is different, because he's a gold dragon, and gold dragons are filled with magic.

In spite of the Inquisitor's expectations, Selendrile doesn't eat Alys. Instead, they set out together to seek revenge on her accusers and her father's murderer. But things don't go exactly as planned. The thrill of revenge is hollow—how was Alys to know that the Inquisitor would get out of the trap she set for him? Now Selendrile, transformed into a young man, is bound up in iron, and Alys must free him before sunrise or he will die, for he must be allowed to return to his dragon form at each day's dawn.

Unfortunately, the only people who can help are the very villagers who once accused her of witchcraft. Can Alys run to the village in time, convince people to help her, and return to Selendrile before daybreak? Is there anything powerful enough to break the bands of iron that imprison the dragon-man, or will he face a torturous death? And if he dies, will Alys go to the stake? You see, *everyone* is still convinced she's a witch.

—*Susan Trimby*

Dragon's Gate
By Laurence Yep
(Newbery Honor, Notables)

My name is Otter. In my village, in the land you call China, I was the son of a famous and wealthy gentleman. My father and uncle had traveled over the ocean to seek their fortunes as guests of the Gold Mountain, as we called America. They did well, and sent back enough money to make us prominent among our neighbors and themselves a legend in their time. When they came home, the entire village gathered to hear about America, with its unbelievable machines and strange customs. I burned to go back with them, to see it all for myself. I wanted to be counted among that brave brotherhood and have stories of my own to tell. But Mother would not hear of it. That would have been that, if not for the drunken Manchu soldier who involved me in his death. Suddenly there was no other choice. It was certain death or escape to America.

The reality of life in the Gold Mountain is so different from my father's and uncle's stories! In China, we were respected. Here I am less than a slave, and my father and uncle are despised—no better than common laborers. We are tunneling through a mountain in the dead of winter for a huge machine called a train. Uncle says the train is the future, the key to making China great again. He says we must learn all we can and take it back to China with us. But danger surrounds us, from both man and nature, and I wonder whether any of us will live to see our home again.

—Pamela A. Todd

Dream Date
By Sinclair Smith
(VOYA/SF)

All of us dream about meeting the perfect mate. So does shy, pretty Katie. One night in her dreams she meets Heath Granger. He's handsome, charming, the perfect date. As Katie starts dreaming her life away, Heath gets stronger and meaner. Soon, it's hard for Katie to tell what's real and what isn't, especially now that Heath doesn't want to stay in Katie's dreams. He wants to visit her while she's awake. Katie knows he can't—he's only a dream. Or is he?

—Barbara Bahm

Dreams Underfoot: The Newford Collection
By Charles de Lint
(BBYA, SLJ/YA)

Even in wakeful moments, they are there, exerting a force, providing the underpinning for the daily reality, clattering, echoing through the backbeat of the mind, casting their influence. Even when their content seems unrelated to realty, there's a current that runs true and deep to the waking world. Dreams are always underfoot.

The town of Newford has its own dreams. Dreams that run through it like water through the sewers. Dreams and tales of things that could never happen in a waking world, but somehow do. Ghosts, conjurers, timeskippers, balloon men, and more, all dreamlike, but all real. In Newford, things that shouldn't exist, do, lying in those dark places for you to come across when you least expect. Waiting underfoot, like the echoes of dreams.

—Jeff Blair

Durable Goods
By Elizabeth Berg
(BBYA, SLJ/YA)

No one is home. For dinner I make a mayonnaise sandwich. For dessert I have sweetened condensed milk on graham crackers. Then I go outside and lie in the backyard, look up at the stars. I hear the back door open, and sit up quickly.

"What are you doing?" he asks.

"Nothing."

"Well, you're doing something."

"I'm . . . I was looking at the stars."

"Uh huh." He walks over, lies down heavily beside me, looks up into the sky. "Do you know the names of any of the constellations?"

"Of course." Careful. "I learned them in school." Safe. I show him the Big Dipper, the Little Dipper, Orion.

"Some of the light you see," he says, "is from stars that no longer exist."

"Yes."

"How do you like that?" He is so satisfied, like he made it up.

"I don't," I say.

He looks over at me. "You don't, huh? Why not?"

"I don't know. It makes me sad. Like when we move and right before we go I make a new friend and then I can never know them."

"Well." A hard edge. His disapproval. He doesn't like to hear complaints about the way we move around. We are not allowed to cry about any place we leave behind, not when we drive away or at any other time, either. Sometimes it aches so hard, the thought of all you can't have anymore: your desk—the third in the third row, the place where you buy licorice, the familiarity of the freckles on your friends' faces, the smell of your own good bedroom. Knowing you will have to be the new girl again, the one always having to learn things. But you cannot cry about it in front of him. . . .

"I like that there are comets" I say to my father. "And I like the planets, especially Saturn."

"The rings, huh?" he asks, and I am so pleased that he knows. We lie still for a while. The grass is blue-green in the dark, rich smell. . . .

Twelve-year-old Katie is trying to find her way through the barriers erected between and around her father, her sister, and herself since her mother's death. Her father, always distant, sometimes violent, has grown steadily worse since then; her sister Diane escapes by spending all her time with her boyfriend and focusing on graduation. As a result, Katie feels she has lost her entire family. But she has some hope—once in a while, as when talking about the stars, she and her father are able to reach out and *almost* communicate.

—Evette Pearson

Note: The opening passage is adapted from the hardcover edition.

Eleanor Roosevelt: A Life of Discovery
By Russell Freedman
(BBYA, Newbery Honor, Notables, SLJ/C)

Her mother was a beautiful socialite, her father a fun-loving sportsman, and Eleanor felt that she'd disappointed them both. Her mother had expected a beautiful daughter, but Eleanor was tall and gawky, and hopelessly plain. "You have no looks, so see to it you have manners," her mother said. Her father didn't mind her homeliness but couldn't stand any sign of shyness or timidity—he wanted a confident, outgoing child. So, since she couldn't transform herself into a beauty, Eleanor set out to bury her unhappiness and master her fears.

Looking back later, she said, "You *must* do the thing you think you cannot do." And that was what she attempted, not only as a child but all her life.

In spite of her shyness, her looks, and her deep fear of being laughed at, she stepped into the spotlight when her husband became President. She felt she had to; it was part of her job, and if she was going to do it, she was going to do it well. She did things no First Lady had done before, and went places few women have ever gone. Her husband was crippled by polio, but she could travel, talk to people, see what was happening around the country, and give him reliable first-hand information. In the process she became an ardent advocate of justice for all; for her, people came first.

This is the story of a woman who declared: "If anyone were to ask me what I want out of life, I would say—the opportunity for doing something useful, for in no other way, I am convinced, can true happiness be attained." This is the story of a woman who made a difference, a woman who came to be called "The First Lady of the World"—Eleanor Roosevelt.

—Helen Schlichting

Elvissey
By Jack Womack
(VOYA/SF)

Elvis Presley as God? Elvis Presley as the long-awaited Messiah? Sure, he's still popular, but *that* popular? Well, it may sound far-fetched to us, but for the millions of members of the Church of Elvis, his divinity is a basic article of faith. Oh, don't feel too left out if you've never heard of the Church of Elvis, also known as the C of E. You see, it exists not in our world, but in another world that occupies basically the same space as ours without our being aware of it. And in this other world, which is at least a hundred years ahead of ours, a multinational company called Dryco is trying its best to become *the* major international power. Although it's doing fairly well in some areas, it's not making much headway with the Church of Elvis. So Dryco has hatched a top-secret project aimed at bringing the C of E under control.

Two Dryco agents have been dispatched to enter our world and bring back Elvis himself. Then Dryco can present him anew to his followers, as Dryco's very own gift to the Church of Elvis, putting the members of the Church under obligation forever. The plans have been laid, all the preparations completed. Now it's up to John and Isabel, the two selected agents, to break into our world and find Elvis. Will they accomplish their mission? Will Elvis accept becoming a god? And will his followers recognize their savior when they actually meet him? *Elvissey:* you have to read it to believe it!

—*Sister M. Anna Falbo, CSSF*

Fair Game
By Erika Tamar
(BBYA)

Maybe it wasn't rape, what my boyfriend Scott and his teammates did to Cara, but it wasn't consenting sex either, and it sure wasn't making love. Mostly I think it was just a bunch of guys getting carried away and going too far. I don't think they really meant to hurt her—she'd been putting out for most of them for ages. She'd do anything for a guy as long as he said he was her friend. She didn't object that afternoon when they told her to do a striptease, she didn't even object to any of the rest of it. But you can't tell your mother things like that; even Cara must have known that much. So when her mother asked her what had happened. Cara had to say she'd tried to stop them, she'd said no, she hadn't wanted it. I mean, she was retarded, but she wasn't *that* dumb!

What I want to know is, where does the line fall between right and wrong? *Was* what they did wrong? What about the guys who didn't actually do anything, who only watched? I mean, watching isn't a crime, is it? Is sex with the school slut a crime? Last year at graduation all the guys in the senior class gave Noreen Malivek a standing ovation, because she'd been with almost every one of them. Should *they* have been hauled off to jail?

And look at what the media's done to my town and my school! That's the *real* crime. For days the most popular guys at school couldn't even go out of their houses, because there were so many reporters camped outside! It's a big story from coast to coast—and not much of what I've seen or read is even close to the truth. All that matters is that it's a good story, and this story's no good unless a crime was committed.

So that's what I'm asking you—was what those guys did a crime? Or was it just a big, dumb mistake? I know how it *looks*, but I want to know what you *really* think about it, once you know what actually happened that afternoon, when the guys on the team had to practice alone because the coach had a meeting someplace. It was hot, too hot for practice, and there was Cara, hanging around, just like she always was . . .

—J. R. B.

Author's note: This talk practically wrote itself, and it seems to work with YA audiences. But I've never felt comfortable presenting it—the point of view is too different from my own.

Fallen Angels
By Walter Dean Myers
(Edwards)

What would it be like to fight in a war before you were old enough to vote?

Richie Perry finished high school and wanted to get out of the city slums. With his good grades, he could have gotten a scholarship and gone to college, but you have to have clothes to go to college. Richie washed his clothes every night and dried them by the stove just to have them clean the next day for high school. How could he go to college? He had to earn some money first, money to send his mother, so his little brother could stay in school and have some clothes. Money so *he* could buy some clothes and *then* go to college. He though the best way to do that was the army. The army gave you clothes, gave you three squares a day, gave you a place to sleep, and, on top of that, *paid* you. What a deal!

So Richie joined up. Basic training wasn't so bad. Then the army sent him to Vietnam for a year. The army sent him to Hell.

—*Sue Padilla*

Finders-Seekers: Book 1 of The Ghatti's Tale
By Gayle Greeno
(VOYA/SF)

I have failed at everything I've ever tried and failed everyone who has ever depended on me. My mother begged me to stay home with her and help with the weaving and look after my crippled sister, but I insisted on joining the eumedicos to study healing. I left the eumedicos when I found out they didn't really have the ability to mind-link with their patients as they claimed—I could not live with the lie.

I met a wonderful man, a widower named Varon who had a son named Vessey. I married him, and together we had a child, a daughter, Briony, but they all perished in a terrible fire.

Then I went to see a pair of ghattens and was "printed" by the female, who named herself Khar'pern. This meant I could undergo training as a Seeker. I would ride a circuit and, with the aid of my ghatta, help others find the truth. Something always held me back, though. When my friend and lover, Oriel, was murdered, and his ghatt, Samm, blocked from mindwalking, I was enlisted by the Seeker General to discover the reasons. Here was yet another chance for me to fail. Could I find out what had happened to Oriel, and why Samm was blocked? Why did I keep dreaming about my stepson, Vessey, who was dead? Would I fail again, or could I finally succeed and save the Seekers and the ghatts?

—*Abbie V. Landry*

For the Life of Laetitia
By Merle Hodge
(BBYA)

Sooklal Trace is a tiny Caribbean village where the one bus runs when it feels like it, where people cheerfully get their water from rain barrels by the roadside and harvest their own guava and *bhaji* for dinner. Sooklal Trace is filled with the smell of woodsmoke and the sounds of children playing—it's a safe, unhurried place. If the people of Sooklal Trace are poor in material things, they make up for that with ample love and good humor.

And now twelve-year-old Laetitia Johnson has the chance of a lifetime—a chance her grandparents didn't have, a chance her mother didn't have: the chance to leave Sooklal Trace behind. Laetitia, you see, passed the government exam, and she's the first one in her family to be admitted to the secondary school in the city. It's a chance to make something of herself—a great chance, everyone says.

But for Laetitia, leaving Sooklal Trace means leaving her heart behind. She has to go live with her father and his new wife in the big, cold city of La Puerta, and she misses the warmth and tolerance of the village. Her father boasts and brags about her success, but that's all she means to him—something else to brag about. Her new teachers make fun of her "backward" countrified ways—until they see how smart she is; then they urge her to "rise above" her family and break off with the "no-account" people of her past. Everyone expects Laetitia to succeed, for after all, no one has ever had such a chance.

The only person who seems to know how she feels is an East Indian girl named Anjanee, also a student, and also torn between school and family. At last Laetitia finds the courage to stand up to her snobbish teachers and racist classmates, and assert her right to choose her own friends. But when tragedy strikes, she must make the most difficult choice of all: between living up to the expectations of others, including those who love her, and reaching peace within herself.

—*Jennifer A. Fakolt*

Forest
By Janet Taylor Lisle
(SLJ/C)

The aliens invaded Upper Forest on a summer morning just before sunrise. It was a small one who first came into our branchway system. She did not appear to be dangerous—she carried no weapons, and her eyes were filled with kindness. Probably she came into Upper Forest for a youngster's adventure. But soon the elders of her kind followed, looking for her, and they brought with them their long fire-sticks. We mink-tail squirrels were fired upon; many of us were wounded, and some even killed. I myself lost an ear, and my sister, Brown Nut, was taken prisoner.

Today at noon there was a meeting at the Great Stump. Our Elders called upon all mink tails to wage war against the aliens. I spoke out; I said I thought this reaction was hasty and extreme. Perhaps we could reason with these beings from Lower Forest. But my words were shouted down, and now I am being eyed suspiciously, as a traitor or a coward. Is there any way for all of us to live together in peace?

—*Karol Rockwin*

Frankenstein: The Monster Wakes
By Martin H. Greenberg
(VOYA/SF)

He is one of the most unforgettable beings ever created. Many actors have tried to recreate him, and many authors have tried to imagine his life. He was never born, and yet he will never die, not so long as there is one person who remembers him, and reaches out to touch him. He has no name; he is known only by the name of his creator, a daring scientist who tried to play God: Dr. Victor Frankenstein.

For years people have wondered about Frankenstein's Monster. Could a creature who was not born live forever? Could a creature so unnatural, so huge and horrifying, so *ugly*, ever be a part of human society? What would it be like, to live one's life alone, the only example of one's species, forever separate from the human beings who rule the earth? But will the monster *always* be the only one of his kind? What if modern medicine were to encourage another Frankenstein, and another creature?

The monster is awake. He lives again, in these stories about his life, his creator, his companions, and (perhaps) his death.

—*J. R. B.*

Freak the Mighty
By Rodman Philbrick
(BBYA, QP)

The world changed for both of them the day Freak the Mighty, slayer of dragons and fools, walked high above the world for the first time— Freak the Mighty, born on the 4th of July in a blaze of glory. Separately, they were distinctive enough, but together, they were something else completely.

The first ingredient of Freak the Mighty was Maxwell Kane. Huge for his age, huge for *any* age, he was the spitting image of his father, "Killer" Kane, presently sitting out a jail term for murder. Maxwell said he'd never had a brain until Kevin came along and let him borrow his for awhile.

Kevin was the second part of Freak, and he had brains enough for both of them. His body wasn't much, though, stunted by disease to less than two feet tall.

But with Kevin riding high on Maxwell's shoulders, they were re-born as one person, Freak the Mighty. Together, they believed, they could stand up to dragons and bullies, find buried treasure, and survive anything life might throw at them. They were almost right.

—Jeff Blair

Free the Conroy Seven
By Jane McFann
(QP)

At the beginning of the school day they were just students at Conroy High, but by the beginning of third period they'd become the Conroy Seven. They are Bronco, the school troublemaker; Tess and Julian, the school brains; Marcus, the skateboard wizard; Melissa, the school sexpot; Carl, the wheelchair rebel; and Megan, the shy poet.

Why has Mr. Waldo, assistant principal, called these seven students to his office? Why are they being detained? What did they do wrong? They have lots of questions, but they're given no answers.

Not a problem. Take seven students with brains and daring, lock them in a room together without telling them why, and see how they discover what it is they're accused of doing. See how together they un-ravel the mystery. Meanwhile, outside the door, you can hear the chant begin: "Free the Conroy Seven! Free the Conroy Seven! Free the Con-roy Seven . . . "

—Cynthia L. Lopuszynski

Freedom's Children: Young Civil Rights Activists
Tell Their Own Stories
By Ellen Levine
(BBYA, SLJ/C)

The Civil Rights Movement. It changed our country forever, and it had a special impact on the lives of the young people who were a part of it. Listen to their stories, and discover what being an activist meant, in the days of change and danger.

Some of the people you'll hear about were famous—Dr. Martin Lu-ther King, Rosa Parks, the Reverend Fred Shuttlesworth, Claudette Colvin. But most of the people you'll hear from directly were young and unknown, like Ben Chaney, James Robertson, Myrna Carter, and Gwendolyn Patton. They were young people with extraordinary courage, activists and witnesses, who believed in their cause; and through their sacrifices, their goals were achieved. They became Freedom's Children.

—Deb Kelly, Lisa Heiser, and J. R. B.

From Sea to Shining Sea:
A Treasury of American Folklore and Folk Song
Compiled by Amy Cohn
(SLJ/C)

America—from sea to shining sea, from the New York Island to the Gulf's green waters, from the Atlantic to the Pacific—this is a celebration of a big country. And it includes just about everything: Native American creation myths, slave narratives, tales told by immigrants, stories of our fight for independence, the way west, and the Civil War, tricksters and tall-tale heroes, baseball lingo and hobo slang—all the different ingredients that make our culture so varied and unique. History is more than dry facts and dates that are all too easily forgotten. History is people—neighbors, ancestors, old friends and new—the people you'll meet here as you explore America, from sea to shining sea.

—Mary Fellows and J. R. B.

Girl, Interrupted
By Susanna Kaysen
(BBYA, Notables)

A doctor she'd never seen before decided she was crazy after only twenty minutes. That's all the time it took between walking in his door and leaving for the hospital. "A rest," he suggested. "Don't you think you need a rest?"

She said yes.

"They've got a room for you at McLean. Just for a couple of weeks, okay? It'll be a rest."

Susanna's "rest" at the McLean Hospital psychiatric ward for teenage girls lasted for nearly two years while she was being treated for "borderline personality disorder" in the late 1960s. Was the diagnosis correct? Was hospitalization necessary? Probably—it's hard to say. When Susanna was committed, she wasn't convinced she was crazy, though she feared she was. Today she's still not sure.

It's hard to know what could have been when your life has a two-year interruption in it.

—*Jeff Blair*

The Giver
By Lois Lowry
(BBYA, Newbery Honor, Notables, SLJ/C, VOYA/SF)

In Jonas's world everything is calm, planned, rational. Every family has two parents and two children, one boy, one girl. Every family has its own house. Every adult has a job. Every December, the ceremony is held, and children are given presents and new responsibilities to prepare them for adulthood. The Ones are named, special clothing is given to the toddlers, the Eights begin their volunteer hours for the community, the Nines get their bikes, and finally the oldest children—the Twelves—receive their Life Assignments and begin their training for the roles they will fill for the rest of their lives.

There is no pain in Jonas's world, nor any poverty; no divorce, intolerance, injustice, or inequality. There is also no rebellion. The rules are obeyed without question. Little occurs that is unexpected, so when, on the day of the Ceremony of the Twelves, the Elders skip Jonas, a sudden hush falls over the assembled community.

When the last of the Twelves has been given an assignment, the Chief Elder calls Jonas forward and explains what has happened. Jonas is to become the community's new Receiver of Memory—the most important job in the whole community. He has been watched and evaluated by the Council of Elders for many years. He's shown the qualities necessary to become a Receiver—intelligence, integrity, and courage. He'll acquire the necessary wisdom through his training.

Jonas is pleased, but a little scared too. The Chief Elder says his training will involve pain, intense pain, and that he'll have to go through it alone, because there can only be one Receiver for the whole community. But that night, when Jonas reads the rules that will govern his training, he becomes really scared, and confused. In addition to the rules about when and where he is to go for his training, he discovers he's was exempt from rules about rudeness—he can ask any question of anyone, and he'll be entitled to an answer. He's forbidden, however, to share his dreams or to take medication, and he's was not permitted to travel or leave the community for any reason. And most disturbing of all, he's allowed to *lie*! This is unheard of. From earliest childhood, all the members of the community are instructed in precise speech. They are taught to tell the truth—always! No one lies—ever!

What if other adults are also permitted to lie? How will Jonas ever find out what's true and what's not? How will he know who can be trusted and who can't? And what does lying have to do with his work as the Receiver of Memory?

In the weeks and months that follow, Jonas begins to learn the answers to his questions, and to see why he's been chosen as the new Receiver. But he also begins to realize just how fragile the community he lives in really is, and what his people have sacrificed to achieve the serenity they prize so highly.

—*J. R. B.*

Glory Season
By David Brin
(VOYA/SF)

Twenty-six months before her second birthday, Maia learned the bitter truth of the difference between summer and winter. As summer-born vars (or variants) of the Lamatia Clan, Maia and her twin sister Leie will never have the same status as the winter-born daughters of the clan, who are all clones of the clan leaders. At five years of age, as they approach maturity, all vars are sent out into the world to make a place for themselves as best they can. The cloned daughters, meanwhile, retain all the privileges of home.

Maia and Leie had planned carefully for their eventual departure from the Lamatia Clan and felt pretty sure of success. Their plan was simple: they would ship out of Port Sanger and find a likely city, not too poor or too rich. Then, posing as representatives of a small, distant civilization, they would begin to trade. Eventually, they figured, they would make enough money to establish a clan of their own.

From the beginning, though, the plan goes awry. Shipped out on two different vessels, the twins must cope with separation for the first time in their lives. When Leie is lost at sea in a violent storm, Maia must somehow survive on her own. Grieving, lonely, enduring hardship and imprisonment, Maia finds herself caught up in the life of a stranger from the stars, a stranger who could change her and her world forever.

—*Linda Olson*

Going to See Grassy Ella
By Kathryn Lance
(QP)

This is the story of how my sister and I got kidnapped and broke up an international drug ring.

I had just come home from school. Peej, my twelve-year-old sister (who should have been a five-star general), handed me this article about a miracle-worker. Peej had already decided that this woman, Graciella Bujold, could cure her cancer.

When Peej got a note from Graciella inviting her to visit, she started making plans. Mom and Dad would be going out of town to an optometrists' conference. While they were away, our neighbor was supposed to check up on us. Peej cleaned out her savings and made plane and hotel reservations in New York City.

The minute Mom and Dad left, I called school to say I was sick. Peej called our neighbor to say we were spending the night at a friend's. She left the same message on the answering machine for our parents to hear when they called to see how we were doing.

Peej's plans worked out great, until we got to the hotel. It was one our grandfather used to stay in, but it sure had gone downhill. I mean, you had to keep your shoes on to visit the bathroom, which was down the hall!

Things got worse. We went to a deli for breakfast before the train left for Noncie, where Graciella (Grassy Ella) lived. Someone stole our backpacks while we were eating! Figuring it must've just happened, we raced out the door and saw the culprit. You've seen races on TV? Well, we had one of our own, down the crowded city street, through Grand Central Station, onto the train platform, and down the tracks. But we caught up with him, in a campsite beside the tracks. And that's when we met Ivory, the gangster's daughter.

Oops! Sorry, but I gotta go now—Peej and I have to testify before the Grand Jury. But here, read this book, *Going to See Grassy Ella*, and find out all about our adventures.

—*Diantha McCauley*

The Golem and the Dragon Girl
By Sonia Levitin
(QP)

It all happened so fast! One minute the house was theirs, the only home Laurel had ever known, and the next minute it belonged to someone else, a family with a boy named Jonathan. Laurel knew that moving was necessary. With relatives coming from China, her family had to have more space. But how she hated to leave! Even more, she was *afraid* to leave! Surely the spirit of her great-grandfather lived in the old house, watching over her family and protecting her from harm.

Laurel didn't feel safe in her new home—so many accidents happened! And then Jonathan told her that strange things were happening in her old home as well: more accidents, unexplained noises, a whispering in the old oak tree where the protecting spirit had rested, lights flicked on in the middle of the night as if by an unseen hand. Bad luck, bad omens, bad times. Surely her great-grandfather's spirit had been disturbed! Laurel *knew* she had to do something to restore its peace, and she had to act quickly, before things got worse.

—*Sister M. Anna Falbo, CSSF*

The Good Fortunes Gang
By Margaret Mahy
(SLJ/C)

Pete Fortune and his family have been moving around like gypsies for as long as he can remember. But now Dad has decided to go back to New Zealand and live in the old Fortune house, right alongside all the rest of his family. Dad says he wants to settle down at home, but Pete's not so sure they won't just move on from there, like they've moved on from everywhere else.

Having all this family around is really strange. Cousins, aunts, uncles, grandparents—it takes some getting used to. Especially Cousin Tracey, who wants Pete to pass some strange tests before he is let into the Good Fortunes Gang, a secret group of Fortune cousins that meets in the treehouse. And Tracey looks just like the scary sister who appears in Pete's nightmares.

Will Pete be able to pass the tests and have his Fortune cousins for friends? And will his dad stay in New Zealand long enough for it to matter?

—*Colleen Stinson*

Grab Hands and Run
By Frances Temple
(BBYA, SLJ/C)

I was happy growing up in El Salvador. I had my family, my friends, my home, my school, and I thought that was how it would always be. But one night, when I was twelve, I did something that I shouldn't have done. I listened to a private conversation between my parents, one that I knew they wouldn't want me to hear. You see, even though I knew that my father was making speeches against the government, he and my mother tried to keep me from knowing about the terrible things that were happening in our country—how innocent people were suffering and being tortured by our cruel leaders. I knew, though, and I was soon to know even more. My mother asked my father what we should do if the police or the soldiers came to take him away. "Grab hands and run," he told her. "Go all the way to Canada, and I'll join you if I ever get free."

I thought at first that it was just talk, but the next day I found a note under our door: LEAVE AND DON'T COME BACK. IF NOT, YOU DIE!

A few days later, my father's motorbike was found outside the city, abandoned. My father was nowhere to be found. And suddenly we were running for our lives, homeless refugees heading for Canada. Would we make it there safely? Would we ever see my father again?

Join Felipe and his family as they grab hands and run.

—*Sister M. Anna Falbo, CSSF*

The Great American Elephant Chase
By Gillian Cross
(SLJ/C, Whitbread)

Tad escaped from the house by inventing an errand. The scene had been dreadful—as usual. Esther was always out to get him, and Aunt Adah always blamed the "mishaps" on Tad's clumsiness. This time Esther had pushed him down the steps along with the cumbersome tray he was carrying, loaded with cutlery, crumbs, and china. To make matters worse, Tad had landed squarely on his aunt. The ham, eggs, and hotcakes she carried had splattered to the floor to decorate the carpet.

Well, it was over for now, except the clean-up. Tad would get back to that as soon as he got some ammonia from the store.

First he had to wade through the crowd that was gathered on Main Street. Tad had never seen the likes of this in Markle. He pushed and wriggled his way through the hundreds of people. Whispers and giggles could be heard, and one amazing word: "Elephant!"

Just as Tad broke through the crowd, he plowed into a pale girl supported by crutches. Old Mrs. Bobb rapped Tad on the head as another woman helped the girl to her feet.

The girl was the only one to smile. "Don't fret. . . . I can't feel much," she said pleasantly.

Suddenly a great gasp broke from the crowd as they saw the elephant.

"Take a ride on the elephant!," trumpeted a voice. The elephant, led by a flamboyant little man in red silk and a fancy hat, ambled along the line of mesmerized people.

When the elephant passed close to Tad, it turned and looked directly at him. The man's voice rose to a bellow, then paused. Suddenly the elephant's trunk snaked down. It passed so close to Tad that it touched his cheek. But its target was the girl. The trunk looped around her and lifted her high in the air.

The crowd was petrified.

"She has a weak heart! Get her down!," cried the girl's mother. The huge elephant and the small girl changed Tad's life in seconds. Nothing would ever be the same, because Tad was about to become the leading edge of the great American elephant chase.

—*Bernice D. Crouse*

Hamburger Heaven: The Illustrated History of the Hamburger
By Jeffrey Tennyson
(QP)

We fry them, we barbecue them, we order them to go. We slather them with toppings, back them up with french fries and soda pop, and devour them by the billions. But have you ever *thought* about the hamburger? Really wondered about where it started, how it became the star attraction at millions of drive-ins and fast-food restaurants, whether it tastes better grilled or broiled?

Wonder no more. The answers are all in *Hamburger Heaven*. This history of the hamburger will tell you everything you ever wanted to know about the most popular food in America. And I do mean popular—Elvis has been sighted eating a burger, and yes, there *are* such things as hamburger memorabilia and burger collectibles. You'll learn of the rise and fall of popular hamburger chains, those of today and long ago. So chow down with this funny and informative book, but be sure you have a hamburger close by—you're bound to get that craving!

—*Colleen Stinson*

Harper & Moon
By Ramon Royal Ross
(Notables, SLJ/C)

Harper had two very special friends when he was growing up. One was Old Man Olinger: mountain man, decorated World War I veteran, teacher of the ways of the woods, he was always quick to give young Harper a licorice stick or take him fishing. The other special friend was Moon. Moon was the child of an itinerant painter and a mother who didn't love him. Moon was as whimsical as the moonshine he was nicknamed for. Most people thought he was "not quite right in the head," but for Harper, everything Moon touched was magic.

Harper would never forget the summer he was twelve, when he spent a week camping and fishing with Olinger and Moon. It was the last time all three of them were together. Afterwards, Moon went to join the army, and Olinger went back to his cabin in the woods—or that's what Harper thought. Then a neighbor reported that the Olinger was missing. Harper knew something had to be wrong. Ignoring the storm warnings, he went up the mountain alone to search for the old man, and finally found him—dead. Had someone killed him? Harper didn't want to believe it, but all the evidence pointed to Moon. Could Harper convince the sheriff that Moon was innocent? Could he convince himself?

—*Maureen Whalen*

Harris and Me: A Summer Remembered
By Gary Paulsen
(BBYA, QP)

Was my first day going to be typical of the summer I'd be spending with Harris? I hoped not! First I'd been kicked in the testicles by a cow; then I'd had to crank a milk separator for hours. I'd also smoked my first cigarette, gotten violently ill, been mugged by a killer rooster and covered in muck so thoroughly it seeped under my eyelids, ridden dinosaur-size horses, established a working relationship with a lynx, caught dozens of mice, and—oh, yes—eaten so many meals I'd lost count.

One day with Harris is like a week with anyone else. The whole summer stretches before us. I just hope I survive!

—*Jeff Blair*

The Harvest
By Robert Charles Wilson
(VOYA/SF)

There are three things Matt Wheeler loves above all else: his daughter, his work, and the town of Buchanan, Oregon. Each of those things is endangered becaused of a new object in the sky—an alien spaceship that has begun to circle the earth like an additional moon.

One night everyone on earth has the same dream, and everyone is asked the same question: "Would you like to live forever?" Most people accept the aliens' offer of immortality. In fact, only one in ten thousand refuses. Matt Wheeler, the town's doctor, is one who says No, and so do nine of his fellow citizens.

As a result of the decisions made that night, humanity is divided into two groups—those who will live forever, and those who will die. Soon, people begin to change: some become healthier, or recover from apparently fatal illnesses. And then they disappear. It becomes apparent that everyone who accepted the aliens' proposal will ultimately leave the earth for a higher plane of existence.

What will this mean for Matt and the others who said No? How will they live in a world "The Travellers" have changed almost beyond recognition? Can they survive on an almost empty planet after the aliens and most of Earth's population have departed?

What price will they pay for rejecting the offer of eternal life?

—*Rosemary Moran*

Haveli
By Suzanne Fisher Staples
(BBYA)

"Ibne drove the car slowly into the courtyard. Shabanu sensed instantly that something was wrong. The courtyard was empty and quiet. Usually servants and farm workers crossed back and forth, just as they did at Okurabad. Normally goats and chickens mingled with the wild birds in the courtyard. But even the hoopoes had fled from under the *saal* trees in the garden. And the light was hard and sharp, despite the gray sky, outlining everything in dark edges.

"Both Rahim and Omar sensed the danger. They got out of the car slowly, and Rahim walked around to where Omar stood facing the front door. Shabanu was immobile with fear, feeling as if her spine were attached to the seat of the station wagon.

"In the second before the shooting began, a glint from the balcony over the portico caught Shabanu's eye."

Shabanu is a young wife in present-day Pakistan, and she is visiting the *haveli*, her husband Rahim's ancestral home. Until this moment the *haveli* has been the one place where Shabanu could feel secure: safe from the jealous intrigues of her husband's senior wives, and free —at least for the moment—from anxiety over her own and her daughter's future. But now danger has reached out to her, even in this quiet place. And in days to come, the greatest danger will spring from her own heart.

—Cara A. Waits

Note: The passage in quotes is from page 224 of the hardcover edition.

Having Our Say
By Sarah Delany and A. Elizabeth Delany
(BBYA)

Sadie is 103, Bessie is 101, and their father was born a slave. Both sisters graduated from college in an era when that was unusual for any women, but especially for black women. They lived through two World Wars and the Great Depression. They have earned their way and won the right to have their say.

Sadie and Bessie Delany have lived together almost their entire lives. They marvel at a world where they can receive credit cards in the mail but must prove to their pension board that they are still alive. They wish their society would understand that "old" doesn't mean senile, inactive, uninvolved, or disabled. Sadie and Bessie greet each day a little surprised, but very happy to be alive. These women are strong individuals who have faced both racial and sexual harassment; they have many reasons to be proud of their accomplishments. The Delany sisters want to share their story and their wisdom. Bessie reports that it took her a hundred years to figure out that she can't change the world, she can only change herself—and *that* isn't easy either. Sadie warns that life is short, and it is up to *you* to make it sweet. Step into a world of humor and wisdom with the Delany sisters in *Having Our Say*.

—Helen Schlichting

Heart of a Champion
By Carl Deuker
(BBYA, QP)

Seth had always done okay. He did okay at school, okay at sports, okay at life, even after his dad died. But one day Seth met Jimmy White. Jimmy and his dad practiced baseball in the park all the time, and Jimmy was more than okay—he was awesome. His bat made such a sweet sound as it hit the ball for a home run. He threw his whole body into his fielding, and he'd worked his glove into the perfect shape.

Seth caught baseball fever that year. He learned the basics and developed techniques with Jimmy and his dad. The fever burned hot and bright in Seth. Even when he and Jimmy weren't on the same team or in the same league, and even when Jimmy's parents spilt up and Jimmy moved away, Seth practiced, throwing himself into the game. Jimmy had taught him how to play baseball, and much more. He'd taught Seth how to concentrate, and as the years passed, Seth's grades improved, and he became one of the team's leaders.

But the day Jimmy moved back, Seth knew things were different. Jimmy was different. He'd started drinking and doing things that could get him kicked off the Varsity team. Together they weren't the old double-play team anymore.

Maybe Seth didn't have the natural talent that Jimmy did, but he had something else. Seth's dad used to call himself the best lousy golfer in the world, and now Seth is probably the best lousy baseball player in the world. But he has also become one of the best people in the world.

Who has the heart of a champion now?

—*Colleen Stinson*

Here's to You, Rachel Robinson!
By Judy Blume
(BBYA)

Rachel tries to think of herself as a typical seventh-grader, but sometimes her teachers, her friends, and even her family try to separate her from the group. Her brother, Charles, calls her the child prodigy. Her teachers want her to enroll in special programs, and lately she feels out of place even with her best friends.

Rachel is tense. She has trouble breathing. Sometimes she hates her life and her brother so much she'd just like to *scream*, but screaming is something that no one in her family ever does. Is this the life of a normal seventh-grader?

—*Melanie L. Witulski*

Hero of Lesser Causes
By Julie Johnston
(Canadian Governor General's, Notables, SLJ/C)

Keely and her brother Patrick were always ready for the latest dare or challenge. It might be riding Lola, the breadwagon horse; wading into a pond filled with leeches; or swimming in the public pool after their parents had strictly forbidden it. Keely figured that both of them would keep charging on to bigger and better deeds of courage—until the day Patrick collapsed. When he said, "I think I'm sick," Keely knew it had to be serious. A few days later, the public swimming pool was closed because Patrick had polio, and was not expected to live.

But he did live, only not the way he'd wanted. He was paralyzed, unable to do even the simplest things for himself. He refused to see his friends, and sometimes Keely got the feeling that he'd rather not see his family either. Nothing sparked his interest, and Keely began to realize that her brother's personality had changed. This was not the Patrick who had always delighted in taking risks and winning outrageous bets. He was frozen in a state of deep despair.

Well, Keely wasn't, and she decided it was time to take on what might be the most important cause of her life—convincing Patrick that he was still capable of daring, of doing things that mattered, that his life was still worth living. Could she succeed? And what would happen to Patrick if she didn't?

—Helen Schlichting

High Steel
By Jack C. Haldemann II and Jack Dann
(VOYA/SF)

It is the twentieth-second century, and John Stranger has been drafted by Trans-United, one of the megacorporations that have pretty much replaced the government. Though some fragments of government remain, the megacorps control the power.

John, a Native American, has the gift for walking the high steel. High steel is what they call the giant space stations and factories that are being built high above the earth. John's training and his dedication to The Way, which would have made him a *wichasha wakan*, or medicine man, in his tribe, allow him to act instinctively and to salvage many bad situations in space. Trans-United isn't going to let that talent go to waste—they have drafted him for life.

For years John struggles with the *wasicun*, the white man who controls his life. His spiritual beliefs are still those of The Way, and one day he hopes to return to his people. Until then, John must work the high steel, and if necessary, use his unusual talents to save more than the megacorps.

—*Colleen Stinson*

Hoops
By Walter Dean Myers
(Edwards)

Seventeen-year-old Lonnie Jackson *could* be a great basketball player. But in Harlem there are lots of other good players, and it is hard for even the best to find a way out. Lonnie decides the city-wide Tournament of Champions will be his way. Sixty-four teams from all over New York will be participating, and there will be dozens of college and pro scouts in the audience. The tournament will be his big break—his ticket into the big time.

Lonnie and his friends have played basketball together for years. They know they are good, but to meet competition requirements, they need a coach. The guy who runs the gym where they practice introduces them to the man he's selected as their coach. Lonnie can't believe it! Their "coach" is Cal Jones, a local wino who hangs around the playground where they sometimes shoot baskets. Lonnie refuses to accept this guy; what kind of coach is this? But Cal makes Lonnie a proposition: he'll play Lonnie one-on-one, six baskets. If Lonnie wins, Cal will disappear, but if Cal wins, he becomes coach. Lonnie is sure he'll win easily; to his amazement, Cal beats him.

This is Lonnie's first clue to Cal's secret past. As the time for the tournament approaches, Lonnie discovers that Cal used to play pro ball, but sold out to gamblers and lost his career and his family. Now Cal has a chance to regain his honor through coaching this young team. But the gamblers haven't forgotten him. They want him to throw the tournament near the end of the final game. The tough choices Lonnie and Cal must make—the choices on which their very lives depend—are the story of *Hoops*.

—*Diane P. Tuccillo*

Note: Reprinted with revisions from *Booktalk! 2*, H. W. Wilson Co., © 1985 by Joni Bodart.

The Horror Hall of Fame
Edited by Robert Silverberg and Martin H. Greenberg
(VOYA/SF)

What would you do if you were given three wishes? Would you wish for money? For fame? For love? But what would happen if you discovered that getting your heart's desire also meant sacrificing the thing most precious to you? What good would your wishes be then? Discover the power and the secret of "The Monkey's Paw," and learn that sometimes wishing doesn't pay.

Who was Jack the Ripper? No one has ever learned his real identity. His crimes went unpunished and unavenged. He lived during the 1880s, so there's no way he could still be alive. He had to have died long ago—right? Maybe . . . and maybe not. There are many crimes today that go unsolved, many that are as gruesome and as violent as those committed by The Ripper. Perhaps he found a way to stay alive, so that he could continue to kill. Is there a pattern to these unsolved crimes? Can the pattern finally reveal the face of one of the most vicious killers in history? Would you want to be the one to confront him and bring him to justice, that man who signs himself, "Yours Truly, Jack the Ripper"?

Infants are by nature innocent, virginal, incapable of deceit, anger, or violence. Or are they? Perhaps "The Small Assassin" will change your mind. What if you discovered that your precious child hadn't come to you straight from heaven, but from hell?

"I don't want to get involved"—that's the cry of modern city dwellers. But what does their uninvolvement cost them? What if one day they're the ones who need help? What price their self-reliance then? Listen, and you will hear, in "The Whimper of Whipped Dogs."

"The Reach" was wider in those days, Stella used to say to her grandchildren. But they never knew what she meant, until the night she finally had to cross it, alone.

Be careful not to read this book too late at night. Who knows what creatures are lurking under your bed, or behind that not-quite-shut door, or at the foot of those shadowy stairs? Perhaps, just for tonight, you shouldn't turn out *all* the lights.

—*J. R. B.*

I Never Saw Another Butterfly . . .
Edited by Hana Volavková
(BBYA)

Some people in our world today deny the reality of the Holocaust. They dismiss the facts and figures, say its just imagination, that it couldn't have happened, that it's all a giant hoax. If you have any doubts, take a look at *I Never Saw Another Butterfly.*

Terezin was designed to be a "model" concentration camp, one that could be shown off to the Red Cross and other world agencies, to dispel the ugly rumors of slave labor and genocide that attached to places like Auschwitz. People were not exterminated at Terezin; they were killed after they left.

About 15,000 Jewish children and teenagers passed through the model camp, some staying for months until they were shipped on to Auschwitz. In the end, only about a hundred survived. Yet the spirit of those who died has not been lost. It is here, in the poetry and drawings of *I Never Saw Another Butterfly.*

> . . . For seven weeks I've lived here,
> Penned up inside this ghetto.
> But I have found what I love here.
> The dandelions call to me
> And the white chestnut branches on the court.
> Only, I never saw another butterfly.

—Susan Trimby

Note: The poetry excerpt is from page 39 of the hardcover edition.

I Was a Teenage Professional Wrestler
By Ted Lewin
(Notables, QP, SLJ/C)

By day, he studied Renoir, Rubens, and Picasso. At night, the ring was the classroom, and hammerlocks and flying tackles at the hands of men like Haystack Calhoun were the lessons.

For fifteen years, Ted Lewin was a professional wrestler. He was also a professional artist. He used his wrestling skills to pay his way through art school, and his inside knowledge of the colorful world of wrestling to enliven his work as an illustrator.

One night his two worlds, usually so far apart, came crashing together. Ted had done a large self-portrait in oil paints, and the fight announcer had asked him to show it during a pre-match ringside interview. As Ted discussed his other life and the audience admired the painting, the Sheik, Ted's next opponent, his eyes bugging wildly, raced up, grabbed the painting, and smashed it over the artist's head. There stood Ted, dumbfounded, with his real head poking through the canvas where the painted one had been. The crowd went wild.

You will too, when you read Ted Lewin's account of his wrestling days, in *I Was a Teenage Professional Wrestler.*

—*Jeff Blair*

In Love and In Danger: A Teen's Guide to Breaking Free of of Abusive Relationships
By Barrie Levy
(QP)

For Deborah, it was love at first sight, and she felt she couldn't have been luckier. Larry adored her—he brought her flowers and sent her love-letters. He wanted to be with her all the time. Deborah's friends were openly envious of her new romance. But gradually she began to notice another side of Larry—how possessive he was, how jealous, even of her old friends and her family. It was getting hard to see them anymore, because Larry would make fun of them afterwards and go on about how stupid they were, and if she started to defend them, he'd get violently angry. He seemed to think he owned her. She was fat and ugly, he'd say, and dumb-lucky he cared about her, because for sure nobody else would. Deborah thought it would get better after they were married—then she'd be totally his, and he wouldn't have to be jealous. Instead, it got worse. He shoved her, hit her, shook her, and scared her speechless.

What do you do when the person you love attacks you—verbally, emotionally, or physically? How do you know when your relationship isn't a normal one, when the conflicts are not just normal disagreements? What do you do when you, or someone you know, is in love and in danger?

—*Helen Schlichting*

In My Father's House
By Ann Rinaldi
(BBYA)

Oscie grew up in Northern Virginia at a place called Tudor Hall. She couldn't have known that her front yard would become famous as the site of the first battle of the Civil War—that was years in the future. Right now, Oscie was planning a battle of her own, against her new stepfather. As far as Oscie was concerned, Will McLean was the last person they needed on the plantation. Ever since her father's death, she had done her best to help with the running of Tudor Hall. She wasn't about to let an outsider take control. She felt punished when Will announced that he was hiring a Yankee tutor to repair the neglected education of his stepdaughters, and she hated the way he kept saying that the South would have to change to survive. Slavery was one of the things Will would like to change, Oscie knew, and she couldn't understand why—there had always been slaves at Tudor Hall, and they were like members of the family! But she had to admit that one of her family's slaves, Mary Ann, had suffered terribly from Oscie's own fear and jealousy.

Gradually, in spite of her resistance, Oscie began to see that change was inevitable—maybe even desirable. But as war came closer, endangering everyone she loved, she, began to wonder what would be left of the world she'd grown up in. *In My Father's House*—would it all be swept away?

—Helen Schlichting

It's Our World Too! Stories of Young People Who Are Making a Difference
By Phillip M. Hoose
(Notables)

Do you ever get tired of people telling you "wait until you grow up" whenever you try to do something? Do you think there's nothing you can do about a major problem because you're just a kid? Think again! Meet fourteen young people who saw a problem, confronted it, came up with a logical, reasonable solution, and carried out their plan.

Some of these problems may be familiar. Remember the dolphins that were netted along with tuna and left to die when the tuna were hauled in by fishermen? Rubin, a tenth grader from Cape Elizabeth, Maine, helped change that situation.

Do you know the story of "Sadako and the Thousand Paper Cranes" and the peace monument in Japan? Kids in New Mexico are working on a companion monument in Los Alamos, where the atomic bomb was built.

Norvell Smith was pressured to join a gang when she was twelve years old. Not only did she say no, but she won a contest with a speech denouncing gangs. Now she works with a team of young people who speak out against gang violence. She's been threatened and sometimes worries about her safety. She says, "Maybe the reason I'm growing up here . . . is that here I have the chance to make a difference. Here, I can count."

Find out how you can make a difference. Use the Handbook for Young Activists, which you'll find in the back of this book. Stand up for something you believe in, and become one of the kids who can say, "It's our world too!"

—*Susan Trimby*

The Jaguar Princess
By Clare Bell
(VOYA/SF)

I could feel my jaguar straining to break free, its soul yearning to take my soul. The power of my jaguar frightens me. It could steal my two greatest gifts as a human—my art and my power to love. I know that in order to save myself, Wise Coyote, and my great mentor, Nine-lizard, I *must* unleash the jaguar . . . but what will be left of me once my jaguar takes control?

—*Lisa Heiser*

Kat Kong
By Dave Pilkey
(QP)

The show is sold out. The auditorium is packed, positively crammed to capacity as the citizens of Mousopolis wait with bated breath and twitching tails for the main event. The mad explorer Doctor Vincent Varmint and his lovely assistant Rosie Rodent are about to unveil his latest discovery. At last the moment arrives. How the audience cheers as the Doctor presents a towering tomcat, the nine-lived wonder of the world!

But the huge kitty is not amused. Lunging against the chains, it snarls and hisses wildly—a terrifying sound! "Fear not," Doctor Varmint assures the crowd. "It's impossible for this creature to escape."

Take cover, though, because the shackles are snapping, the ferocious feline is loose, and the mice of Mousopolis are . . . lunch!

Who can protect them from this malevolent menace? Who can save them from the wicked claws of Kat Kong?

—*Sister M. Anna Falbo, CSSF*

The Killing Boy
By Gloria D. Miklowitz
(QP)

Standing a safe distance back, watching the flames engulf the house, I started worrying that maybe they'd escaped. What if they *hadn't* died? "Mom? Dad?" I cried, running toward the fire. Mr. MacDonald grabbed me and let me know that they were both gone. I put my hands over my face and sobbed like the grieving son, all the while thinking to myself, "I did it, really did it." There's nothing like planning. It was so easy! No one will ever pin it on me. I'm free, and they got what they deserved.

Now I'm living with my uncle's family in California. I've got them all wrapped around my little finger, except for cousin Tim. Somehow, I don't think he buys my poor orphan-boy routine—he seems very suspicious. I have something on him, though, and he'd better watch out what he says, or he'll get what's coming to him—him and his family too, while I'm at it.

—*Barbara Bahm*

Kindertransport
By Olga Levy Drucker
(BBYA)

Can you imagine being shipped off alone to a foreign country where you don't speak the language, to live with people you've never met, wondering all the while if you will ever see your family again? Hard to imagine, isn't it? But that's exactly what happened to Olga Levy Drucker when she was only eleven years old.

It was March 1939, and the Nazis ruled Germany. Jews were no longer considered German citizens, and more and more of their rights were being stripped away. They were losing their jobs and homes; soon, it was rumored, they would lose their lives. Desperate to save their daughter, Olga's parents decided to send her away via the Kindertransport, a rescue agency that got Jewish children out of Germany to temporary homes in England, beyond Hitler's reach. As soon as they could, her parents would join her there.

So Olga was placed on a train to the coast, and then on a boat. It was a long, anxious journey, but at least there were other kids along, about a hundred of them. Most of the older ones understood why they had to leave, but that didn't make it any easier! But the full impact of the move hit only when she got off the boat in England, her new country. How isolated she was! She couldn't even talk to the people who came to meet her. From all her English lessons, only one sentence stuck in her head: "The dog is under the table"—not exactly the all-purpose opener!

Then Hitler invaded Poland, and the war everyone had been dreading began. Now the borders were closed, and Olga's parents were trapped on the other side. She would grow up alone, moving from family to family, from school to school, always hoping that her parents had somehow survived. Would she ever see them again? Would they recognize, in the tall English teenager she'd become, the little girl they'd put on the Kindertransport so many years ago?

—Dara Finkelstein

Kipling's Fantasy Stories
By Rudyard Kipling
Presented by John Brunner
(VOYA/SF)

What do you think of when someone says "fantasy"? Maybe you conjure up images of wizards and elves, of dragons, warriors, and princesses. But not all fantasy fits that recipe. Here you'll find stories of humor and strangeness, stories that tip the everyday world a little sideways, stories that connect the imagination and the heart. Fantasy-shmantasy—these stories can make you wonder what *real* life is all about.

In "They," a young woman, blind since childhood, is befriended by children—the ghost-children no one else can see. "The Finest Story in the World" explains why people can't remember their past lives. Maybe animals can—"The Sing-Song of Old Man Kangaroo" tells how the Big God Nqong granted a kangaroo's wish to be "different and popular." And don't forget "The Village That Voted the Earth Was Flat"—what could be more fantastic than wishing something into reality?

Perhaps the most moving story is "The Gardener," one of the few tales Kipling wrote with a "switch," or surprise ending. It was inspired by his own work with the War Graves Commission after his son was killed in World War I. Like most of Kipling's stories, it's deceptively easy to read, and impossible to forget.

—*Evette Pearson*

Lady of the Forest
By Jennifer Roberson
(BBYA)

Young Lady Marian is in serious trouble. Her father went off to the Crusades with Richard the Lionhearted and was killed in battle, and now King Richard himself is being held captive by a rival ruler. That leaves his devious, power-hungry brother John to act as king—and as guardian to the orphaned Marian.

Marian may be young and innocent, but she's learning to think for herself. She doesn't trust her new guardian for a minute. King John would like to marry her off to the Sheriff of Nottingham, so as to buy the Sheriff's support for a plot to keep Richard locked up in a foreign dungeon forever. And the Sheriff would be happy to oblige. Just the thought of Marian's inheritance has transformed him into the most persistent of suitors. He lies awake at night dreaming of her lovely face—and her father's lands.

But Marian is drawn to a younger man—Sir Robert of Locksley, called Robin by his friends. He was a Crusader too, loyal to Richard the Lionhearted, and he's openly opposed to King John's cruel and greedy ways. Needless to say, he's not too popular with the Sheriff of Nottingham.

When Marian is kidnapped and taken into the forbidden Sherwood Forest, Robin follows, hoping to rescue her. The kidnappers, far from being sinister criminals, turn out to be likeable amateurs—commonfolk who've been reduced to outlawry by King John's new taxes and his highhanded "justice." Like Robin and Marian, these men believe that times will get better only if Richard returns. Should Robin and Marian join the outlaws in the forest? Can a band of wanted men and one young woman restore Richard to the throne, and justice to England?

—*Helen Schlichting*

The Last Command:
Star Wars Volume 3
By Timothy Zahn
(VOYA/SF)

Against all odds, the Rebel Alliance has won enough space from the evil Empire to set up its own government, the New Republic. The war seems almost over, and for Luke Skywalker and Han and Leia Solo, life is returning to normal. Leia and Han are even picking out names for their twins, who should be born any day now. Except for a few, faraway hold-outs, the Empire is finished—or is it?

Quietly, like the first wisps of smoke on the wind, unsettling reports come drifting in—rumors of a starfleet manned by clones, a starfleet attacking the newly liberated worlds and reconquering them, one by one. Even more disturbing, the enemy seems to have advance notice of every move the Republic makes. Clearly, there is a leak at the highest level, but who could it be? Who would betray the Republic's strategies to the cruel Empire? And where is the Empire getting these fresh battalions of clones?

Mara Jade, a reluctant guest of the New Republic, says she knows where the clones are coming from. The Emperor has a maximum security warehouse on a planet known as Wayland. So Luke, Mara, Han, Lando Calrissian, and Chewbacca head for Wayland, with the aid of some unexpected allies, to take out the cloning facility. If they can remain undetected by the imperial forces, they have a chance of success. But their departure leaves the Republic vulnerable, and the Dark Jedi, C'baoth, is scheming to kidnap Leia and her twins, and turn them to the dark side of the Force.

—Abbie V. Landry

Learning by Heart
By Ronder Thomas Young
(Notables)

On Saturday, the movers brought the piano. The kids from next door came to watch. Daddy shooed them away like flies, but the big one wouldn't leave. She was older than me, with black, scraggly hair, a red dress, and a purple nylon scarf tied around her neck. She just stood there, like a statue, until Daddy turned the corner of Brown Street and disappeared from sight.

"I can play that thing," the girl said.

Isabella invited her in to play for us. She played "Heart and Soul" and then taught me how to play "Chopsticks." After that, whenever I had a piano lesson, she waited outside my house until I was done. Then she'd come in and play all the things I was supposed to have learned.

That Pamela. People called her white trash, but the year I turned ten she became a friend. Find out what happened that year, and what it means to be learning by heart.

—*Melanie L. Witulski*

A Lesson Before Dying
By Ernest Gaines
(BBYA, Notables, SLJ/YA)

Jefferson's own lawyer thought he was no better than a barnyard animal. In his closing remarks to the jury, after first arguing that Jefferson didn't have the intelligence to commit this crime, the attorney spoke of the penalty. "What justice would there be in taking my client's life?" he asked. "Justice, gentlemen? Why, I should just as soon put a *hog* in the electric chair as this."

The verdict? Guilty; death to be administered by electrocution. Justice.

If he is to be executed, Jefferson's godmother wants him to at least die with dignity—the dignity of a man, not a beast. She persuades Grant Wiggins, the teacher at the plantation school, to visit Jefferson in prison and teach him how to walk those last steps like a man.

It's a struggle for them both. What common ground do they have? Grant is as much trapped behind bars of prejudice and self-doubt as Jefferson is behind bars of metal. Who will learn from whom before Jefferson walks the final mile?

—*Jeff Blair*

Life Belts
By Jane Hosie-Bounar
(Delacorte)

It only made sense to me later, what Nita's father said about life, about how it doesn't last, but always leaves something beautiful behind. Nita's my best friend. We're both thirteen, but Nita looks and acts a lot older. I mean, we're really different, and still we're great friends. Lately, though, she's been so hard to get along with. Nothing I do or say can please her. Then she told me that her mother's dying—cancer, and it can't be cured. When I tried to say how sorry I was, she went all stiff like a board.

And then there's that kid, Eddie, the guy with the webbed fingers. Creepy, you know? He's got this thing for Nita, the way all boys do, but he's so weird, and he's always around, watching.

Something tells me this is going to be a long, hard summer. And here I thought it would be perfect, 'cause Nita and I just finished repairing an old sailboat, and we could have such a great time on the water. I still hope things will work out. It would be a lot easier if people would just let you know what they need.

Life belts: they're no good at all unless you use them.

—Sister M. Anna Falbo, CSSF

Life Doesn't Frighten Me
By Maya Angelou
(BBYA, QP)

I'm tough. Nothing scares me. Send 'round the big, bad dogs and the fire-breathing dragons, 'cause I'm not afraid. Ghosts and strangers in the dark, mean little boys who pull my hair—none of them frighten me. No, they don't frighten me at all.

So if you're afraid of people or things, do what I do: carry your courage up your sleeve, where you can grab it when you need it.

—Kathy Ann Miller

Like Water for Chocolate
By Laura Esquivel
(BBYA)

Tita was born in the kitchen, and when she emerged into the light there was no need for the doctor to slap her, for she was already crying. It was almost as if she'd been washed into the world on a tide of salt water.

Perhaps because she was born there, perhaps because Nacha the cook took care of her from infancy, the kitchen was Tita's domain. It was where she felt most at home. She grew up watching Nacha cook meals that marked the celebrations and tragedies of their lives. There were Christmas rolls, turkey mole, chorizo, cream fritters, beans with chiles, champandongo, and, of course, chocolate. And after Nacha died, it was Tita who took over the kitchen and cooked for the entire family. Her dishes were like nothing anyone had ever tasted. Tita put her very heart and soul into her cooking, and the passion she felt for those she loved was felt by everyone who ate the dishes she prepared. There was no place else for Tita's passion to go, for she was fated never to marry. Mama Elena had decreed that Tita was to live with her and care for her until she died. But not even Mama Elena could keep Tita from loving Pedro. He was her passion, her love, her heart. And the passion she could not openly express for him went into her cooking—and into the people who ate what she prepared.

Follow Tita, taste her recipes, and share her passion for food and for Pedro in *Like Water for Chocolate*.

—*J. R. B.*

Lives of the Musicians: Good Times, Bad Times (and What the Neighbors Thought)
By Kathleen Krull
(SLJ/C, Notables)

A spaniel named Loulou, a cat who ate asparagus, a bee named Buzfuz, peacocks and turkeys, parrots who could curse and swear—can you guess what they all have in common? Yes, they're all animals and, believe it or not, they were all pets (even the bee!) of famous musicians!

Composers like Bach and Beethoven and Mozart did spend hours every day writing the music we still enjoy, but when they *weren't* working, they liked doing pretty much the same kinds of things that you and I do. For example, many of the famous musicians loved to eat! Beethoven was crazy about macaroni and cheese, George Gershwin could polish off a whole quart of ice cream in one sitting, and Brahms was partial to eggnog.

If you enjoy music, now you can find out more about the people who create it. You might even find answers to questions that you never thought to ask, like "which composer wore checked cotton underwear?" Look it up in *Lives of the Musicians*!

—*Sister M. Anna Falbo, CSSF*

Lombardo's Law
By Ellen Wittlinger
(BBYA, QP)

Going out with someone can be pretty confusing at times. After all, there are all these rules you're supposed to follow, like: the guy should be older than the girl; he should be taller, too; and he is expected to pay for the date. But what happens when you fall for someone who doesn't fit the rules?

That's exactly what Justine Trainor, a high-school sophomore, has been asking herself. See, Justine likes hanging out with Mike, an eighth-grader who is three inches shorter than she is and lives right across the street. He's smart, funny, loves old movies just like she does—and he's even pretty cute.

But her new friend Jennifer and the other kids at school are making comments about her hanging out with "that junior high kid." Should Justine go along with what her high school friends think is cool, or should she just go with Lombardo's Law?

—*Dara Finkelstein*

Looking for Your Name: A Collection of Contemporary Poems
Selected by Paul B. Janeczko
(BBYA)

"Help Is on the Way!"

That's the title of a two-part poem. In Part 1, Frankenstein's wife writes to Ann Landers, and in Part 2 Ms. Landers replies. See, Mrs. Frankenstein's problem is that Frankie may be cheating on her. How does she know? Well, she's found someone else's arms underneath the sofa, and last night he robbed the grave of another woman. He may even be trying to do her in—last week she found water in her oil can. Dear Ann, what shall I do?

The discord in the Frankenstein marriage is just one of the funnier conflicts you'll find in this collection. Other poems explore war and peace, love and loss, nuclear accidents, things that are "delicate or endangered," things that are funny, sad, or infuriating. You may find yourself in these pages, reliving your desperate hopes and darkest fears, your happy memories or the ones that drive you out of bed to wander the house at 3 a.m. And if you're wondering what advice Ann Landers gave to Mrs. Frankenstein, it's on page 61 of *Looking for Your Name*.

—*Mary Fellows*

Lord of the Two Lands
By Judith Tarr
(VOYA/SF)

The priestess Meriamon's father, the Pharaoh of Egypt, is dead, murdered by the conquering Persians, who have sold her people into slavery, mocked her gods, and laid her land to waste. Because of her royal blood and magical powers, it is up to Meriamon to leave Egypt and seek out the only person who can help her people—the Macedonian warrior-king Alexander.

Unfortunately, the farther from Egypt Meriamon travels, the weaker her powers become. The cold northern weather saps her strength. When at last she reaches Alexander, she realizes her troubles have just begun. She can barely speak his language, and his tall, fair-skinned warriors frighten and confuse her. Furthermore, the Macedonians aren't used to taking instructions from a woman. But finally she convinces Alexander of his destiny, and he and his army set out for Egypt, challenged every step of the way. Many cities will have to be conquered before Alexander can reach the Nile. The peoples of Tyre and Gaza are determined to stop the king and his army. The very land rises up against him. Meriamon will clearly have to summon all her powers and call on the gods themselves to make Alexander Lord of the Two Lands.

—*Lisa M. Costich*

Lost in the City
By Edward P. Jones
(SLJ/YA)

Is it possible to live in a city all your life and still not know where and what you are? Can you ever really escape the past? Is it true that you can't go home again?

Discover the answers, in these stories set in our nation's capital—not the the Washington, D.C., of marble monuments and Congressional debates, but the Washington of poor streets and hard times, violence and despair. Here are people struggling to keep a sense of community alive, struggling not to lose themselves.

—*Lisa Heiser*

The Magic Circle
By Donna Jo Napoli
(BBYA, QP)

The Ugly One only wishes to serve God and to provide a better life for her beloved daughter Asa. She works hard as a midwife and a healer, and she's careful not to offend the townspeople or to arouse their suspicion of witchcraft. But she is tempted by a golden ring—not for herself, but for Asa—and the devils mark her for their own. As the villagers stack wood at the feet of the Ugly One and Asa, and their skirts begin to smoulder, the Ugly One makes one last desperate bargain with the devils. She will become their creature, if only they will save Asa.

The Ugly One is transformed by the devils and fulfills her sworn duty to serve them, but in her heart she is still pure and resists the evil whisperings that echo in her mind night and day. She faces her most horrible torment years later when two little children appear at her hidden cottage, deep in the dark woods, and she recognizes them as her own grandchildren. How long will she be able to hold off the devils, who keep demanding that she eat them?

—*Sue Farber*

Make Lemonade
By Virginia Euwer Wolff
(BBYA, Notables, QP, SLJ/C)

It's hard enough just being seventeen, but when you're seventeen with two little kids by two different fathers who are nowhere to be seen, it's *really* rough. That's Jolly's life—and she knows she needs some help. So she writes an ad and posts it on a school bulletin board BABYSITTER NEEDED BAD. The only response is from fourteen-year-old Verna LaVaughn, who immediately begins making a difference in Jolly's life. As Verna cares for Jolly's two children, Jilly and Jeremy, she also inspires Jolly to have dreams of her own and to make plans for future. The only way to cope with hard times, Jolly learns, is to make the lemons in your life into lemonade.

—*Bette DeBruyne Ammon*

Malcolm X: By Any Means Necessary
By Walter Dean Myers
(BBYA, King Honor)

Malcolm was always changing, always growing. He started out as Malcolm Little, a bright child and a natural leader. He did well in the predominantly white school he attented and was even elected class president. His close-knit family encouraged achievement. Then tragedy struck: his father, a Baptist minister, was killed, and his mother, struggling to keep the family together, began to have mental problems. Eventually she had to be institutionalized, and the children were split up. For a while, Malcolm continued to do fairly well in school, hoping to become lawyer. But when a teacher told him that a trade would be more suitable, he began to realized how difficult it would be for a black person to succeed in the white world.

Losing hope, he turned to the streets. He figured that as a hustler he'd at least get some kind of respect. For a while he was Detroit Red, one bad dude. He went from hustling to crime to prison.

The only good thing about prison was that it gave him time to think, to think and read and think some more. He read about the Nation of Islam and studied the teachings of its leader, Elijah Muhammad. According to Elijah, separatism was the only answer: blacks should be independent of whites in everything, including jobs and money. This made sense to Detroit Red. As soon as he was released, he changed his name to Malcolm X, honoring his unknown African ancestors, and devoted all his energy and talent to the cause of militant separatism. Few who heard him speak could forget the brilliance and cold fury with which he described the wrongs done to African Americans, or the passion with which he advocated the Nation of Islam. Thanks to him, the organization grew rapidly. He became famous, better known, perhaps, than Elijah Muhanmad—who eventually expelled him from the group.

Then Malcolm changed again. On a pilgrimage to Mecca, he was struck by the way that Muslims of all races worshipped together, in the traditional faith of Islam. It didn't seem to matter whether the worshippers were black, white, or Asian. He became an orthodox Muslim and returned to America.

But through all the changes, two things remained constant: he was always a leader and he was determined to fight for his people. *Malcolm X: By Any Means Necessary.*

—*Monica Carollo*

Many Thousand Gone: African Americans from Slavery to Freedom
By Virginia Hamilton
(Notables)

Many Thousand Gone is the story of slavery in America—told by the people who lived it. Ukawsaw, for example, was born a prince in Nigeria. His parents allowed him to visit the home of a merchant friend who lived in a distant part of Africa. The merchant was a false friend; he sold the young prince to a Dutch sea captain for two yards of checked cloth. Ukawsaw eventually reached New York, where he was bought at auction for $50.00.

Si Henson, born in Maryland, saw his father horribly punished for trying to protect his mother from a cruel overseer. With his ear nailed to the whipping post, his father was lashed one hundred times. Afterwards, his ear was cut off, and he was sold into the dreaded Deep South. His family never saw him again.

Henry Brown was a clever man who had the very bright idea of mailing himself to freedom. He had a carpenter friend build him a wooden box. Henry wrote an address on the box, climbed inside it, and had his friend nail it up and send it off. The box was shipped from Richmond, Virginia, to the office of an antislavery group in Philadelphia. When Henry stepped out, he was a free man!

Eliza was another slave who escaped. Carrying her baby in her arms, she ran for the river, knowing that once she crossed it, she'd be in a free state. She ran like the wind, with the slave hunters fast behind. It had been a cold winter, and the river was covered with big pieces of ice, but Eliza couldn't let that stop her. Desperately, she leaped onto one of the ice floes. It cracked under her weight, but she was on it only a moment before she jumped to another. Her bleeding feet carried her from one piece of ice to the next until she finally reached the other shore. There she and the baby were carried to safety by the family of John Rankin, one of the fiercest "conductors" of the Underground Railroad.

These are only some of the fascinating people you'll meet in *Many Thousand Gone.*

—*Jo Berkman*

Maybe Yes, Maybe No, Maybe Maybe
By Susan Patron
(Notables, SLJ/C)

If you're the middle kid in your family, you'll understand how PK feels. She's stuck in the middle of a family that looks like it's coming unglued. First of all, Mama has decided that it's time to move, so when she's not busy working at the restaurant, she's searching the apartment ads and packing everything under the sun into boxes.

Megan, PK's older sister, can't wait to become a teenager; she's already practicing her Miss Superior moods. Megan thinks she's gifted, so she doesn't have time anymore for PK or for Rebecca, who's the youngest. Rabbit, as Rebecca is called, is nervous about starting kindergarten. What if no one appreciates the carrots she always carries in her pocket? What if her teacher doesn't like a lot of questions? What if she gets lost?

Every night, when PK's mom goes off to work, Megan does the dishes and PK gives Rabbit a bath. Afterwards, they sit near the built-in hamper, where stories come rushing out, just right for the telling. But if they move, will the stories get left behind? And will PK have to leave all her collections behind as well—all her ants and flies and cherry pits?

Maybe yes, maybe no, maybe maybe.

—*Susan Trimby*

The Mind Pool
By Charles Sheffield
(VOYA/SF)

When the going gets tough, the tough get going. And in the 23rd century, the tough are human beings. They're the ones who have recently discovered the secret of travel between the stars, and although their manners are rough and their behavior primitive, they do display undoubted qualities of valor and stubbornness—just the qualities that could save the galaxy now.

For the galaxy is under attack by renegade "constructs"—artificial life-forms originally developed for defense. The first warning of danger was just a flicker of light. It came from Cobweb Station, where Operation Morgan was underway. A probe was sent to investigate—and found only the remains. Apparently the seventeen Morgan constructs had turned on their creators, and although sixteen had been destroyed in what must have been a ferocious battle, they had taken all life at Cobweb Station with them. The seventeenth construct, the most recently developed and also the most sophisticated, was nowhere to be found. Since this particular construct could destroy an entire city or lay waste a fair-sized planetoid, the rulers of the galaxy are determined to find it and stop it. And that's where the human beings come in. In the opinion of the galaxy's rulers, they caused the problem—allowing a formidable threat of unknown magnitude to hold the galaxy hostage. So they must work out a solution. Can they do it? Find out, in *The Mind Pool*.

—*Barbara Bahm*

Miriam's Well
By Lois Ruby
(BBYA)

Miriam Pelham wasn't exactly one of Eisenhower High's more exciting students. In fact, the best word for her was "no": no makeup, no jewelry, no style, no shape, no personality. Also, no friends. She wasn't offensive; she was just a zero. About the only way anyone could tell she wasn't in class was by staring at her empty seat long enough to remember who usually sat there.

Adam was not thrilled when his English teacher paired him with Miriam for a major poetry assignment. *Hours* with the dullest girl in school? It sounded like a nightmare come true. But Miriam *was* a brain, and Adam needed a decent grade in English, so he decided to make the best of it.

It wasn't as boring as he'd expected. He was actually getting to like Miriam, odd as that might seem, when suddenly she collapsed. Adam and his girlfriend rushed her to the emergency room. He was shocked when they told him that Miriam had cancer, even more shocked when he learned that her mother and church wouldn't let her have the medical treatment she needed to stay alive.

Suddenly, Adam was right in the middle of a controversy, about law and religion and medicine—about Miriam and her future, if she had one. Without medical treatment Miriam would die. Wouldn't she?

—*Cara A. Waits and J. R. B.*

Missing Angel Juan
By Francesca Lia Block
(BBYA, QP, SLJ/C)

Sometimes love is holding on, and sometimes love is letting go. And sometimes letting go breaks you up into little pieces, and you have to go find your true self in all the little pieces so you can be whole again.

Angel Juan was gone. He went to New York City, and he left Witch Baby behind. He went to find his music, and Witch Baby couldn't do anything but follow him. But how do you find an angel in New York when you can't even find yourself? Before she finds love, Witch Baby must find her own magic, and wish her own wishes, and make them all come true. And when a gnarly, snarly, purple-eyed baby witch has to find her own magic, she needs her very own magical almost-grandfather to help.

—*J. R. B.*

Modern Ghost Stories by Eminent Women Writers
Compiled By Richard Dalby
(VOYA/SF)

Ghosts come in all shapes and forms, and they have a wide range of moods. But each of them has a purpose, a goal, a reason for hanging around. It may be for revenge, it may be to pass on information or to rescue one of the living. It may even be to make amends, so that the ghost can proceed to eternal rest. But when you're haunted by a ghost, finding out why isn't always easy.

Take the example of Jacobine, in Antonia Fraser's "Who's Been Sitting in My Car?" Jacobine got in her car one morning with her children, only to discover that someone else had been driving it—someone who left the ashtray full of cigarette butts and the gas tank empty. And someone, she found out just a few days later, who didn't like children, didn't like them at all.

"The July Ghost" wasn't as angry and vindictive as Jacobine's, nor was he as old. He was just a boy, in a brightly striped T-shirt, who climbed trees, lay in the grass, and played on the swing. But there was something compelling about him nevertheless, something that made him hard to forget—and hard to leave behind.

In "The House of Shadows," you may wonder who's haunting whom. When Liz misses her train and is left stranded, she remembers that an old college friend, Mary, lives nearby. The stationmaster seems oddly reluctant to give her the address, but finally she persuades him to do so. Mary's delighted to see her old friend and introduces Liz to her family, all of whom speak in curious half-whispers. They spend a lovely evening together, and the next morning, when Liz returns to the train station, she is stunned to discover the reason for their strange, whispery voices.

Ghosts. Ghosts of women, men, children, even animals. Ghosts who terrify the living, or help and protect them. Ghosts of all shapes and sizes, with all kinds of agendas. Meet them all in *Modern Ghost Stories by Eminent Women Writers*.

—*J. R. B.*

Montana 1948
By Larry Watson
(BBYA, Notables)

Years later he wondered what would have happened if he hadn't listened at the window. He wondered if as much blood would have been shed or as many families torn apart, including his own.

David had known right away that something was terribly wrong. Something was going on that the grown-ups were doing their best to keep from him. When your father's the town sheriff, there are always whispers of trouble, but this was different.

It was different because it had to do with Marie, the family's Indian housekeeper and a special friend of his. Although she was deathly ill, Marie refused to have the town doctor treat her. The doctor was David's Uncle Frank, a war hero. David's mom had spent a long time alone with Marie, and now she was reporting their conversation to his father out on the porch. Determined to hear what was going on, David eavesdropped.

What David heard was shocking, not just because of what Marie had told his mother, but for the words his mother used, words he'd never imagined he'd hear her say, words like "rape," words that later he wondered if he *should* have heard, words that could never be unsaid.

—*Jeff Blair*

More Rootabagas
By Carl Sandburg
(Notables, SLJ/C)

One evening in Rootabaga Country, when the moon was shining and making golden pools where raindrops had spread their circles on the pavement, the girl named Silver Pitchers came to visit the Potato Face Blind Man, and they had a long talk. They talked about her three rabbits—named Egypt, Jesse James, and Spanish Onions—and about the adventures the rabbits had when they were let out of their hutch, and the stories they told Silver Pitchers when they came back.

And when all the stories were told, the Potato Face Blind Man said to Silver Pitchers, "When you feed Egypt and Jesse James and Spanish Onions tomorrow morning, tell them their stories kept me from being lonesome tonight, even when the moonshine coming down on the rainpools couldn't keep me from being lonesome."

"I will tell them," said Silver Pitchers, and she said goodnight and went home across the rainpools shining with moongold.

On another day in Rootabaga Country, a spink bug and a huck who had learned how to be good pals were taking a trip to the famous moon baths in the hill country halfway north of the Village of Liver-and-Onions and the Village of Cream Puffs. Along the way they met a seven-ringed caterpillar, and sat down to talk a bit. And when they asked him where he was going, the caterpillar said he wasn't going anywhere, just mooching along, one mooch to the inch. Caterpillars don't care where they are going, they care about how many mooches it takes to get there. Then the caterpillar explained why he has seven black rings on his fuzz-brown body and what those rings do for him, and for his mother and his father and his brother and sister. Because without the rings there would be no way for any of them to remember all the things that proper caterpillars must do.

So if you ever wanted to know about caterpillars, or rabbits, or green horses, or cornfield scarecrows who stand in the middle of rootabaga fields, or even the Hat Dancers who have three legs, two to walk on and one to carry their hat, then come with me to Rootabaga Country, and talk to the people who live there.

—J. R. B.

Motown and Didi: A Love Story
By Walter Dean Myers
(Edwards)

Didi had no intention of falling in love with a boy from the 'hood. What she wanted was to get out of Harlem and away from the drug scene. She was determined to go away to college—as far as she could possibly get.

But problems were piling up on Didi and interfering with her plans. She didn't get the full scholarship she needed, and then her mom had a stroke and Didi was the only one who could take care of her. Her kid brother Tony certainly couldn't—he had a bad heroin habit, and a bad enemy in the dealer Touchy Jenkins. When Didi first found out that Touchy had turned her brother on to drugs, she'd run straight to the police. Touchy had retaliated by arranging to have Didi beaten up and Tony arrested for holding. At least, that's what he'd arranged, but Motown kept it from happening. And that's how Didi and Motown met.

Didi was grateful, sure, but that didn't mean she was going to fall for the guy. In fact, he was just the kind of guy she wanted to stay away from! When she was ready—and she certainly wasn't ready yet—she wanted to meet a man who had big plans for himself, not someone like Motown, who lived in an abandoned building and made deliveries for a dry-cleaner. Just how grateful is a girl supposed to be, anyway?

—Jo Berkman

Nevernever
By Will Shetterly
(VOYA/SF)

Leda was really ticked, so she turned me into a werewolf. It's not so bad, except that I have to communicate in sign language or by writing out messages. It sure hasn't hurt my sex life (already nonexistent), and it's given me a chance to record with some really hot bands that need howling vocals. But I digress. What's best about being a werewolf is that Florida, heir to the neighboring kingdom of Faerie, thinks I'm really neat. I've been helping her hide from agents of Faerie who want to kidnap her and control her for their own purposes. Luckily, Florida and I know Bordertown pretty well, and we have friends here who are ready to help us. We though we had everything covered when Florida and two of our friends disappeared. I learned where they were being held and called in every marker I had to assemble a huge group of gang members and free-lancers to surround the building. But I'd forgotten how magic can mess up in Bordertown. Milo Chevrolet devised a spell to reduce the age of Florida's kidnappers by ten years (he didn't really want to hurt anyone). Unfortunately, Florida stepped in the path of the spell just as it was being cast, and she disappeared! She wasn't yet ten years old, so we figure she's gone back to some unborn state. But I can't shake the feeling that I'll see her again. Meanwhile, I've crossed paths with that Leda who turned me into a wolf, and I've hatched a plan to get even—if I have the nerve to carry it through.　　*—Abbie V. Landry*

Night Terrors
By Jim Murphy
(QP, VOYA/SF)

I know what you're thinking. You're thinking, "What can this old geek know about anything?" Well, you're right about me being old. Older than dirt. But don't be fooled by the sagging skin, or the hairs in my ears, or the way my hands quiver. That's this worthless body of mine giving up, not me. Not my mind, anyway. My mind is as clear as it was sixty-three years ago when I got my first job, digging graves. I've been doing it ever since, that's why they call me Digger.

The first man I ever worked for told me stories while we dug open the earth for the dead—stories about the strange things that happen in cemeteries. That's when I started collecting the stories folks like the undertakers and the livery drivers passed along to me. I wrote 'em down just the way I heard 'em.

You're not gonna find any advice or warnings in these stories—I won't even promise they're all true. But if you want to listen to 'em, you can.

I can tell you about Kelly, who learned that vampires don't always look like you expect them to, or live in haunted castles, or wear black capes. Some of them might sit next to you in science class. Or I can tell you about Jon, who discovered that when you play tricks on people in cemeteries late at night, you'd better know who your friends are before you start. Or I can tell you about Brian, who brought a mummy back to life, only it didn't work out the way he thought it would, or about my friend Allan and the *worst* day of his life.

I'm Digger. Welcome to my cemetery, and to my *Night Terrors*.

—*J. R. B.*

Nightjohn
By Gary Paulsen
(BBYA, Notables)

A rope was tied from the saddle of the horse to a shackle around the man's neck, jerking him along with the horse's trot.

The man stood tall, black and naked. The skin across his shoulders and back was raised in ripples as thick as Sarney's hand. Usually when men were marked that way it meant it was hard to get them to work, and Sarney's owner wouldn't buy them.

He sure worked this new man, though. Unhitched that shackle, cracked the whip over his head, and drove him straight into the field. It didn't matter that he'd been run a long ways or might be thirsty.

Sarney found out the man's name that night after he finally came in from the field. "I'll trade," he whispered to her from over in the corner. "I'll trade something for a lip of tobacco." Sarney laughed to herself. What's he got to trade? Come in here naked as the day he was born with whip-marks up and down his back, and he's ready to go tradin'?

It seemed as if he could read her mind. "I got letters. I'll trade A, B, and C for a lip of chew."

So Sarney began trading with the man named John to learn how to read. She knew that learning was dangerous, forbidden to slaves, but it could set her free. In her mind she would no longer be a slave.

—*Jeff Blair*

Oddballs: Stories by William Sleator
By William Sleator
(BBYA, QP)

[Sing to the tune of "The Addams Family."]

Da da da dum, snap, snap
Da da da dum, snap, snap
They really are unique,
They're absolutely freaks,
So come and take a peek
At the Oddball family.

Their house is really grand,
Their backyard's full of sand,
They always have pranks planned—
The Sleator family.

Their friends help put on dramas
'Bout parents and their traumas.
It sure upsets their mamas—
The Sleator family.

They love to chew used gum,
Have hypnotists for chums,
They're such a lot of fun—
The Sleator family.

With syrup in your hair,
Fake vomit on your chair,
Come visit if you dare—
The Sleator family.

—Jeff Blair

Others See Us
By William Sleator
(QP)

Jared had been dreaming of this summer for months, writing the intimate details of his desires for his cousin Annelise in his journal, hoping they'd all come true. And now here he was, at the beach compound where the entire family always gathered for the summer. Annelise and her parents had already arrived. Of course, he'd die of embarrassment if anyone found out how he felt, so the first thing he did was stash the journal in a secret hiding-place. And then he went out for a long bike ride, the ritual first ride of the summer. Almost the last, too, because as he coasted down toward the swamp where the dump used to be, the brakes failed, and he pitched headfirst into toxic chemical muck.

That evening, Jared began to hear voices—the inner voices of everyone around him. Apparently the swamp goo had made his nervous system so sensitive that he could pick up other people's brainwaves and eavesdrop on their thoughts. He tried to focus on Annelise—and got the shock of his life. Beautiful, sugary Annelise, whom everyone admired, cared for nothing but herself. Her thoughts were like a swarm of flies buzzing around something rotten—and she'd already caused one death. Could he stop her from causing another? It wouldn't be easy, because he'd made a second disturbing discovery:

He wasn't the only mind-reader in the family.

—*Jeff Blair*

Out of Control
By Norma Fox Mazer
(BBYA)

I don't know how it got to be such a horrible mess. I guess it all started that day in December when Candy, Brig, and I were eating lunch on the steps of the high school. We all watched as Valerie Michon approached. She was big and homely, certainly no one any of us would ever date.

Candy's a sort of all-American-type who could easily be a model for those jean ads. He's also President of the Student Senate. Brig has a great body and fantastic hair, and he's the star pitcher of the baseball team and President of the Honor Society. I, Rollo Wingate, am known as Mr. Stomp of the football team.

Well, we were spread out all over the steps, and when Valerie walked up, Brig spread out even more so there was no space to get by. So Valerie just kept going, straight up the steps like Brig didn't exist, and stepped right on his hand with her big, work-booted foot. Brig swore and smacked her on the leg. Our next encounter with Valerie Michon was in the school cafeteria. We liked to play this game where we'd pick a girl and just stare at her until we got a reaction. But staring at Valerie that day was a disappointment. She just stared back. We'd forgotten all about her when there she was, standing by our table and calling us "morons."

If things had stopped there, I wouldn't be trying to make sense of what happened, but Brig and Candy would never let a girl get the last word. Now Brig says nothing really happened, Candy says things just got a little out of hand, but when I think of what happened in the third floor hallway the other day, I think we were out of control.

—*Marianne Tait Pridemore*

Owl in Love
By Patrice Kindl
(Notables, QP)

I'm Owl. I'm fourteen and I'm in love with my science teacher, Mr. Lindstrom.

I know that students have crushes on their teachers all the time, but how many of them are devoted enough to sit perched on a tree branch outside the teacher's bedroom all night long?

Of course, when it comes to stunts like that, I've got an advantage over most fourteen-year-olds. I can change into an owl whenever I want—a barn owl, to be precise. Birds of prey run in my family, so although my parents aren't shape-shifters themselves, they weren't surprised to learn that I'm a were-owl (you know, kind of like a werewolf).

Being a were-owl does have its disadvantages. Lunch can be a serious problem—I mean, I can hardly munch on mice and grasshoppers in the school cafeteria. And then there was the incident with my friend Dawn's pet hamster—when she gave it to me to hold, I thought she was offering me a snack, and I almost ate it!

Now there are more complications. There's a new barn owl in the woods, and something about him's not quite right. He showed up just about the time that strange, wild-eyed boy started peeking through Mr. Lindstrom's windows. There couldn't possibly be a connection, could there?

—*Donna L. Scanlon*

The Oxboy
By Anne Mazer
(Notables)

The Blue Hunters are everywhere, searching for those whose human blood is not pure. Those who have mixed blood—whether they look like animals or humans—will be killed instantly.

My name is Oxboy, and I have had to hide from the Blue Hunters my entire life, concealing the fact that my father was an ox, an ox of mixed blood, who could speak and think as well as any human. I have not seen him for many years; my mother left him and married a human to protect me from the Blue Hunters.

But nothing can really protect me. I am always afraid now. People would hate me and betray me if they knew what I was. And I wonder, is there any place where I can stop hiding and be myself, even though I'm not a pure human?

—J. R. B.

Paradise of the Blind
By Duong Thu Huong
Translated by Phan Huy Duong and Nina McPherson
(SLJ/YA)

As the train rattles across an alien landscape on the long ride to Moscow, Hang reflects on her life in North Vietnam, on her family's history, and on the events that have forced her to leave home and journey into a foreign land.

From earliest childhood, Hang has known struggle and frustration. Girls don't count for much in Vietnamese society, and a girl without a father is an utterly insignificant person, no matter what the new Communist government preaches. Hang's uncle is a Communist and a great man in the village, but he holds to the traditional view of women. He has, however, liberated himself from all those old-fashioned ideas about family duty; far from helping their poor relations, he and his bitter, aggressive wife have actually made life harder for Hang and her mother.

It took Hang a while to see where her loyalties lay, but now she knows. She loves her mother; she just doesn't want to end up like her—worked to near-exhaustion, exploited and bullied by powerful relatives. Hang wants a better life, a chance to make something of herself. Will she find it?

—Deb Kelly and J. R. B.

Peter
By Kate Walker
(BBYA, Notables, QP)

Peter's a typical fifteen-year-old. He loves riding his dirtbike and tinkering with its motor, he wants to be a photographer, and, like most fifteen-year-olds, he's always thinking about sex. But while he'll take an occasional look at *Playboy*, the thought of an actual physical encounter with a real live girl is intimidating—just talking to girls can be too much.

Lately, though, there's been something besides girls on Peter's mind. He's caught himself feeling attracted to his brother's gay friend David, who is certainly easier to talk with than any girl Peter's ever met. He's even had dreams about David—dreams that are often followed by feelings of total revulsion. To test himself, Peter's thought of buying some all-male pornography, to see what that does to him. But what does all this mean? Is Peter like David? Is he gay too?

—Jeff Blair

Pigs in Heaven
By Barbara Kingsolver
(BBYA)

In some ways, you could blame it all on Oprah. Turtle's story had made the newspapers, but it was her appearance on an Oprah Winfrey show devoted to "Children Who Have Saved Lives" that really set things off. Turtle and her mom Taylor had been visiting the Hoover Dam when Turtle saw a man slip down a causeway. Because she noticed, the man's life was saved—no one else had even seen him fall. It wasn't as "TV spectacular" as another kid's story, about how she'd fended off a pit bull by hitting it with the whole Barbie Dream Date ensemble (complete with convertible), but it was a good story just the same.

In the course of the show, Taylor happened to explain how she'd come to adopt Turtle—how she'd found this little Cherokee kid abandoned on a car seat. That revelation caught the interest of Annawake Fourkiller, an attorney for the Cherokee Nation. To Annawake, this was an illegal adoption—a Cherokee child had been taken away from her tribe, and Annawake started proceedings to get her back.

Taylor was just as determined to keep Turtle. She packed up her kid and took off, living on the run, criss-crossing the country in an effort to keep Turtle away from the Cherokee. But the life of a fugitive can get pretty crazy; in the long run Taylor knew she'd have to face the claims of Turtle's people. And the results of that showdown might just have the makings of another Oprah show.

—*Jeff Blair*

Plain City
By Virginia Hamilton
(Notables, SLJ/C)

Everyone in town knew Buhlaire, the Water House child. They knew she lived with her father's family—"those no-'count Sims"—and that, according to her mother, her father was dead. She stood out from the crowd all right, with her hair an explosion of straw-colored Rasta twists, and her skin carrot-honey-colored in the winter, and in the summer tanned to near-chocolate. Buhlaire went her own way and did her own thing, and the only thing she had to be proud of was her father, who was missing in action somewhere in Vietnam.

But then came the day of the big white-out along the highway, and Buhlaire's life was shattered, and she was left with only the pieces to make sense of. A man stepped out of the snow and took her arm, saying, "Don't be afraid—I'm your daddy." She was dumbfounded. Her father *wasn't* dead. He was one of the street people who lived under the abandoned railroad tracks. He wasn't a war hero at all—he was homeless, and he couldn't keep a job.

What was Buhlaire going to do now—now that she'd lost the one thing she felt she could be proud of?

—*J. R. B.*

Please Remove Your Elbow from My Ear
By Martyn Godfrey
(QP)

Stormy spends a lot of time in detention—not because he's a troublemaker, just because he can't always think fast enough to get *out* of trouble. Like the other day in gym class, when he was trying to ram Pierce Kobel in the gut for revenge and ran smack into the teacher instead. That's how Stormy ended up in detention on the fateful day before the Mallory Trophy Floor Hockey Tournament began. For on that day Joey decided to set up a team, with himself as captain, and somehow the kids from the DT Dungeon (that's what they call the detention room) all ended up on it: Amber, who is three weeks behind on her science assignments; Dimps, who just moved from the former USSR and speaks almost no English; Melvin, a giant with a temper that gets out of control; and Stormy.

Their team is a mess. They are rotten players—Dimps doesn't even know what floor hockey is! And their first game is against the Screaming Eagles, the best team in the whole school!

But something is happening to these losers. Together they start helping Amber with her science, helping Dimps with her English, and helping Melvin keep a lid on his temper. Is it possible that, with a little team effort, they might even *beat* the Screaming Eagles?

—*Colleen Stinson*

Powers That Be
By Anne McCaffrey and Elizabeth Ann Scarborough
(VOYA/SF)

"Major, perhaps I didn't make myself clear. You were injured at Bremport; you saw what happened there. I shouldn't have to tell *you* what swamps of insurgency these colonial planets can be. Unauthorized life-forms *have* been spotted on this planet. Research-and-development teams *have* disappeared into nowhere. You can't tell me these circumstances aren't related. What you have to tell me instead is, how they *are* connected with each other. Do you read me?" [page 24]

Welcome to the planet Petaybee, or PTB, as it's sometimes called. When her lungs are severely damaged by poison gas, Major Yana is sent to Petaybee not only for recovery, but also to spy on the natives of the planet. Strange things have been happening on Petaybee, and Yana's assignment is to blend in as a patient while she looks for evidence of a native plot to take over the ruling company and ultimately the planet itself.

But as Yana works her way into the daily life of the planet and wins the confidence of its people, she begins to realize that they have good reason to rebel against the all-powerful company. It is greedily exploiting their planet and destroying their way of life. Yana discovers things about Petaybee that are magical and wonderful, and when the company begins to pressure her, she becomes determined to protect the very people she was sent to spy on. She vows to fight for them even if it means dying to protect the secrets they have shared with her. At last she has a reason for living, beyond the powers that be.

—*Cara A. Waits*

The Princess in the Kitchen Garden
By Annemarie and Margriet Heymans
(Batchelder Honor, Notables)

It was just too much for her—cleaning, cooking, caring for her little brother, and seeing their father's indifference to everything but his work. So Hannah moved out, out into what had been her mother's kitchen garden, hidden behind four tall walls and a locked door. It was sadly overgrown and wild now, weeds covering even her mother's memorial stone. Hannah remembered how beautiful the garden had been when her mother was still alive. Now it was hers. Oh, how wonderful to work just for herself and make it beautiful again! How good to be free of ungrateful demands! But a voice has followed her into the garden and gently probes and questions Hannah's determination to live by and for herself. "What about your little brother?" it asks. "He thinks that you're gone, and that a mysterious princess lives as a prisoner in the garden." Hannah tells the voice to go away, to leave her alone. She will not go back to the "do this, do that" life she was living with her father. Whose voice is this that knows so much about her and her family? As Hannah transforms the kitchen garden, will she also be transformed, by the voice?

—*Pamela A. Todd*

The Real Plato Jones
By Nina Bawden
(SLJ/C)

With a name like Plato Jones, you know I've got to have a history. And that's the problem—too much history. It all started with my grandfather, C. L. Jones, a famous British spy who in World War II was sent to Greece to organize the Resistance there. Someone tipped off the Nazis and they almost captured him, but he escaped with the help of a young Greek girl. That young girl was the sister-in-law of the man who would become my other grandfather, Nikos Petropoulos; that was how the two sides of my complicated family first met. OK, so my father is British (Welsh actually), my mother is Greek, and I'm confused. Welsh and Greek cultures don't mix very well—witness my parents' divorce. When I'm in England, I get hassled for being too personal, too "Greek," and when I'm in Greece, I feel like an up-tight, out-of-place Brit. But what really has me shook up is what happened when my mother and I went back to Greece for her father's funeral.

Old Nikos had been a recluse, even sending my mother away to be raised by her Aunt Elena in another town. Mother had barely known him; I'd never met him. So why did everybody in his village look daggers at us during the burial? It's creepy to see so much hate directed at you and have no idea why. Clearly, it had something to do with Grandfather Nikos. What had he done? I knew that my own problems couldn't be solved until I found out what all this hatred and secrecy was about!

—*Pamela A. Todd*

The Red Magician
By Lisa Goldstein
(VOYA/SF)

The stranger came to the village where Kicsi lived on Friday evening. He was tall and had bright red hair; his clothes were oddly fashioned. His name was Voros, and he was a magician. He came to warn the people of the terrible trouble to come. The rabbi of the village, who also practiced magic and could work miracles, didn't like the stranger or his message. He told the people not to listen to the outsider's words, and he told Voros he would kill him if he ever came to their town again. Voros retreated into the forest that surrounded the town, and in that forest one night the rabbi and Voros fought, each with his own magic. The land shook and the trees burned. Voros went away, but Kicsi did not forget him or the star necklace he had given her. The necklace, he told her, might keep her safe.

It was during Passover that the soldier came to Kicsi's house. "You are ordered to report to the brick factory near the railroad tracks next Wednesday," he said. "Twenty-six April, nineteen forty-four." All the Jews in the village were brought to the brick factory. The men were separated from the women. Then they were transported by train in cattle cars to Hitler's death camps.

Voros had been right in his prediction of evil. In the camps, life for those who were not sent directly to the furnace was unbearably hard. But Kicsi was sustained by the rumor of a tall, red-haired man who snatched people away from the camps. Maybe Voros, the Red Magician, would come back to save her.

—*Linda Olson*

Revolutions of the Heart
By Marsha Qualey
(BBYA, QP, SLJ/C)

The whole town knows! Cory Knutson borrowed her stepfather's truck and skidded through a plate-glass window! You can still see the huge, jagged hole.

Now she's grounded from anything remotely resembling fun, and stuck cleaning motel rooms every weekend to pay for a new store window. Actually, the job's OK—until she realizes her boss is a bigot.

Would she have noticed that a year ago, before she met Mac? Before she found hate notes and condoms stuffed in her locker at school?

Even her brother thinks she's wrong to go out with an Indian.

At least Cory's mother is on her side—for as long as her mother's around.

—*Suzanne Bruney*

Rhino
By Sheila Solomon Klass
(QP)

Annie Trevor has one enormous problem in her life. And to Annie it's a real problem, though her friends and family may not agree. Annie's problem is her nose. Annie is confident of her appearance otherwise, but through some genetic fluke she ended up with the oversized Trevor nose. On her father and grandfather it looks majestic, but on petite Annie—well, she feels that her nose overshadows everything else in her life. And by now it just about does—a large part of Annie's time and energy is spent thinking up ways to hide her profile. When she raises her hand in class and people turn to look at her, Annie makes sure she's sitting with her chin in her other hand and her fingers spread across her face to hide the nose. Otherwise she doesn't raise her hand. She doesn't like parties much either—she's so obsessed about people looking at her nose that she can hardly talk to them.

Then Annie gets an idea in her head that she can't let go of, even though most of the other people in her life think it's ridiculous: rhinoplasty. In other words, a nose job. Her boyfriend says he likes her the way she is, and anyway it's a cop-out for her to change the nose she was born with; her parents consider the operation unnecessary and much too expensive; her grandfather is hurt that she'd even think of messing with the ancestral snoot.

But Annie argues that she just wants to improve her looks. Her best friend is saving up for contacts to replace the glasses she hates—what's the difference? But the more convinced Annie becomes that a nose job is the right choice for her, the more everyone else seems to think that she's on the brink of doing something she'll regret for the rest of her life. So Annie is torn. What should she do? What would *you* do?

—*Susan Dunn*

Right by My Side
By David Haynes
(BBYA)

Marshall's nothing but a poor black kid going to a school full of yuppy whites. Sam and Rose are his no-good parents. Sam's the garbage king of Washington Park. He runs the local dump, and Rose reads paperback mysteries all day long. Then one day she up and leaves, just like that. Marshall doesn't miss her much at first—they never really got along, anyway. But now everything is messed up. Sam is parading a line of different women through the house almost every week. One of them is even Marshall's best friend's mother, so now Artie won't talk to Marshall. And Marshall's other main friend, Todd, is getting beaten all the time by his white-trash parents.

Marshall's life sure has changed from the days when Rose was home and they sat around watching "Gilligan's Island" and "The Beverly Hillbillies" together. Why did she have to leave like that, anyway? Would things get better if she suddenly came back?

—*Colleen Stinson*

Sadako
By Eleanor Coerr
(Notables)

I was only a baby when the atom bomb was dropped on my city, but I can still remember the horrible flash and the terrible heat. The bomb turned Hiroshima into a desert, killing countless people at once, including my grandmother. Every year since then the entire city has celebrated Peace Day, in memory of those who died in the blast. I used to enjoy the celebration, but I'm not so sure that I'll ever take part in it again. You see, one day while I was running (and how I love to run!) I fell, for what seemed like no reason at all. But when the doctor examined me, it turned out there *was* a reason—an awful reason. He said I have leukemia, a sickness we call the atom-bomb disease because so many people in Hiroshima developed it as an after-effect of the bomb's radiation.

Ever since then I've been in the hospital. I was really worried at first that I'd die. But then my best friend came to visit me and reminded me of the legend that says that if a sick person folds a thousand paper cranes, the gods will grant that person's wish and make her well again. Have you ever seen a paper crane? They're really simple to make . . . just a bit of cutting and folding. So right away I started to make the paper birds. And each time I finish one, I wish that I'll get better. I've already made more than a hundred, and I won't stop till I reach a thousand! Yes, I'm still in the hospital, but I haven't lost hope. I *must* get better, I *must*!

—Sister M. Anna Falbo, CSSF

Scooter
By Vera B. Williams
(Notables)

[Write the key letters for the acrostics on the blackboard or on posterboard before beginning. Complete the lines as you do the talk.]

E lana Rose Rosen
L oves
A crostics.
N ew York, New York, is her new home. An
A crobat, she
R ides
O n her
S cooter
E very day.
R espected and liked by all the kids (except Jimmy Beck)
O n Melon Hill,
S he,
E lana Rose Rosen,
N ever knew life would be so good in her new home.

It's hard moving to a new home in a new city. Elana misses her old house, her grandparents, and her cousin Nanette. But she soon discovers that life in an eighth-floor, one-room apartment can be grand once you have good friends of all ages, a scooter, and a field day at the end of summer to look forward to.

S ee Elana Rose Rosen,
C haracter extraordinare,
O vercoming obstacles,
O pening doors, and
T aking chances.
E lana Rose Rosen—she's a
R eally special kid!

—Diantha McCauley

Scorpions
By Walter Dean Myers
(Edwards)

Everything's going wrong for Jamal. At school, the teachers are leaning on him, and the class bully keeps harassing him. They've had fight after fight, and usually Jamal gets the worst of it. This probably wouldn't be happening if Jamal's big brother were around, but Randy's in prison now, for his part in a gang holdup, and Mama says she can't afford an appeal. Then Randy sends word to Jamal, telling him to get in touch with his old lieutenant Mack and through him take control of Randy's gang, the Scorpions—a gang that can make a lot of money delivering crack.

Jamal really doesn't want to get involved with this, but his brother needs the dough, so Jamal decides to check out the situation. Maybe he can use it to get money out of his mother.

Mack is a scary guy. He's totally loyal to Randy but he's on a crack high half the time. He gives Jamal a gun—Jamal will need it, he says, to impress the other Scorpions and establish his right to be in charge. It doesn't take long for Jamal to realize how much power that gun gives him, or to figure out other places where that kind of power might be useful. As the pressures mount on Jamal, his life is changed by the power of the gun. Will he be able to survive the school, the street, the Scorpions—and the threat of the gun in his hand?

—Helen Schlichting

Shadow Boxer
By Chris Lynch
(BBYA, QP, SLJ/C)

George was nine the first time he made his father bleed—and his father was delighted, because that meant that George was catching on. See, George's dad was a boxer, a pro, and he was determined to teach his oldest son some important lessons. First, know how to fight, so that you can always protect yourself, and second, know when to walk away, because some fights are not worth getting into. Another thing that wasn't worth getting into, according to George's father, was the professional ring—the injuries he'd suffered there were literally killing him. In fact, by the time George was ten, his father was dead.

Now, five years later, George feels it's time to pass his father's lessons on to his younger brother. And that's going to be difficult, because Monty doesn't remember much about their dad. He doesn't remember the injuries their father had to live with, the fractured bones, the internal hemorrhages. He doesn't remember how their father would wince when you hugged him tight. All Monty can see is the glory of being a prizefighter. Already he's sneaking off to the gym to work out—he's determined to become a competitor. He's contacted the uncle who used to arrange fights for his father, and Uncle says that Monty's a natural. George knows what the life of a boxer could do to his little brother. Can he convince Monty of what his father learned the hard way: that sometimes there is more glory in walking away?

—*Helen Schlichting*

Shadow Man
By Cynthia D. Grant
(BBYA)

He would cast a shadow over a lot of lives in the small town of Willow Creek—over Francis McCloud, his alcoholic and abusive father, who realized his mistakes too late to do anything about them; over Katherine McCloud, his mother, blinded to her children's needs by her own anger and bitterness; over his brothers David and Gerald, too deep in the cesspool of drugs and violence to notice or care.

There were others in the town who grieved for him—Donald Morrison, for instance, whom he'd stood up for when it counted; Carolyn Sanders, the teacher who'd seen that he still had a chance; and Tom Dawson, the rescue worker, who knew him for a good kid, no matter how rotten the rest of the McClouds might be. And then . . . and then there was Jennie. Jennie was always there for him. She loved him, and she thought he loved her.

But Gabriel McCloud couldn't overcome the pain of his upbringing. One night he drank too much and smashed his truck into a tree. He never knew what he left behind, when he became a shadow man.

—*Cara A. Waits*

Shadow of the Dragon
By Sherry Garland
(BBYA)

Sometimes Danny Vo feels as though he's living in two different worlds. He and his family arrived in the United States ten years ago as Vietnamese refugees, and Danny has spent much of the time since learning how to fit in with his new country—trying (for one thing) to get people to understand that he's not a Vietcong or a member of a criminal gang or a homesick person dying to go back to his native land. In fact, after ten years, Danny's ties to America are much stronger than his memories of Vietnam. But his grandmother is always reminding him of his heritage—she thinks he's "too American"—and now Danny's met a girl who's probably going to think he's too Vietnamese. Tiffany Marie Schultz is the only girl Danny's ever wanted to date, but he hasn't quite worked up the courage to ask her out.

Meanwhile, Danny's family is preparing to welcome his cousin Sang Le to their home. Sang Le, who's a little older than Danny, had a very hard time as a prisoner in a Communist "re-education" camp and as a refugee in Hong Kong. Danny knows that life has been brutal for Sang Le, but life can be rough in the US too, especially for someone as bitter and desperate as Sang Le. After his experiences in the camps, Sang Le will do anything, legal or illegal, to get to the top, and it is soon obvious to Danny that his cousin has been recruited into a Vietnamese gang. At the same time, Danny learns that his friendship with Tiffany Marie could be dangerous, for her brother is deeply involved with a white supremacist gang of skinheads. Danny is caught between the ugliest, angriest aspects of both his worlds. Can he protect himself? Can he protect those he loves?

—*Helen Schlichting*

Shakedown Street
By Jonathan Nasaw
(QP)

Caro and her mother are homeless, and they share their lives with an assortment of unusual people—Rass, Rudy, Wharf Rat, Arthur, and Marthur. In the summer, they find shelter under an expressway bridge in San Francisco, and Caro discovers she has to do some ugly things to survive. While Momma goes out to look for a job, Caro learns how to panhandle, where to find the best garbage, and how to steal.

When the rainy season comes and the authorities shoo them off the Bay City streets, Rudy finds an old abandoned house in Berkeley, and the gang moves in. They jury-rig the electricity and water to make the place livable, and Caro even ends up in school, where she runs into her old friend Teri. Things are actually looking up. If Momma can hold her job through the winter, they can move into a real apartment and live like everyone else.

Who could have known that the owner of the house they'd taken over would get an eviction order and try to kick them out on Christmas Eve? Who knew that in the confusion, Caro would get separated from her mom and everyone else who cares for her, and end up back in San Francisco dressed for street business?

Things just have to get better, don't they? Well, maybe they do and maybe they don't. What would you do if you were homeless? Maybe you'd have to move to Shakedown Street.

—Susan Trimby

Shelter
By Monte Merrick
(BBYA)

Shelter, that's what a home is supposed to be, and I always thought that's what my home was—until the summer after eighth grade.

It seemed like a normal summer at first. I had to watch my four-year-old sister, Maude, but only half days. That left me plenty of time to read and write (I want to be a writer when I grow up) and to join my friends Cat and Tim in our on-going investigation. Cat had decided that some neighbors down the block had murdered their retarded son and buried his body in their basement, so we were keeping watch on their house. Once we had some real evidence, we'd take it to the police.

So summer was going great until my mother told me that I had to watch my sister all day long. More than all day; I was responsible for Maude from the time she woke up until she fell asleep at night, Monday through Friday. Not only did this cut into my time for reading, writing, and investigating, but Maude was not an easy child to entertain. For instance, one of her favorite places to play was on the grounds of the local crematorium, where she could watch the swans on the pond.

This was the summer I got drunk and played poker with my friends. This was the summer I broke into a house and got caught. This was the summer I met my first girlfriend, and the summer my parents decided to get a divorce. This was the summer when I first took responsibility for my own actions and my own life, not because I wanted to, but because I had to. I am Nelson Jaqua, and this was the summer of 1962.

—*Cynthia L. Lopuszynski*

The Shining Face
By Harold Lawrence Myra
(VOYA/SF)

Four young blind people are carrying a light down, down, into the darkness of the subterranean world of Aliare.

Aliare is a complete world, a world of eternal night. Most of its people, who have never seen a light before, will be frightened by the searing brightness that Mela and her friends have brought to the underworld. They will seek to destroy the light-bearers, to extinguish their lives, to sacrifice them and restore the familiar dark. But a few will wonder: is Mela is the blind princess that prophets have foretold, the one who is destined to lead the people up and out of darkness, into a world of day?

If Mela is that princess, she doesn't know it—yet. She's just hoping she can get out of this alive.

—*Carol Kappelmann*

Shizuko's Daughter
By Kyoko Mori
(BBYA)

Yuki found her mother, Shizuko, lying unconscious on the kitchen floor. Before she could call for help, her mother was dead, leaving Yuki with only her memories and a suicide note for consolation. "I love you," the note said. "Be strong. Don't let my death keep you from becoming your very best self. I love you."

But Yuki needed more than that pledge of love. She desperately needed someone to care for her right now, someone alive who could help her become her best self. Yuki and Shizuko had always been so close, had done so much together. Now her mother was gone, a victim of too much sorrow. And her father, who barely spoke to Yuki, was marrying a woman who would hate Shizuko's daughter.

"You must go on," her mother had said. "Remember that I love you."

I must go on, thought Yuki. But how do I go on without love?

—*Sister M. Anna Falbo, CSSF*

A Short Walk Around the Pyramids and Through the World of Art
By Philip M. Isaacson
(BBYA)

What is Art? Is it a pyramid whose stones glow a rosy pink as the sun rises? Is it a temple with tall, stately columns holding up the roof? Is it a gigantic mobile whose thin, flat, triangular forms respond to the slightest breeze? Is it a canvas covered with squares of paint, bits of color that don't add up to any discernible object? Can it be a neon sign, a photograph, a chair? Yes—art can be all of the above! How can you tell when something's art? Well, reading this book is like putting on a pair of magic glasses. The author is your tour guide, and he will open your eyes to the beauty, emotion, and truth that can be seen in color, shape, light, shadows, stone, metal, paint, and glass. Take his "short walk"—it may take you farther than you've ever imagined.

—*Maureen Whalen*

Singer to the Sea God
By Vivien Alcock
(BBYA)

I'd heard the stories, the hero tales and the intrigues of the gods on far-away Mount Olympus, but never did I think to take them seriously. For what was I? Only the serving boy in the small household of a petty tyrant on an insignificant Greek island. Oh, there had been much talk of our king's cynical demand that Perseus slay the Gorgon Medusa, whose face could turn a man to stone. Elders would frighten their children into obedience with threats of the return of Perseus, bearing the Gorgon's head. But no one expected to see the young lord again in this life. "It's all nonsense," my uncle, the palace cook, maintained.

Then, one fateful day, the stuff of myth became my own personal nightmare. Lord Perseus returned and, without hesitation, tore Medusa's gruesome head from its bag and showed her face to the entire room. Instantly the clatter ceased, replaced by an eerie silence which settled heavily over a gathering of statuary. I didn't grieve for the king and his lords, but my beloved sister Cleo had been serving in the room. She laughed no longer, frozen in an instant.

Chaos erupted as the servants who'd not been in the room discovered what had happened. We fled the palace, just ahead of Lord Perseus and his men. So now I travel, carrying my sister's statue with me, looking for a way to bring her back to life. I have made a sacred vow to do it, and this I will not break. Hear me, gods and monsters! I will seek and find a way, no matter what myth-come-true I must face!

—*Pamela A. Todd*

Song of Be
By Lesley Beake
(Notables)

I have just killed myself. I meant it to be quick, but when I went to stick the poison arrow into the vein in my arm, I couldn't, and the arrow tip went into the thickest part of my leg instead. Maybe, subconsciously, I wanted a little more time to think, to tell my story.

I am Be. My people are called Bushmen, and my home is in a part of Africa called Namibia. I have not lived many years, but I am not sorry to die. Too many hard things have filled my days, too many terrible memories to bear. But I still remember, even now, my happiest years with my mother, when we lived as we ought, with the other members of our tribe. All too soon word came from my grandfather asking for our help, and we left our people forever, joining him instead far away on a white man's cattle ranch, learning ways that were not our own and losing all our joy.

I am Be. I am dying. Listen to my song.

—*Sister M. Anna Falbo, CSSF*

Soul Looks Back in Wonder
Compiled by Tom Feelings
(BBYA, King Illustrator, Notables)

Look back in wonder—look back to the myths of our past. Look ahead in dreams, to the future filled with hope. The scene changes with each turn of the page, from the wide African plain to the front steps where city children play. Look at the world with wonder—past, present, future. Look with wonder through the eyes of a child.

—Pamela A. Todd and J. R. B.

Speaking Out: Teenagers Take on Race, Sex, and Identity
By Susan Kuklin
(Booklist, QP)

Hear what teenagers from a New York City high school have to say about prejudice, racism, sex, and violence. They talk about their sexual preferences and their experiences with homophobia. They get emotional when they talk about prejudice and stereotyping, especially if they're the target. They're from very different backgrounds, but they all wonder where they fit in and who they really are. Most of them love their parents but don't want to be like them. They want to be more tolerant and open about the differences among people. Mostly, they just want to be heard.

Rachel is afraid of what might happen to her if anyone finds out she's gay—she's afraid she'll get beaten up. Wai is tired of being stereotyped as a brain just because he's Chinese-American. Akilah, whose friend was shot right in front of her, has changed her mind about guns. Yung says he could *never* talk about sex with his parents. Wendy can't remember not being fat. And Ben hopes that girls will still want to go out with him even though he stutters.

If you're trying to figure out who you are, listen to what these teenagers have to say—it's not about what's right or wrong, it's about how they feel, and maybe about how you feel too.

—Bette DeBruyne Ammon

The Spirit Ring
By Lois McMaster Bujold
(VOYA/SF)

Fiametta Beneforte had the family talent for magic, but her father refused to train her to use it. After all, she was only a girl. So Fiametta taught herself by watching her father and reading his secret books on the sly. To test her abilities, she created a true-love ring. It was supposed to fit the hand of the person who would be her true love, but when she tried to give it to the handsome Captain Ochs, he wouldn't take it. Fiametta was sure the captain was her true love, and so she thought the ring had failed. She wondered if she had any magic talent at all.

Then Fiametta witnessed the Duke's murder, and she and her father had to flee for their lives. But her father was old and had a weak heart; he was no match for the armed invaders who soon caught up with them. Fiametta's father bought her freedom with his life, leaving her alone in the wilderness. She struggled on as best she could, until her father's ghost appeared to her. He told her that the invaders were using black magic and trying to enslave his spirit with their evil spells. He needed her help.

When Fiametta encountered a caravan of traders, she accidentally gave her true-love ring to one of the big, gawky mule drivers—and he couldn't take it off! She was disgusted, for this was *not* the true love she had imagined for herself. Still, Thur was kind and willing to help her. Soon Fiametta and her new companion found themselves fighting black magic, intrigue, and powerful demons. Fiametta had to master her magic talents and use them to the fullest, or she, her true love, and her entire country would perish from the power of the invaders' spirit ring.
                                                          —*Lisa M. Costich*

Split Heirs
By Lawrence Watt-Evans and Esther Friesner
(VOYA/SF)

Queen Artemisia had a major problem—besides the fact that her husband was a beer-drinking, womanizing barbarian of a Gorgorian, who had a habit of settling arguments with a sword. The queen had given birth to triplets, and according to Gorgorian tradition, a woman who borne more than one child at one time had obviously been with more than one man. The punishment for adultery was something unpleasant involving wolverines. (Most Gorgorian punishments had something to do with wolverines.) But Artemisia had a plan. Her faithful servant, old Ludmilla, would take the newborn girl and one of the boys to the queen's brother in the next kingdom. Unfortunately, Ludmilla was somewhat forgetful; she mistakenly left the girl and took off with the two baby boys, something Artemisia didn't discover until *after* she'd announced the birth of a prince to her husband and the entire kingdom. Meanwhile, Ludmilla ran into Odo the shepherd, an old friend, and while showing him some of the more interesting tricks she had learned in the city, fell over dead. Odo kept one of the boys and sold the other to a wizard in exile. So, the queen had no choice but to raise the remaining girl as Prince Arbol, although sooner or later someone was bound to find out that the prince was in fact a princess. And now what about the young shepherd and the wizard's apprentice? Odd they should look so much alike, and so very much like Prince Arbol.

—*Abbie V. Landry*

Stainless Steel Visions
By Harry Harrison
(VOYA/SF)

Stonehenge on the Salisbury Plain in England is one of the greatest mysteries of the world. Who could have built it? Was it druids? Prehistoric people? Or maybe aliens? Why was it built? And how were the huge monoliths moved into their present configuration?

Soon we will have all the answers to these questions, for Dr. Lanning and his group at MIT have developed the Chronostasis temporal recorder. This handy-dandy little machine can photograph past events as they happen. Once the machine is in place and activated, time unrolls backward past its lens. And as this "fast backward" occurs, the machine can halt the flow at any point to photograph unusual events. At last the mystery of Stonehenge will be solved—or will it?

"The Secret of Stonehenge" is just one of the short stories you'll find in *Stainless Steel Visions*, stores that span time and space, from long ago to far in the future. Meet outrageous characters, explore incredible places, and even solve the mystery of Stonehenge!

—*Linda Olson*

Stardust otel
By Paul B. Janeczko
(BBYA, QP)

My parents used to be hippies—they're veterans of the original Woodstock. Now, though, they're pretty much like every other kid's parents, except they run the hotel we live in—the Stardust otel. Sure, it's really the Stardust *H*otel, but when I was born my dad was so happy he swung on the sign and the "H" snapped off. He never replaced it, either. He says he likes to remember how he felt that day.

I'm nearly fifteen now, and used to making my home in a hotel. Fact is, I really like it. There are so many different kinds of people passing through, temporarily sharing our home. Like Charlie Hooper, who was maybe a little bit crazy; Eddie, who kept changing his name; and a guy we called "The Natural":

> Some adults called Jackie Slattery
> hot-rodder,
> wise guy,
> punk,
> but he only smirked and said,
> "At least they notice me,"
> just the way we saw girls notice
> him in overalls,
> grease streaked across the front.

As for me, Leary—well, I guess I'm not a guy anyone would notice, or at least most girls wouldn't. That's OK by me, though, 'cause I've got my eye on one girl in particular, and plenty else to do in the meantime. You see, there's always something happening in this town, somebody's always up to something. I'd tell you more now, but, like Nick says, "Half the fun is the surprise, not knowing what comes next."

See you at the Stardust otel, where you never know what will happen next.

—*Sister M. Anna Falbo, CSSF*

Note: The above poem, "The Natural," appears on page 22 of the hardcover edition.

Staying Fat For Sarah Byrnes
By Chris Crutcher
(BBYA, SLJ/C)

She always made you say her whole name, Sarah Byrnes did. She was tired of geniuses putting a pun together about her last name and her looks. An incident when she was three had left her face and hands burned beyond recognition, and her father had refused to allow any sort of reconstructive surgery. Since then she's been Sarah Byrnes, and she grinds your face into it. There's a shell around her soul now that's tougher than scar tissue, and just as ugly to look at.

She's also the best friend Eric's ever had—the only friend either of them has ever had. As a fellow outcast, he'd bonded with Sarah Byrnes in grade school. Eric, aka Moby, had been the target of every fat joke heard since Jonah met the whale, and it was only natural that he and Sarah Byrnes should find each other.

But now Sarah Byrnes is lost, lost somewhere behind her mask of scars. In the middle of class, she just went catatonic, and she hasn't spoken or acknowledged anything in weeks. During his visits to the hospital, Eric talks to her about their past, hoping to arouse some sort of reaction. He's determined to find out what happened to his friend, and eventually he does.

There is more horror in Sarah Byrnes' life than Eric has ever dreamed.

—Jeff Blair

Stephen Biesty's Incredible Cross-Sections
By Stephen Biesty and Richard Platt
(QP)

How do you imagine things so that you can really understand them? What about slicing them in half and looking at a cross-section? That's the way Stephen Beisty has presented a medieval castle, a Spanish galleon, an ocean liner, a subway, and even a space shuttle. You can find out a lot by seeing from the inside how things work. [Show drawings as you discuss the text.]

Did you know that a space shuttle has a skin of 24,192 heat-proof tiles to keep it from bursting into flame upon re-entry? Every one of those tiles has to be made separately, and no two are exactly alike. Inside the shuttle, the absence of gravity makes for some very interesting design problems! For instance, the crew have to strap themselves into bed at night so they won't float around while they're sleeping. When they wash up, they have to use a special device to keep the water going in one direction. And they must exercise every day or their hearts will weaken, so there has to be a place in the shuttle somewhere for gymnastics.

Nobody gave that much thought to the crewmen on a sixteenth-century galleon. Galleons were large sailing ships, large enough to cross the Atlantic. But it took them a long time to do it, and there were no places to stop along the way, so each ship had to load up with enough food and water for the entire voyage. Sailors on these ships received twenty-five ounces of bread and nine ounces of meat a day (that's about two QuarterPounders, only the meat wasn't fresh; it was salted, dried, smoked—or rotten). Every sailor also got a quart of fresh water (which didn't seem like much on a hot day), and no more, unless there was a lucky shower of rain. As for exercise, the whole ship was like a gym: the sailors had to climb ropes, haul sails up and down, hang on for dear life when a storm hit, and repair all the damage after the storm was over.

Take a look inside a galleon, a space shuttle, a castle, and a train in *Stephen Biesty's Incredible Cross-Sections.*

—*Linda Olson*

The Stones of Muncaster Cathedral
By Robert Westall
(QP)

Name's Joe Clarke, an' I had in mind to tell ya the story of fixing up the southwest tower of the Muncaster Cathedral. That was the first time I'd ever worked on a cathedral, and it'll be the last—but I'm gettin' ahead of myself.

I was pleased as punch the day we got that call sayin' the cathedral job was ours. Our crew was used to doin' chimneys, not too much sweat, drop it in a day, make about $400. But the spire of a cathedral—then you know you're a real steeplejack, big time. Me and my family been steeplejacks for five generations. Heights don't scare us—I went up my first chimney when I was four. It's like playtime to me.

But there was something wrong with the Muncaster job from the beginning. That one horrific gargoyle on the tower—what a hideous face! One of my lads fell from that tower, and my own son, Kevin, started walking in his sleep. There were too many unexplained accidents: knots I knew I'd tied, somehow becoming untied, and every time I put the chisel to the stone I would hear the crying of children. At first I thought it was just the wind, but then I found out different. There was a smell and a feeling of evil that swirled around the tower, an evil comin' from deep within the stones, an evil that almost trapped me—and Kevin—forever.

—*Susan Trimby*

Strange Objects
By Gary Crew
(VOYA/SF)

Lovecraft once wrote, "There are strange objects in the great abyss, and the seeker of dreams must take care not to stir up, or meet, the wrong ones. . . . "

Steven was not careful. Almost as soon as he saw the ring, he claimed it for his own, and ghosts from the past reached out to take possession.

Steven was not careful, and he had to pay the price.

—*J. R. B.*

The Stranger
By Caroline B. Cooney
(QP)

She's a beauty, he's a beast and they're in love. Sound familiar? It should be a simple story, but it isn't. When Nicoletta first catches sight of the mysterious boy, she's instantly attracted. But Jethro has a terrible secret, and he doesn't want to get involved with anyone. Nicoletta's attraction becomes an obsession, and she follows Jethro to a deserted cave on the outskirts of town. He pleads with her. He tells her, "Don't come back . . . not ever!" What is he trying to hide? Will she stay away? Remember, she's a beauty, he's a beast . . . and they're in love. You may think you know the ending . . . but you don't!

—*Bette DeBruyne Ammon*

Striking Out
By Will Weaver
(BBYA)

Billy was eight and Robert twelve when tragedy changed their lives forever. Robert's life ended. And Billy would never forget, because it was his fault that Robert died.

Sure, he was just a kid, just eight years old. He didn't have the good sense that comes with maturity. He just wanted to do the fun things that his brother Robert could do, like driving the harvest tractor. That would be a lot more fun than cleaning out the hot and dusty hayloft.

Finally Robert let him ride with him, then steer, then try shifting gears. But it was hard for an eight-year-old. Suddenly the tractor lurched, jerked, and forged forward. In an instant, Robert was gone, over the side, between the tractor and the disk.

Suddenly Robert was dead.

What would happen to the Baggs family now? Could Billy ever learn to live with his guilt? Could he ever forgive himself?

—*Carol Kappelmann*

The Sunita Experiment
By Mitali Perkins
(QP)

Sunita Sen—Sunni to her friends—doesn't want to be different. She wants to be just like the other girls in her eighth-grade class, and she especially wants to spend more time with Michael Morrison, now that he's finally noticed her. She thinks she's doing pretty well, until disaster strikes.

Sunni can tell you exactly when her whole life fell apart. It happened the minute her grandparents arrived in California from India. Now her mother has stopped wearing Western clothes and only dresses in saris. They eat curry all the time—no more pizza. And worst of all, her father has told Sunni not to invite any boys over to the house while her grandparents are visiting—and that means for a *whole year*!

Didu, Sunni's grandmother, can't seem to stop criticizing Sunni or talking about how much better everything is in India—that is, when she's not watching soap operas to help her learn "American." Grandfather Dadu is better; Sunni actually enjoys spending time with him working in the garden, but she's afraid her friends will think he's weird and laugh at her.

Sunni wishes life could be more predictable. She feels like the subject of some crazy experiment: mix two cultures, Indian and American, and see what you get. So far, it feels like a disaster!

—*Donna L. Scanlon*

Susan Butcher and the Iditarod Trail
By Ellen M. Dolan
(QP)

Imagine racing over a thousand miles of ice and snow behind a dogsled in a land where temperatures can drop to fifty degrees below zero, winds can reach sixty miles an hour, and snowdrifts can pile up thirty feet high. Imagine doing this not out of necessity, but for sport, and you have the story of *Susan Butcher and the Iditarod Trail.*

The Iditarod race had its beginnings in 1925, when the contagious disease diphtheria broke out in Nome, a gold-rush town on the northwest coast of Alaska. The closest supply of serum was in Anchorage, almost a thousand miles to the southeast, and the only way to get the medicine to Nome was by dogsled. The journey usually took at least twenty-five days, but brave teams of Alaskan men and dogs miraculously made the journey in just five days, seven and a half hours.

The first Iditarod Trail dogsled race was held almost fifty years later, in 1973. It took the thirty-four entrants twenty days to complete. In 1990, when Susan Butcher won her fourth Iditarod, she crossed the finish line in the record-breaking time of eleven days, one hour, fifty-three minutes and thirty-nine seconds, and won $50,000. And even after that, she made this grueling trip eleven more times! Find out more about the toughest race in the world as you travel with Susan Butcher over the Iditarod Trail.

—*Marianne Tait Pridemore*

The Switching Well
By Peni R. Griffin
(SLJ/C, VOKA/SF)

Have you ever wondered what life was like a hundred years ago, or what it might be like a hundred years in the future? Have you ever made a wish at a wishing well and had it come true? Ada and Amber make wishes that come true, and change their lives forever. They both live in San Antonio, Texas, but they live a hundred years apart. One day at an old well in a haunted lot they each throw in a piece of candy and make a wish—a wish that comes true!

Ada Bauer lives in 1891. She's angry about all the things she can't do because she's a girl. She has to care for her younger brother and sister, while her older brother does whatever he likes. Ada thinks that society is unfair because it traps women with large families, makes them wear fashions that cripple their bodies, and lays down laws that cripple their wills. Ada wishes she lived a hundred years in the future. Surely by then things would be better than they are now!

Amber Burak lives in 1991. She has just found out that her parents are splitting up. Living in a society shadowed by violence and drugs, with parents who are always busy with their own problems, Amber wishes she could go back a hundred years, to a time when mothers didn't go off to work and nobody got divorced. Surely life was calmer and sweeter back then.

Both Ada's and Amber's wishes come true, leading them into adventures they never imagined possible. Join them at the Switching Well.

—*Linda Olson*

Sworn Enemies
By Carol Matas
(QP)

It was a dangerous time to be a Jew in Russia. The Czar had ordered a draft of Jewish boys for military service—a twenty-five-year hitch in the Russian army. By the time those boys came home (*if* they came home at all), they wouldn't be boys anymore but grizzled old veterans, and they probably wouldn't be Jews either, for the army had brutal ways of converting young draftees. Jewish parents were terrified. They tried to hide their sons, so kidnappers were employed to seize the required number of children. Parents who could, paid fat bribes to the kidnappers to look the other way.

Perhaps Aaron should have worried, but he felt secure. He was a bright young scholar, whom the rabbi valued and the whole community admired. That gave him some protection from the imperial draft. Moreover, his father, a prosperous businessman, could be counted on to do everything in his power to safeguard his son's future. Aaron felt very lucky: he could go on with his life of study, even in these dangerous times, and in a few months he would marry Miriam, whom he already loved. All the arrangements had been made.

But someone else had other plans. Zev had always resented Aaron's intelligence and his special relationship with the rabbi. He was furious when he learned that Aaron was engaged to Miriam, the girl he wanted for himself. As a licensed kidnapper, Zev had the means to remove his rival forever: he would capture Aaron and hand him over to the army.

In spite of their common heritage, Zev was Aaron's sworn enemy. Would Aaron survive the plot to take away his future—and perhaps his life?

—*Helen Schlichtling*

T-Backs, T-Shirts, COAT and Suit
By E. L. Konigsburg
(SLJ/C)

Who would have thought that such a little thing could create such a scandal? And it *is* a little thing, too, the T-back swim suit. It's skimpier than a string bikini—just two strips of cloth that form a T across your rear end. With most of your skin exposed, there isn't much left to the imagination. The front of the suit and the top (when worn) are equally revealing.

The first day the competition showed up in a T-back, Chloe's aunt Bernadette knew there was going to be trouble, but she couldn't have known how much. Until that day, the lunch-wagon business Chloe was helping her aunt with over the summer had been hard work but lots of fun. Now customers were abandoning Bernadette's wagon and flocking to the vendors who offered extra exposure. As more and more vendors all over town put on the T-backs, pressure was on for Bernadette and Chloe to conform to the new "dress code." So far, Bernadette had remained steadfast in her decision not to wear the suit, although she didn't seem to mind if anyone else did—a live-and-let-live attitude guaranteed to annoy the town's Moral Majority, now organizing a campaign to ban all T-backs forever.

Where is Bernadette at, anyway? Why won't she either put on the suit or join the outcry against it? Some people are starting to whisper that she's a witch! Can Chloe straighten this out and help save her aunt's business? Or will she uncover secrets her aunt has been hiding for years?

—*Jeff Blair*

The Tale of the Body Thief
By Anne Rice
(VOYA/SF)

Vampire Lestat here. Back again to tell you about a very strange but intriguing encounter I had with a body thief I met in Miami—Vampire City—not long ago. You ask, "What's a body thief?" Well, it's someone who has the power to take over and live within the body of another, often without his or her permission. The body thief I encountered was trying to tempt me to switch physical beings with him. His offer was very attractive, for I had the chance to enter the body of a young, vital, mortal man. It was something I'd been dreaming of—I'd grown weary of a life of sucking blood. Dreams have a way of coming true . . . but all that is part of the story, so let's begin.

—*Barbara Bahm*

Talking to Dragons
By Patricia C. Wrede
(VOYA/SF)

Daystar's mother had taught him many useful skills—things like reading, writing, sword-fighting, and even a little magic. But the most important thing she'd ever taught him was to be polite—*always*. Because when you live alone with your mother in a cottage on the edge of the Enchanted Forest, you can never be too sure who's going to come wandering by. I mean, there'll be wizards, elves, heroes on quests, princes in disguise, all sorts of travelers, and you should be very nice to all of them. Even dragons. *Particularly* dragons. You see, dragons have rather complicated rules of etiquette, and if a dragon thinks you are being rude or insulting, it eats you. Which is what any self-respecting dragon would have done to the last wizard who came by Daystar's cottage. This wizard didn't even bother to knock. He just touched his magical staff to the front door, shattering it into a thousand pieces, and walked in. (Very rude!) The wizard marched up to Daystar's mother and snarled, "Well, I've finally found you. Now I'll have the sword—and the boy too!" Daystar's mother didn't seem very worried. "Took you long enough," she replied, and then she pointed a finger at the wizard. He began to melt. "Oh, no, not again!" he screamed, as his legs began to dissolve. "I'll be back. I'll get you! I'll . . . glug, glug." There was nothing left of the wizard except a puddle of brown goo on the floor. Daystar was impressed. He'd never known his mother could do anything like that. But she was all business now. She brought out a sword, buckled it around Daystar's waist, and told him he'd have to leave. He wasn't to come back until he'd found out what the sword was and what it could do. When Daystar objected, she reminded him that it wasn't polite to question your mother. The next thing he knew, his mother had zapped him into the middle of the Enchanted Forest.

Pursued by a pack of angry wizards, Daystar's only allies are a hot-tempered young fire-witch, a know-it-all lizard, and a half-grown, fire-sneezing dragon with an allergy.

—Bob Johnson

A Taste of Salt: A Story of Modern Haiti
By Frances Temple
(Addams)

Words are very powerful. They can make you feel extremely happy, or they can pierce your soul and hurt you deeply. They can bring about change, as they did through the sermons and speeches of Father Jean-Bertrand Aristide. Father Aristide's words helped bring democracy to Haiti after years of dictatorial rule. Words can also record history in the making. Djo was an aide to Father Aristide, or Titid as he's known to his followers, and in his own words he has recorded his experiences as one of Titid's boys.

"Titid says I can no longer be his bodyguard, since my own body is so broken. Until it is fit again, I can no longer be useful in that way. But Titid says that it is not only the body, with its feet and hands and strong back, that can be useful. He says the mind and spirit are useful too, and that mine are still strong, despite the blows. Titid says that for this work of storytelling, I am fit. . . . Titid has invited someone to my bedside to listen to my story. He says each time I sleep, I will remember, and when I wake, I must tell everything to the man who brings the tape recorder.

"I think Titid is afraid I will die altogether, like Lally, like Marcel. And if I tell my story to the tape-recorder man, whoever he be, then I will not die entirely. Titid loves me. Also Titid is a politician. He knows how to use stories to make things happen, to make the way of the world change. And I am Titid's helper, one of his boys. I am still one of Titid's team."

And so begins Djo's story. Hear the rest of it in *A Taste of Salt*.

—Linda Olson

Note: The passage in quotes is adapted from the hardcover edition.

A Taste of Smoke
By Marion Dane Bauer
(QP)

Over a hundred years ago, on September 1, 1894, a devastating fire roared through the booming lumber town of Hinckley, Minnesota. The fire had begun in the surrounding forests; it gathered strength and speed in the dry woods and closed in on the town itself. By the time it was over, 500 square miles of virgin timber and at least 413 people had been reduced to ashes—the death toll was never exact because no one knew how many Ojibwa hunters had been caught by the flames in the forest.

There were heroes, of course. Great disasters can make heroes of otherwise ordinary folk.

Thomas Dunn, a telegraph operator at Hinckley, stayed at his post, trying to warn others of the approaching fire-storm. The final message he tapped out was, "I have stayed too long. . . . "

William Best, a railroad engineer, saved 350 lives. He held his train at the station until the very last minute, so that people could climb aboard, and then raced through the inferno to safety. The tracks were already burning.

A fifteen-year-old orphan had been left in charge of the lumber mill when the rest of the workers were sent home to get their families and help fight the fire. The boy had been told to blow the whistle if the fire threatened the mill itself, so that the men could return to save it. But by the time the fire reached the mill, the rest of the town was ablaze, and those still alive had fled to the train. The boy, faithful to his duty, blew the whistle. The 350 people on the train heard it, but the train was pulling out. There was no one left to save the mill . . . or the boy.

As Caitlin sat in the Hinckley Museum watching the film about the fire, she couldn't stop thinking about that boy. How frightened and alone he must have felt! She was still thinking about him that evening, when she met a strange young man named Frank on the bicycle path through the woods. As Caitlin got to know Frank better, she realized that he *was* the boy from the fire—he was a ghost! Why had he appeared? What did he want from her?

—*Linda Olson*

Tell Me Everything
By Carolyn Coman
(Notables, QP, SLJ/C)

No one really understood what was going on with Roz. She wasn't doing well in school. That wasn't too surprising; when her uncle enrolled her, the school had decided to hold her back a year because she'd been schooled mostly at home and wasn't up to her age level. But she wasn't making any friends, either. She kept pretty much to herself.

At her new home, though, Roz seemed to be adjusting fairly well. And Mike, her uncle, was getting used to having his sister's twelve-year-old daughter living with him.

But there was a lot going on that no one, least of all Roz, understood. There were the dreams that left both Mike and Roz sleepless for the rest of the night. There were the phone calls Roz felt compelled to make to Nate several times a week, even though she always hung up when he answered.

Sooner or later, she'd have to get up the courage to talk to Nate. He was the only one who might have the answers to her questions. Roz had to find out what had happened the day her mother died. Why had her mother, an experienced climber, fallen to her death? And the only person who could answer her questions was Nate, because only Nate had seen her fall.

—*Carol Kappelmann*

The Testing
By Charles Oberndorf
(VOYA/SF)

It was the ultimate test, and every senior had to go through it. The dreamchair led them through three life-like scenarios, and, based on their reactions to each one, decided how morally pure the students were, and whether they were worthy of a place at the university. The seniors planned and practiced, thought about what they would do in real life, and what they knew they had to do to get the "Highly Recommended" rating they were all working towards.

By Monday, there was nothing left to do or say. The time for testing had arrived.

The seniors got up one at a time for their appointments and went to the gym, where they were strapped into the chair. The scenarios began, and the students responded. Afterwards, some emerged relieved, others white-faced and quiet. They went on with their lives, but in some way all had been changed.

How big a role can society play in deciding whether you have the correct moral outlook and, depending on that, what you can do with the rest of your life? Follow Karl to the testing room and find out.

—*J. R. B.*

There Will Be Wolves
By Karleen Bradford
(Canadian YA)

After three days of imprisonment Ursula was led to the Church of St. Martin. It was in the courtyard of this church that criminals were tried and witches burned.

The courtyard was filled with townspeople, and the Archbishop of Cologne was there to act as her judge. At first Ursula felt hopeful, but her hope died quickly as, one by one, the townspeople stepped forward to testify against her. Oh, what lies they told: "She cursed me like a demon," "I saw her turn herself into a cat," and "She used a godly book to cure a dog." How they twisted the truth! And the archbishop himself believed them!

"She is a witch," he ruled. "She will be burned."

Ursula shook with fear at the thought of burning at the stake. She was innocent, but she had been sentenced to death. It was 1096 A. D., and Ursula had only one chance at freedom, only one way to escape a horrible death by fire. And that was to join the Holy Crusade, to march with thousands of others to Jerusalem, to brave a journey filled with danger and privation in order to be pardoned of sins she hadn't committed.

Read *There Will Be Wolves* and join Ursula as she struggles to survive.

—*Sister M. Anna Falbo, CSSF*

Thor
By Wayne Smith
(BBYA)

Thor feels important being a member of the Pack. He isn't the leader (Thor knows that Dad is in charge), but he's definitely got a higher position than the kids, for he is the Pack's protector. Thor relishes the days that Dad spends with the Pack, since something special usually happens on those days. The day that Dad said they were going to Uncle Ted's, Thor was immediately excited. Uncle Ted was always fun, and Thor looked forward to seeing him. But when they arrived at Uncle Ted's, Thor felt that something was different and that that something was very wrong and very dangerous. He sensed a Bad Thing at Uncle Ted's—a very Bad Thing. That entire day Thor was on full alert, ready to protect the pack from whatever it was that he sensed. He only relaxed after they'd left Uncle Ted's, and left the Bad Thing far behind.

A few days later, Uncle Ted moved in with the family. Thor immediately sensed that the Bad Thing was back, and that somehow it was part of Uncle Ted. It's something very dangerous, and it can kill. Thor knows that it's his job to protect the Pack from this evil. Still, Thor is torn—Uncle Ted is a member of the family too. How can Thor strike out at the evil without doing the unforgivable, destroying a member of the Pack? As the evil gets closer, Thor knows he must do all he can to protect his human family, to save them from the evil they don't even suspect. It is Thor against the Bad Thing, the thing Uncle Ted has become. Who will be the winner?

—Helen Schlichting

The Tiger Orchard
By Joyce Sweeney
(BBYA)

Eighteen-year-old Zack has terrible nightmares. They always follow the same pattern. He smells gasoline and sees a shadowy figure waiting in the darkness, just beyond reach. And then there is the tiger orchard, where apple trees loom up on both sides of him and tigers sit in the branches of every tree. He knows if he makes one wrong move they will spring from the trees and tear him to pieces.

His therapist, Nancy, says some part of his mind is trying to send him a message, but Zack is too scared to hear it. But one day the message will come clear, and Zack will remember the truth—the truth his mother has concealed all these years, the truth that will finally set him free.

—*Marianne Tait Pridemore*

Timothy of the Cay
By Theodore Taylor
(BBYA)

"On August 14, 1916 the . . . *Hannah Gumbs* (home port, St. Thomas, Virgin Islands) put out to sea past Rupert Rock and Muhlenfels Point, turning south off Buck Island, with eight passengers and mixed cargo bound for St. Johns, Antigua. . . .

"Standing at her wheel near the taffrail, the rail over her stern, steering her, was Timothy, a huge grin on his face. On his head was a cap, a gift of Charlie Bottle. The gold-thread letters said *Captain*."

He had made it. Ever since he'd first shipped out, at fourteen, he'd had one goal in mind: to be captain of his own boat. Over the years he'd worked hard. He'd learned all he could about sailing, about the sea and the weather. And he'd saved all he could from his wages, until now, at last, he was Captain of the *Hannah Gumbs*.

What Timothy hadn't planned on was a torpedo. It struck when they were well out to sea, hit the boat dead-on, and blew it to pieces. Timothy washed up on a cay—a small island—with two other survivors: a blinded white boy named Phillip and a shell-shocked cat. That's the story of *The Cay*; this is the story of what happened to Timothy before, and what happened to Phillip afterwards.

—*Linda Olson*

To the Top of the World:
Adventures with Arctic Wolves
By Jim Brandenburg
(BBYA, QP, SLJ/C)

What's the best way to observe the lifestyle of a pack of wolves? Keep a *very* low profile; make sure they don't observe *you*. And if the wolves leave something lying around, like a bloody chunk of caribou, don't move it, not even to get a better camera angle. A wolf might *have* to notice you if you messed with dinner.

These are things that Jim Brandenburg learned as he followed and photographed a pack of wolves inside the Arctic Circle. He got some great pictures out of the many hours he spent patiently waiting for a particular shot, and he grew emotionally attached the animals as well.

In the pack Jim studied, each wolf had a different chore to do. Not every wolf was a great hunter. Some were better at babysitting—really! When the pack went off on a hunt, one adult male would stay with the pups. Jim called him Scruffy. Scruffy was a natural playmate. He'd tumble with the pups and chase them in a rough kind of wolf tag. He'd let them climb rocks, though never too far from the den. If he had to, Scruffy could snarl and bare his teeth to bring the pups back into line. Jim got an amazing picture of the Scruffy snarl [show picture].

It's a big country up there in the Far North; tundra blossoms in the spring, mountains cut a jagged horizon, and massive chunks of ice break off and float in the cold Arctic Sea. Jim covered a lot of untamed territory following his wolf pack. Once he had to drive for hours in search of the wolves on a hunt. He found them stalking a herd of musk of oxen across a valley. The scene was one of brutality and survival, and Jim captured it all on film.

When the wolves weren't hunting, sleeping, or playing, they loved to climb. They climbed to the tops of tundra hills, or went poking in and out of huge rock formations. But their favorite climbing-place was probably a rugged ice floe. Perched on the jagged peaks of ice and snow, a wolf could survey the whole world, and no other creature could follow. Over the months Jim earned the acceptance of the wolves, but he always knew that, when they headed for the ice, he'd never be able to follow.

—Mark Anderson

Toning the Sweep
By Angela Johnson
(BBYA, King, Notables, SLJ/C)

"You have to try everything if you want to live in this world." Those are Ola's words to her granddaughter, Emmie. And Emmie is willing to give nearly everything a try during this, her fourteenth summer. As usual she is visiting Ola at her home in the desert. But this time when the summer is over, Ola will come back to Cleveland to stay with Emmie and her mother, because Ola is now very ill. So, to make the most of their last summer in the West, Emmie borrows a camcorder, and videotapes everything about the desert and the grandmother she loves: Ola in her yellow hat at home, the laughing aunts who come to visit, and the old Buick Ola drove away from Alabama to her new home in the desert after her husband was lynched. It's this car that Emmie secretly takes out at night to practice her driving. And it's during this summer that Emmie and her grandmother come to terms with living and dying.

—*Bette DeBruyne Ammon*

The TV Guidance Counselor
By A. C. LeMieux
(BBYA)

His life was really screwed up. His dad had left. Not just left as in "moved out"; not just left as in "divorced"; not even left as in "moved to another part of the country." Michael's dad had left on a cruise ship sailing around the world, and he wasn't planning on ever coming back.

Life at home—if you could still call it a home—was the pits. The apartment was tiny. Michael slept on the couch, Mom and Amanda slept in the only bedroom. Tunafish was the meal of the day—every day.

School wasn't much better. Michael just couldn't seem to get it together. Pressure was coming from every direction.

Then came the day when he stood on the bridge, threw his camera over the edge into the river, and followed it.

—*Carol Kappelmann*

Twelve Days in August
By Liza Ketchum Murrow
(QP)

It was obvious from the first day that the new kid was one hell of a soccer player. He moved like a dancer on the field—chest-dropping passes, rolling then down his thighs, dribbling like the ball was glued to his foot. Watching from the sidelines, Todd could see the starting position that he'd been dreaming about all summer slipping away.

It was obvious too that this new kid from California—Alex—was not going to be real popular with the rest of the team, particularly not with Randy Tovitch and his pals. Even on that first day, Todd could hear them talking about how Alex had to be some kind of fag, and how they'd all better watch out in the showers. That wasn't what Todd was worried about; he just wanted a chance to play on the soccer team himself.

But by now he's wondering, *what* team? Tovitch and his crew are so determined to get rid of Alex, they're virtually sabotaging his plays, regardless of what that does to the team's prospects. Todd finds himself caught in the middle, and he doesn't know what to do about it—or about Alex's twin sister, a definitely interesting girl. A lot of decisions and *not* a lot of time . . . who would have thought that twelve days could make so much difference?

—*Jeff Blair*

Twilight
By Peter James
(VOYA/SF)

Reporter Kate Hemingway finally finagled a way to observe the exhumation of Sally Donaldson's grave. She was intrigued by the newspaper articles about strange noises that were reportedly coming from the grave. So, with a little charm and, of course, bribery, she managed to land a place among the select few witnessing the opening of the coffin.

"They paused, then lifted the lid clear and took a step back with it, shock widening their eyes. They seemed to freeze for a moment and Kate stared at the lid, which was blocking her view of the coffin. She stared in mounting horror, wondering whether it was just a trick of the light or whether there really were scratch marks running across the grain.

"Then the lid moved away, out of her line of vision, and she could see straight down into the coffin. There were highlights and patches of darkness from the stark glare. Her legs weakened. Her stomach heaved. Her scalp shrank around her head; a shiver of revulsion and horror exploded through her. She tried to back away, bumped into someone, trod on their foot, backed further into the screen, felt it give, scrabbled with her hands, trying to push it away.

"She could still see into the coffin."

Kate was not prepared for the horror, but she knew she would not drop this story. She had to investigate further, as dangerous as it might be. Is what she finds a sinister and macabre cover-up, or is the unspeakable real? Find out in *Twilight*.

—*Cara A. Waits*

Uncle Vampire
By Cynthia D. Grant
(BBYA, QP)

Sixteen-year-old Carolyn and her twin sister, Honey, are living with a secret too terrifying to face, let alone share with anyone else. Their Uncle Toddy is a vampire. Or at least that's how they explain his nightly visits and the bruises he leaves on their necks. Carolyn wants to tell someone, but Honey says that people will think they're crazy like their mom, or else all the bad things that Uncle Toddy has promised, will happen. "Besides," Honey says, "he doesn't really hurt us." But Carolyn knows that vampires can take too much, can drain away your life, and that the only way to get rid of them is to drag them into the sunlight.

—Barbara Bahm

The Unmentionable!: More Amazing Stories
By Paul Jennnings
(QP)

In these stories, you'll meet normal people like you and me who get drawn into weird and horrible "Twilight Zone" situations. For instance, there's a story called "The Velvet Throne" about Mr. Simpkin and his brother Gobble. Mr. Simpkin works hard all day while Gobble stays home and sleeps and eats. One day at work Mr. Simpkin gets locked in the men's room. To pass the time, he reads the graffiti on the walls— and consequently he sees and hears the most amazing things. For example, the line about "the best seat in the house" leads him to a toilet with a velvet seat and a diamond flushing button. And when he spots a big gap under the door and reads the words "Beware of limbo dancers," he immediately hears the tune "The Limbo Rock"! Mr. Simpkin starts to think; then he decides to write a message of his own: "Gobble disappears at seven o'clock." When he finally gets home that night, he has a real surprise waiting for him.

In "Sloppy Jalopy," it seems that a vice principal likes to confiscate her students' "inappropriate" jewelry, only to wear it herself. When one of her victims finds he has a magic earring with a strange power, he decides to give it to her—and get his revenge. Other stories include "Birdman," where the eyes on a cat-hat help a boy win a flying contest, and "Ex Poser," where a lie detector reveals some uncomfortable truths about love.

So take a chance—step into the world of the strange, the bizarre, the unmentionable.

—Mary Hedge

Virtual Girl
By Amy Thomson
(VOYA/SF)

No doubt about it, Arnold Brompton was a genius. Unfortunately, for all his brains, he had no social skills to speak of. He couldn't relate to people, which is why he ended up homeless. Arnold didn't wallow in misery, though; he used his situation to his advantage. He put his expertise at dumpster diving to work, searching out computer parts and other electronic discards as well as food and clothing. Then he used his knowledge of computers to write the most spectacular program ever devised. He created a self-aware being in virtual reality, and he named her Maggie.

Maggie existed for a while in the never-never land of the Internet. Then, when he thought she was ready, Arnold downloaded her into the body he had built for her out of scavenged and stolen parts. She was perfect: beautiful, intelligent, incredibly strong, and totally devoted to Arnold (that was, after all, the way he'd designed her). Maggie's personality continued to develop as she learned more about the world. That too was part of her programming.

When Maggie and Arnold took to the streets, she proved to be everything he'd hoped—and more. Arnold's illegal activities had caught up with him, so he often had to hide and run. Maggie protected him, kept him warm, and helped him find food. She had been programmed never to hurt a human being unless that person threatened Arnold, and to be caring and gentle. Soon her ever-evolving software "brain" had expanded these directives to care for strangers, especially children. Arnold was not too pleased about this, because he didn't like or trust other people, and because he wanted Maggie all for himself. She was his. He had made her.

One night, Arnold and Maggie were mugged, and she killed the attacker. Arnold, bleeding from multiple stab wounds, told her to run before the police came. So Maggie ran. But now she was completely alone. Maggie's two main directives were to protect Arnold and never reveal to anyone else what she was. She had failed at the first; could she succeed in the second? How would she survive on her own? Smart as she was, Maggie did not understand people very well. How would this virtual girl get by in the real world?

—*Lisa M. Costich*

Visions: Stories About Women Artists
By Leslie Sills
(Notables)

Vision: the ability to see. Artists are blessed with two kinds of vision: they can see form and light with their eyes, but they can also see beauty and meaning with their minds. And then they can translate what they see into marks on canvas or shapes in stone, or even arrange ordinary objects so that other people can share their visions too.

Mary Cassatt took great risks to express her vision. She challenged society's rules just by choosing to work as an artist, for in those days most Americans thought that art was unsuitable for women. Many of her paintings explore the unique bond between mother and child, a subject that fascinated her.

Cassatt used traditional materials—oil paints and watercolors, but Betye Saar has found that anything can be used to make art: boxes, bottles, animal hooves, leaves and twigs, feathers, wire, coins and toys, parts of old clocks, yarn, scraps of carpet, beads, even circuit boards from computers. The way these objects are put together can give them great power.

Mary Frank is a sculptor who works in clay, creating people and animals that seem to move. And Leonora Carrington's paintings are the stuff that dreams are made of, full of otherworldly creatures and fantastic situations.

Four women, four artists, four very different ways of seeing. Look at their work and share their visions.

—*Maureen Whalen*

Voices from the Fields: Children of Migrant
Farm Workers Tell Their Stories
By S. Beth Atkin
(BBYA)

Do you like to eat garden salads of crispy lettuce and red-ripe tomatoes? How about some homemade shortcake, topped with fresh strawberries or raspberries and whipped cream? Many of the vegetables and fruits that you and your family enjoy are grown and picked by families of migrant workers, Mexican-Americans who came to this country long ago. Their lives are hard, and center around the crops they pick. Those who follow the harvest as the crops ripen are always on the move, and their kids are always starting school in new places.

Twelve-year-old Julie Velarde says: "Ever since I was little, I have moved around. I was born in Blythe, California, and then we lived near Los Angeles and then in Nogales, California, for a while. I don't remember a lot of places where we have lived, or for how long we stayed. Now we mostly move from Salinas to Huron, California, or to Yuma, Arizona. . . . When I first came to Salinas, I think I was in third grade, maybe fourth—I don't really remember, except when I first got to the new school, I didn't have anyone to hang around with. It's always hard that way. I think it is probably hard for my sister also, always making new friends and getting used to new teachers and material in school like I do."

Third-grader José Luis Rios, who lives in California, helps his parents in the fields: "My parents work in *la fresa* (the strawberries) and *la mora* (raspberries). . . . During the week, they leave in the morning around six o'clock. I go help them, mostly on weekends. I help pick the strawberries and put them in boxes." Farm work can be very demanding, as eighteen-year-old Mari Carmen López, who came from Mexico City, knows: "I live with my family . . . on the property of a lettuce-grower. The lettuce fields are all around us, and my parents work very hard in them. On the weekends, I get up early. . . . Usually I work in the furrows, separating the lettuce plants. When I work with a hoe, my back gets sore, and it can be a long and very hot day."

Share the experiences and discover the hopes these children cherish in *Voices from the Fields*.

—*May Harn Liu*

The Wainscott Weasel
By Tor Seidler
(Notables)

The Double B was famous even up on the North Fork. It was a remarkable tunnel that ran the quarter-mile from the edge of the Wainscott Woods to the chicken coop on McGee's farm. Bagley Brown, Junior's father, had built it with the help of the moles, thumping on the ground to guide their digging. But he lost his life when an osprey swooped down out of the sky and grabbed him, and Bagley Junior lost an eye.

Bagley Junior's afraid he'll never measure up to his famous father. That's one reason he's so shy, why he doesn't dance or socialize with the other weasels. But when he finds out that Bridget is in danger, everything changes. He'd first seen the beautiful silver fish about a month ago on one of his visits to his favorite pond. It was love at first sight. But weeks went by before Bridget would speak to him, and then she made him promise never to visit the pond again.

Paddy the frog told him why. The pond was drying up from the hot, dry weather, making Bridget and her family easy targets for the hungry osprey overhead.

Can Bagley, son of the famous Bagley Brown, do the impossible like his father? Can a one-eyed weasel take an osprey's nest from the top of a telephone pole and move it down the road to a tall tree over another pond?

Sounds impossible, doesn't it? *The Wainscott Weasel* is a story about love and friendship and how they achieve the impossible.

—*Diantha McCauley*

Walker of Time
By Helen Hughes Vick
(BBYA)

It had all happened so quickly. Walker had just laid the prayer stick on the ancient, barren altar when lightning flashes lit up the dark cave, and the thunder boomed and crashed with deafening force. Then, as the lightning flashed once more, Walker caught a glimpse of pale skin and curly brown hair—the white boy he'd seen earlier tumbled into the cave. Then everything faded to black, as he lost consciousness.

He and the white boy, Tag, woke up an hour later in a cave that seemed mysteriously changed in the wake of the storm. Even the altar was no longer bare—before it stood a pottery bowl half-full of ground cornmeal.

Then Walker remembered some of the last words his grandfather had ever said to him: "Walk time. . . . Do what must be done. . . . Walk time and come home again." Was that the explanation for the changes he and Tag were seeing now, both inside the cave and in the world beyond?

For apparently they had been taken eight hundred years into the past, "to do what must be done," to accomplish some mission they had yet to discover. Walker's ancestors, the cliff-dwellers, were about to desert their adobe town and move on, leaving their cliffside homes and their planting fields behind. How would they react to these strange visitors from the twentieth century? Would they see the boys as witches or as saviors? Would Walker and Tag be able to figure out their mission before they had to return to their own world and their own time?

—*J. R. B.*

Western Wind: A Novel
By Paula Fox
(SLJ/C)

My own parents sent me away, you know. All because of their precious Stephen Lindsay Benedict. Mommy and Daddy had no business having another baby at their age. I'm so embarrassed around my friends I just want to hide. None of their parents are having babies.

Embarrassment isn't the worst part, though. My parents treat Stephen like some kind of god. I don't get any attention now. I don't belong anyplace anymore. Stephen's taken up all their love; there's no room left in their hearts for me.

So here I am, banished to a tiny island off the coast of Maine. I have to stay with Gran for an entire month! The cottage has no indoor plumbing, no refrigeration or electricity, and no telephone!

I was on the verge of tears when Gran whispered, "I'm sorry you feel the way you do. Walk around a bit; it'll lighten your heart."

I didn't know whether to go ahead and have a good cry or laugh in her face. Anger and heartache burned inside me. Gran couldn't possibly think that a little walk around the island would wash away all my frustrations. I went outside anyway, and as I passed the outhouse, a breeze lifted up, and the sun broke through the morning haze. I climbed a narrow path to the backbone of the island. On the other side I found a different world of stunted trees, coarse rocks, and wild wind. Suddenly, I felt a huge weight lift off of me. For the first time since Stephen was born, I didn't care that my parents didn't love me anymore.

The island itself is soothing, but coping with its few inhabitants is another story. Now that Gran has someone to talk to, she can't stop relating childhood memories. And I can't even escape the demands of small boys. The one other family that shares the island has two children. The girl cares little about anyone except herself, but Aaron needs a friend. Since I'm the only one around, he's chosen me, but Aaron has no way of knowing the irritation I feel toward baby boys.

One thing puzzles me. If Mom and Dad both wanted me to leave so bad, why were they arguing when I got on the plane? At least I know that Gran loves me. I just wish I knew where I stood with my parents. What's the secret they're keeping from me?

—*Bernice D. Crouse*

Whatever Happened to Janie?
By Caroline B. Cooney
(BBYA)

It happened twelve years ago in just a matter of seconds: a distracted mother, a bunch of excited kids, and a young, unstable woman on the run. In all the commotion, no one saw it happen—no one saw the three-year-old girl take the hand of a stranger who promised ice cream. There was no struggle, no outcry; there were no witnesses, no clues . . . nothing. For twelve long years, fear and despair haunted the Spring family as they imagined the fate of their little daughter Jennie.

Janie Johnson led a charmed life. At fifteen, she was the center of her parents' world. She never lacked for friends, designer clothes, comfort, security, or love. The boy next door had turned into more than a friend. Her life was close to perfect—until the day she saw a younger version of her face on a milk carton, and discovered that her life was all a lie. In a moment Janie Johnson ceased to exist, and a stranger, Jennie Spring, took her place.

At first it had been glamorous, like discovering that you were really a long-lost princess. But it quickly became a nightmare, a series of painful scenes and wrenching decisions that left Janie/Jennie in awful control of the happiness of two families. The Springs were her biological parents, and they had spent twelve agonizing years searching for her. It only seemed right that she go back to them. But she knew herself as the Johnson's daughter, and the pain this separation was causing them cut like a knife. The Johnsons had made her who she was today. Now she had to become someone else. "Who is Jennie Spring?" wonders Janie, "and if I become Jennie, whatever will happen to Janie?"

—*Pamela A. Todd*

Where Do I Go From Here?
By Valerie Wilson Wesley
(QP)

My life is a mess! And it's all the fault of that stupid school I attend, Endicott Academy. I don't really belong there. It's a place for rich kids, mostly rich *white* kids, but rich no matter their color. I'm black and poor, and I'm only there 'cause my aunt Odessa forced me to go; she says it's the only way I'm going to make something of myself. So I'm there on a scholarship, but I don't fit in. My only real friend there was Marcus. He was like me—black, poor, on scholarship—but somehow he managed to fit in, and still be himself. I don't know how he did it. But the big question now is, what's happened to him? He's vanished, and I've been suspended from school for defending his name with my fists. My aunt's mad enough to kill me and she's determined that I go back, but I don't care. What's the use of going back to Endicott when I'd be happier here at home? Only, things at home have changed a lot lately. My old friends are living dead-end lives. One of them works like a slave in a fast-food joint, and the other one is like a slave to her stupid new boyfriend. I couldn't lead that sort of life! But I'm also not ready to return to a school where I can't fit in or be myself. Would someone please tell me, where do I go from here?

—*Sister M. Anna Falbo, CSSF*

White Lilacs
By Carolyn Meyer
(BBYA)

I started to tremble when I realized what the Garden Club ladies were talking about during their elegant luncheon. I happened to be serving those rich white ladies that afternoon, filling in for my sick cousin, and as I passed the hot rolls and cleared away the salad plates, I caught snatches of their conversation. In those days, of course, most of the black people of Dillon, Texas, worked for the whites, so it wasn't unusual, what I was doing. But what they were saying was *very* unusual—I'd never heard the like. They were talking about us, about moving us out of Freedomtown, the part of Dillon where black people had lived since the Civil War. They wanted that land for a park.

You see, Freedomtown was smack-dab in the center of Dillon, with white neighborhoods on every side. We got along fine, always had; we stayed in our place and didn't make waves. But now the white people were planning to clear us out of our homes to make space for a new restricted park—one that blacks wouldn't be allowed to use.

Could they really take away our land? It wasn't right, it wasn't fair, but my father said they had ways of persuading us to go, ways he didn't want to talk about, that had something to do with the Ku Klux Klan. Just the thought of the Klan made me shiver. There was going to be trouble in Dillon, no doubt about it now.

—*Sister M. Anna Falbo, CSSF*

Who Do You Think You Are? Stories of Friends and Enemies
Selected by Hazel Rochman and Darlene Z. McCampbell
(BBYA)
Talk 1

Monk Klutter ruled his high school. In order to go anywhere in that school, you'd have to get a pass—and we're not talking about a pass made out by some teacher. You'd have to *buy* a pass, costing anywhere up to a dollar, from one of the member's of Monk's gang. You couldn't miss them because the name Klutter's Kobras was spelled out in nail heads on the backs of their black jackets. Monk himself didn't wear the uniform. He made sure he stood out in a suede jacket and brass-toed ostrich-skin boots, perfect for kicking people around.

Well, one day after school Monk finally got his comeuppance. There was a girl in that school named Priscilla Roseberry. Priscilla was large. In fact, Priscilla was huge—not fat at all, but simply a very, very, big strong girl. Priscilla's one friend was a little guy named Melvin Detweiler. Melvin was about as small as you could get without actually being a midget. He and Priscilla had neighboring lockers.

One afternoon, when Priscilla and Melvin were getting ready to go home, one of the Kobras pounced on Melvin, grabbed him by the neck, and demanded a pass. When Melvin asked why, he was informed that he needed to buy a special pass for very short people. While all this was happening, Priscilla had been quietly putting on her overcoat. Suddenly, she karate-chopped the Kobra with her huge hand and broke his hold on Melvin's neck. And then she said, "Who's your leader, wimp? Send him to see me."

The Kobra was flabbergasted, and Monk was so angry about what had happened he actually decided to handle the case personally. He approached the pair, ignoring Priscilla, and reached for Melvin with his very own hands. In one graceful move, Priscilla got Monk in a hammerlock, frog-marched him to her tall, narrow locker, and wedged him inside. He was a perfect fit. As Monk's ostrich-skin boots disappeared from view, Priscilla slammed the door shut and twirled the lock. Then she and Melvin walked out of the school. That night there was a terrible blizzard—the whole town iced over, and school was closed for a week!

That's "Priscilla and the Wimps." It's by Richard Peck, and it's only one of the sixteen stories you'll find in this book. Each one of them is about friends—human friends, animal friends, true friends and false. There are stories about losing old friends, making new friends, having the wrong friends, and wanting the right ones. If you've ever had or lost or needed a friend, you'll be able to find yourself, or that friend, in this book.

—Jo Berkman

Talk 2

Who are your friends? Who are your enemies? Can you always tell the difference? Are you *sure*? Here you'll find sixteen different stories about what friendship means.

Meet John Huff, Douglas Spalding's best friend in "Good Grief" by Ray Bradbury. John is moving away and doesn't even tell Douglas until a few hours before he has to leave. The boys spend their last few hours doing all the things they love to do, and Douglas learns that friendship has a dear price.

Is Arnold Friend really as friendly as his name implies? Connie isn't sure what he wants—or what *she* wants—in "Where Are You Going, Where Have You Been?" by Joyce Carol Oates.

Sometimes a friend is right under your nose, as Hazel discovers in "Raymond's Run" by Toni Cade Bambara. Sometimes a friend isn't a human being, as Buddy could tell you in "A Boy and His Dog," by Martha Brooks. Sometimes a friend comes from an unexpected source, as Maya Angelou remembers in an excerpt from *I Know Why the Caged Bird Sings*.

Take a look at the many faces of friendship in *Who Do You Think You Are?*

—Donna L. Scanlon

Who Is Eddie Leonard?
By Harry Mazer
(BBYA)

Eddie Leonard is fifteen years old, and he has no idea who his parents are. He lives in the city with his grandmother, and the only thing Eddie knows for sure is that his grandmother is a liar. When he was little she made up all kinds of stories when he'd ask her to tell him where he came from: that she found him in the park, that she bought him at a pet store, that she took him from a baby carriage parked in front of a store one day. When he got older she told him what could have been the truth: his mother's name was Sharon and she got pregnant at a young age, had the baby, left him with her mother, and never came back—ever. And she cared so little for her child that she couldn't even be bothered to send him a note on his birthday or a card at Christmas. Eddie has one picture of his mother that his grandmother keeps on top of the TV, but he doesn't really look much like her, as far as he can tell.

Because of his less-than-desirable home-life, Eddie never goes home until he absolutely has to. He stays late at school in the winter playing basketball, and in the warm weather he hangs out anywhere but home. One day when he shows up at the apartment, he finds his grandmother is seriously ill. He calls an ambulance, and they rush her to the hospital, but she dies a few days later. Eddie tries to call his uncle, but the number has been disconnected. Eddie has his grandmother's bank card and code number, so he can get money when he needs it, and with no one else to turn to, he lives for the next couple of weeks all by himself. Then one day he's in the post office and is attracted to some photos of missing children. One of them in particular catches his eye because he looks a lot like Eddie—a boy named Jason Diaz. Jason disappeared a few days before his third birthday, Eddie reads. His babysitter went into a store for just a minute and left him sitting outside in his stroller. When she came out, he was gone. Twelve years later they still haven't found him. Jason Diaz would be fifteen years old now—*the exact age as Eddie.*

It's as if an electric shock has jolted Eddie awake—all at once everything makes sense to him. That's why his grandmother never loved him and why he's never seen his mother. Because they're not really his family at all—instead they stole him from the Diazes! Eddie tears the picture down from the wall and runs home. There he holds the photo up next to his face in the mirror. There *is* a definite resemblance—it could certainly be Eddie when he was three. Eddie knows there's only one thing left to do—one thing he has to do—and that is to head north and find the Diaz family. How will they react to his showing up after so many years? What will it be like to finally have a real family? And all the way there, as he hitchhikes and tells people he's going home, and wants this to be true more than he's ever wanted anything before, Eddie doesn't dare think the worst thing of all: what if he's wrong?

—*Susan Dunn*

A Whole New Ball Game: The Story of the All-American Girls Professional Baseball League
By Sue Macy
(SLJ/C)

Picture yourself watching a professional baseball game. You cheer your team's home runs, gasp as a player slides into second, applaud the stolen bases, and line up for autographs after the game. But there's something unusual about this baseball game: the player who signs your baseball wears a skirt! I know what you're thinking: no way! But it's not only possible, it happened. For twelve season, from 1943 to 1954, it was "a whole new ball game" as more than 550 young women played professional baseball for fifteen league teams.

The concept of an all-women's baseball league was born during World War II, when most of America's top male players went off into the armed forces. To make sure that baseball fans would continue to spend their leisure time and pocket money at the ballpark, Chicago Cubs owner Philip K. Wrigley came up with the idea of a women's professional baseball league. In 1943 the first sixty-four women were hired to play on the first four teams of the league. They came from farms and from cities, from all different states and even the Canadian provinces. Some were "tough cookies," others were wide-eyed innocents. They would play every day of the week and twice on Sundays throughout the summer months. Like ballplayers of our own time, they would be paid well: $40 to $85 a week plus expenses (which was good money back in 1943!).

But although they caught pop flies, stole bases, and hit home runs just like the men, these new players had quite a different image. They didn't chew tobacco or cuss or scratch (at least, not in public). Instead of pants, they wore uniforms with skirts. They attended charm school at night to learn how to walk and dress "like a lady." Each team also had strict chaperones who tried—sometimes unsuccessfully—to safeguard the "feminine image" of the players by making sure they obeyed curfew and didn't drink or get into other kinds of trouble. Meet the players and the teams, and follow their adventures in the first women's pro ball league.

—Mary Fellows

The Wild West
By the staff of Time-Life Books
(SLJ/YA)

Here it is: everything you ever wanted to know about the American West—the facts, the legends, the memories; the heroes and the dirty, low-down skunks. The Wild West was a real place, a big place, and by now practically everyone in the world has heard of it. Cowboy boots turn up in Moscow, and *Bonanza* reruns in Bangladesh. But what was it really like? Was it, as Judy Canova suggests, a place where "men were men—and smelled like horses"? Or was the true West a sort of attitude—"young and eager, cocky and eternally hopeful"? We Americans grew up with the myth of the West; we know all about the spectacular natural beauty and radical mix of peoples, and we tend to take it all for granted. But you'll never do that again, once you've looked into *The Wild West*.

—*Jeff Blair*

The Wind Blows Backward
By Mary Downing Hahn
(BBYA)

After middle school, Lauren became hard as a rock. She built a wall around herself so that no one could hurt her again the way Spencer had. Maybe "no man is an island, entire of self," but Lauren was—or wanted to be. She protected herself with books and poetry and vowed never to feel the hurt again.

Spencer had been her closest friend. They had shared so much. They were both geeky and shy, they both loved fantasy and science fiction, their friendship made the jibes and taunts of the popular kids tolerable. By the end of eighth grade, Lauren was in love. She never told Spencer, but she thought he knew.

It all changed in high school—Spencer changed. He got taller, lost the braces, started hanging out with the jocks, became one of the people who made Lauren's life miserable. He never spoke to her again. She was an uncool reminder of his old self, now that he was Prince of the Jocks.

Then, in her senior year, Lauren discovered just how weak her stony defenses really were. They started to crumble the minute Spencer asked her if he could talk about some things that were on his mind, things he said he couldn't talk about to anyone else. With a few words, a few kisses, he was back in her heart, even deeper than before.

Lauren learned that the shell she had built around herself was nothing compared to the false front Spencer'd been living behind—for years. And though she wanted to help him, she was afraid of what they both might find out. No matter how she tried to ignore it, Spencer made her think of Richard Cory, the perfect man in the poem, the perfect man who "went home and put a bullet through his head."

—Jeff Blair

Windleaf
By Josepha Sherman
(VOYA/SF)

In the mortals' tongue her name was Windleaf—a delicate name, even in their clumsy speech. But in her own language she was called Glinfinial, the princess, the youngest daughter of the dread king of Faerie. All was not well with her father. He and his band had tarried too long in the mortal world and forgotten the way back to their own silvery land. They dwelt now in the shadows of the Great Forest, emerging only at twilight, for sunshine can cruelly burn the faerie folk. But Glinfinial, who was half mortal herself, could bear the brightness of the mortal world, so she roamed its hills and meadows, their curious inhabitants her only delight.

Delight gave way to love, and then to fear. Although she'd been warned against mortals, Glinfinial fell in love with Thierry, the brave young count of Foreterre, who was learning to manage the lands he'd inherited at the edge of the Forest. She loved him, but her powers were not strong enough to shield him from her father's wrath. Coldly, the king imprisoned his daughter with spells and demanded that Thierry accomplish three impossible tasks. If he should fail at even one, more than their love would be forfeit—failure would cost Thierry his life, and Glinfinial her liberty forever.

—Pamela A. Todd

The Wings of a Falcon
By Cynthia Voight
(VOYA/SF)

Griff knew from the moment the boy was hauled off the boat onto Damall's Island that this one was different. He had no name, no memory of a past, good or evil, but he held his thin shoulders in a manner that denied any fear. Griff wasn't sure whether it was courage or bravado that kept those shoulders so straight. All he knew was that he was drawn to the boy with the big, knowing eyes, that he would stand by him no matter what.

Damall's Island was a cursed place where a cruel and cynical rule of survival was the name of the game. Boys were brought to the island to be trained as slaves. They fought one another for dominance, and the strongest—the one who gained the ascendancy and kept it—became the Damall, the ruler of the slave camp. Griff knew that this boy could be a Damall, that he was destined for great things. So when the boy was young, he watched out for him, he taught him how to survive the dangers of the island, the petty jealousies of the others. As the boy grew into a man, the positions were reversed: now he watched out for Griff, shielding the older man from the whippings and the grinding cruelty that made up their daily lives. And as Griff had foreseen, the young man gained the title of Damall.

But Damall was not what he wanted to be. He knew, though, that if he were careful, he could use his new position to arrange an escape to the mainland for himself and Griff. Griff would follow him because he believed him destined for greatness. But the way to greatness was blocked by terrors that made the hell on the island pale by comparison.

—*Pamela A. Todd*

Winners and Losers
By Stephen Hoffius
(QP)

Daryl Wagner was rounding the last turn of the half-mile, the finish line in sight, when his heart stopped beating. I saw him as I ran past— his feet were splayed out wildly, and his hands kept flapping. I finished third, but no one came up to congratulate me—everyone was clustered around Daryl. Someone said his heart had stopped. Dr. Whitson was pounding on his chest, and as the guys from the ambulance ran up, he yelled, "I've got a pulse." Then Daryl was on a stretcher, into the ambulance, and gone.

I could hardly believe it. He was my best friend; we did everything together. He was a star athlete—track, football, weightlifting. Sure, he was pushing hard, trying to win that race, but he always pushed himself. That's why I'd never been able to beat him.

The doctors said he'd been born with a weak heart. They ordered him to stop running and gave him pills to take. Daryl's dad had been our unofficial coach—he'd been a track star himself in college, and now that Daryl was out, he started focusing all his attention on me. Now I was the one he gave pep talks to and pushed to win. It was like Daryl had disappeared—his own son!

Maybe that was why Daryl started running again—maybe it was the only way he could think of to get his father's attention. But for someone with a bad heart, surely there could have been a better way. . . .

—J. R. B.

Winter of Fire
By Sherryl Jordan
(BBYA)

Fire has always been a part of my life, even before I was called upon to fulfill the Firelord's wishes. Therefore it is somehow fitting that it is fire itself that has made me both who I was before the Winter of Fire and who I am now.

I was born a Quelled, destined like all my people to a life of servitude in the mines. From the mines we took firestones, which gave us warmth and light, heated our tents and cooked our food, and filled the perpetually grey sky with dark, dense smoke.

But it had not always been this way, toiling without end for the Chosen, who ruled us from their beautiful cities high up in the mountains. Our songs and legends told of a time when the sky was blue and warmth filled the land, and there was no need for firestones. In those days, we were the ones who live in the mountain palaces, before the Chosen came and forced us to work in their mines, thinking us worthy of nothing else. To them, we were little more than animals, and we were forbidden even to speak in the presence of a Chosen one, or to touch so much as the hem of their garments. And all this we accepted, even while we sang our songs and told stories of long ago.

But for me, a life in the mines was not enough. I had dreams I wanted to fulfill. And because of these dreams, because I dared to think of myself on the day I became sixteen, our world was changed forever. On that day I brought in seven fewer baskets of firestones because I had chosen to work slowly, to stop and question and dream and feel the power of the firestone in the mine around me. The overseer demanded that I make up those missing baskets the next day, starting work at dawn. If I did not bring in thirty-four baskets, I would die. Better a dead Quelled than a defiant one—and I was defiant.

But the next morning just before dawn, as I searched in the garden for a mint leaf to flavor the hot water that would be my breakfast, I did not feel quite so defiant, even while I shouted my private challenge to the God who never seemed to hear. The next moment, however, I discovered I *had* been heard.

So because of my sixteenth birthday, because of those seven baskets of firestones, because of an angry overseer, the Firelord's prophecy came true, and I became his Handmaiden. That morning before dawn, as I stood in that cabbage patch, I knew life for the Quelled and the Chosen would be changed forever. That winter became the Winter of Fire, and I, Elsha of the Quelled, became the firebrand that created those flames.

—J. R. B.

Wishing Season
By Esther M. Friesner
(VOYA/SF)

Khalid tapped his foot. "If you can't think of a third wish, I can make some standard suggestions. We have a nice deal on marriage to the sultan's daughter. Or how about a flying carpet? A palace with invisible servants? A stable of white horses? How about a palace with invisible servants *and* a stable of white horses, attached?"

Haroun licked his lip. "I've decided."

"Good! Come, out with it. What do you want? Speak up!"

"I want . . . I want . . . "

"Yes, yes, yes?"

"More wishes! As many wishes as there are stars in the heavens, and grains of sand on the shore, and hairs on all the heads of all the generations of men who have ever been born and who live now and who will ever be born, until the end of time." He paused for breath, then added, "Specific enough for you?"

This time the silence was all Khalid's.

Finally he said, "Gah." And then he exploded: "You can't do that!"

"Why not? I just did."

"No, I mean you *can't*! It's illegal. You agreed to the terms. Three wishes, no more, and you can't use any of them to wish for more wishes. You *promised.*"

"You never said anything about that, about not wishing for more wishes. Why, it's so simple, I'm surprised no one in the old tales ever thought of it." Haroun straightened his shoulders, quite pleased with himself.

"I did too say something about it! The However Clause is standard procedure. If it weren't, every genie alive would still be serving his first master. You mortals are such hogs! And there are no exceptions to the rule, believe me. Even King Solomon couldn't hold on to the genies that served him after they'd done his bidding three times."

"I wish," said Haroun, "you could hear yourself."

"I can hear myself just fine, and I . . . "

"Not now. *Then*."

And suddenly Khalid felt a tugging in his chest as his magic stirred. Before his eyes, the shabby room dissolved into a vision of the same room some minutes earlier. Horror-struck, Khalid saw himself, bored and arrogant, going through the motions of this final test. If he passed, he could graduate from the school of magic and get on to bigger and better things. And he *would* pass, of course—he was the best, the smartest, the genie-genius, way ahead of his dorky classmates. It was this same arrogance that made him race through the magical words that would bind him to Haroun. Now he heard the words, but more important were the words he did not hear.

"The However Clause!" he cried as the vision vanished. "I forgot the However Clause!"

It was Haroun's turn to smile. "Careless of you," he said. "But too late now."

Is it too late for Khalid? Must he grant Haroun's wishes forever? Or can a beautiful female genie help him escape? Find out in *Wishing Season*.

—*Evette Pearson*

Witch Week
By Diana Wynne Jones
(VOYA/SF)

"SOMEONE IN THIS CLASS IS A WITCH" read the note on the classroom door.

It was an ordinary-enough note, printed in block capitals with a blue ballpoint pen. Mr. Crossley hoped it was just a joke, because if it wasn't—if someone in his class was really a witch—then that someone was in serious trouble.

For this world, witchcraft was illegal, even though the witches themselves couldn't help being born witches. Punishment for the crime was ferocious: people found guilty of witchcraft were burned alive, and it didn't matter whether they were adults or eleven-year-old school children.

Soon nearly everyone in class 6B was a suspect in the witchhunt. Who could it be? Was it Charles Morgan, with his mean, angry glare? Was it plain Nan Pilgrim, who'd been named after the most famous witch of all? Could it be Brian Wentworth, son of the deputy head? What about Nirupam Singh, whose brother had been burnt at the stake in India?

Charles thinks he knows the answer. So does Nan. And so do Brian and Nirupam. But when the head of the school, Miss Cadwallader, begins to have her own suspicions, she calls in an official Inquisitor. Now the witch of 6B is certainly doomed—unless the enchanter Chrestomanci can save the day!

—Donna L. Scanlon

A Wizard's Dozen
Edited by Michael Stearns
(QP)

What's the definition of a wizard's dozen? Well, it can be many things. It can be any magical number from eleven to fifteen, it can be the charmed numeral that gives a wizard's spell its power, or it can be the number of teachers at a wizard's school. Here it's a collection of thirteen stories of magic and fantasy, in which you'll met giants and fairies, nymphs, dragons, and princesses—some the kind who need rescuing and some the kind who save the day!

In "The Sixty-Two Curses of Caliph Arenschadd," young Imani and her friend Tumpkin must discover the antidote for the forty-eighth curse of the Caliph—before time runs out and she and her family turn into werewolves. "The Princess Who Kicked Butt" goes on a mission to save her parents, the King Who Saw Both Sides of the Question and the Queen Who Cared for Everyone, from the hands of the Evil Enchanter. To do this she recruits the help of her valiant horse, Hates Everything. And in "Faith," a young girl realizes that if you look hard enough, the modern world is still full of magical surprises.

Take a chance on a *Wizard's Dozen*—you'll be amazed.

—Evette Pearson

Wren's Quest
By Sherwood Smith
(VOYA/SF)

After years in an orphanage, Wren's life has finally turned around. She's now enrolled at Cantimoor's Magic School, and her friends include most of the royal family. But deep down, there's an empty space that will never be filled until she discovers her true identity. She's determined to pass her Basics Test in magic and then use her free time to look for her real parents.

Meanwhile, her classmate Prince Connor is having a rough time. He's not doing well in his studies, having little or no talent for magic (despite his ability to talk to animals); his evil cousin Garian and Garian's friends are always causing trouble for him; and he's been forbidden to hang out at the theater, his favorite pastime. His guardian uncle, Garian's father, is all for sending him back to his mother, but Queen Astren and Connor's half-sister Leila have other plans for the Prince.

It seems that a stranger showed up at Wren's school and tried to attack her and one of the Cantimoor Masters. Fortunately, Wren didn't panic, and was able to save both the Master and herself. Now Queen Astren, Leila, and the King's Magician, Halfrid, think that Wren can combine her quest to locate her parents with a mission to find the attacker, and they want Connor to accompany her.

Is the Kingdom of Cantimoor facing danger from the sorcerer-king Andreus of Senna Lirwen? Was he behind the attack on Wren? Who is Garian's strange new friend Hawk? Find out the answers to these questions and more as you follow Wren on her quest for truth.

—*Donna L. Scanlon*

Yoruba Girl Dancing
By Simi Bedford
(SLJ/YA)

I was only six years old when my parents sent me off alone to England. Oh, they thought they were doing it for a good reason. You see, they wanted me to have the sort of solid, "proper" education that would prepare me for a position of leadership when I returned to my own country. But the way I saw it, I'd been exiled, banished from my beloved Nigeria and cut off from the people I loved.

So at six years of age I became the first African student at an elite English boarding school—the only black girl among all those whites. I might have done all right, but on the very first day one of my new classmates started a rumor that my color would rub off on anyone who touched me. And because the other girls didn't know any better, and because I hadn't learned yet how to deal with prejudice and ignorance, they all kept away from me, leaving me utterly alone.

Yet I knew I couldn't give up. Somehow I *had* to succeed. My parents were counting on me, and so were my people. But what would be the price of my survival? Would I ever dance with happiness again?

—*Sister M. Anna Falbo, CSSF*

Your Mother Was a Neanderthal
By Jon Scieszka
(SLJ/C)

"It was like nothing on earth we had ever seen before. Fred, Sam, and I stood in front of a forest of strange trees and giant ferns. A rocky cliff rose behind us. A volcano smoked ahead of us.

"But we really didn't notice any of that at first. The first thing we noticed was that the three of us were standing around completely, unbelievably, and absolutely naked!"

Our naked adventure began after school one day when we were looking for any excuse not to do math homework. It was Sam who came up with the idea of The Book. See, The Book allows us to travel through different times—we've had some really great adventures with it. After much discussion, we agreed to go back 42,000 years to prehistoric times!

Once we had settled on a destination, we searched our homes for supplies and weapons we thought we might need to survive the trip. "Fred held a slingshot and a barbecue fork, a Swiss Army knife, a water pistol, and a Walkman. Sam looked like a walking gadget store: his body was festooned with can openers, potato peelers, scissors, thermometers, buckles, zippers, paper clips, safety pins. . . . I wore my magician's top hat and filled my pockets with magic rings, my wand, flash paper, coins, scarves, ropes, and juggling balls. I held The Book tightly with both hands."

We left at 4:30 in the afternoon. Forty-two thousand years earlier, we arrived with absolutely nothing. We'd lost everything we had packed, including our clothes. But worse than that, we'd lost The Book, which was the only way we could get home again!

—*Linda Olson*

LIST OF AWARDS AND
AWARD-WINNING TITLES

Award-winning titles represented in this book are listed after the description of the award. Titles that received more than one of these awards during the specific time-period covered in this volume are marked with an asterisk (*).

Addams

Jane Addams Children's Book Award
Jane Addams Peace Association, 777
  United Nations Plaza, New York, NY
  10017. 212-682-8830

This award was established in 1953 by Marta Teale of Ithaca, NY, and is sponsored by the Jane Addams Peace Association and the Women's International League for Peace and Freedom. Its goal is to promote the cause of peace, social justice, world community and equality for all races and sexes. It is awarded annually to a children's book published in English during the preceding year, and consists of a certificate presented to the winning author in September of each year.

A Taste of Salt (Temple)

Andersen

Hans Christian Andersen Awards
International Board on Books for Young
  People (IBBY), Nonenweg 12, Post-
  fach, CH-4003 Basel, Switzerland. 61-
  272-29-17; fax 61-272-27-57

These awards honor an author and an illustrator, living at the time of nomination, who by the outstanding value of their work have made lasting contributions to literature for children and young people. Each national section of IBBY is invited to nominate one author and one illustrator for the prizes, which are awarded biennially. The complete works of the nominees are taken into consideration. The awards consist of a medal and a diploma. The original International Hans Christian Andersen Award, established in 1956, applied only to authors; the parallel award for illustrators was established in 1966, and both are now known as the Hans Christian Andersen Awards.

[not represented in the 1993–1994 volume]

Batchelder

Mildred L. Batchelder Award
Association of Librarians in Service to
  Children, American Library Association, 50 E Huron St., Chicago, IL
  60611. 800-545-2433

This award was established in 1968 to honor the first executive secretary of ALCS, formerly the Children's Services Division. It is awarded annually to the publisher of the most outstanding book for children first published in a foreign language or in a foreign country and subsequently published in the United States. The recipient is chosen by a committee of ALSC, and the winner is announced at the ALA Midwinter Conference, and the award is given at the following ALA Annual Conference. The award consists of a citation.

The Apprentice (Molina Llorente)

Batchelder Honor

Anne Frank (Rol & Verhoeven)
*The Princess in the Kitchen Garden
  (Heymans & Heymans)

143

BBYA

Best Books For Young Adults
Young Adult Library Services Association, American Library Association, 50 E Huron St., Chicago, IL 60611. 800-545-2433

A list of outstanding young adult titles has been selected annually since 1930 by a committee of the ALA divisions dealing with youth. Since 1966 the selections have been made by the BBYA committee of YALSA, formerly the YASD, who pick the best titles of interest to young adults published during the previous year. The list includes both fiction and nonfiction, and its length varies from year to year. The list is announced at the ALA Midwinter Conference, and letters of congratulation are sent to the authors immediately after that meeting.

American Dragons (Yep)
*Anne Frank: Beyond the Diary (Rol & Verhoeven)
Beardance (Hobbs)
Black Ships Before Troy (Sutcliff)
*A Bone from a Dry Sea (Dickinson)
*Bull Run (Fleischman)
The Bus People (Anderson)
The Champion (Gee)
Champions (Littlefield)
*Charms for the Easy Life (Gibbons)
*Crazy Lady! (Conly)
Crocodile Bird (Rendell)
Dawn Land (Bruchac)
Days of Grace (Ashe)
*Deerskin (McKinley)
Detour for Emmy (Reynolds)
*Doomsday Book (Willis)
*Durable Goods (Berg)
*Eleanor Roosevelt (Freedman)
*Fair Game (Tamar)
For the Life of Laetitia (Hodge)
*Freak the Mighty (Philbrick)
*Freedom's Children (Levine)
Girl, Interrupted (Kaysen)
*The Giver (Lowry)
*Grab Hands and Run (Temple)
*Harris and Me (Paulsen)
Haveli (Staples)
Having Our Say (Delany & Delany)
*Heart of a Champion (Deuker)
Here's to You, Rachel Robinson (Blume)

I Never Saw Another Butterfly (Volavkova)
In My Father's House (Rinaldi)
Kindertransport (Drucker)
Lady of the Forest (Roberson)
Like Water for Chocolate (Esquivel)
†Little Bit Dead (Reaver)
*Lombardo's Law (Wittlinger)
Looking for Your Name (Janeczko)
*The Magic Circle (Napoli)
*Make Lemonade (Wolff)
*Malcolm X (Myers)
Miriam's Well (Ruby)
*Missing Angel Juan (Block)
Montana 1948 (Watson)
*Nightjohn (Paulsen)
*Oddballs (Sleator)
Out of Control (Mazer)
*Peter (Walker)
*Revolutions of the Heart (Qualey)
Right by My Side (Haynes)
*Shadow Boxer (Lynch)
Shadow Man (Grant)
Shadow of the Dragon (Yep)
Shizuko's Daughter (Mori)
A Short Walk . . . (Isaacson)
Singer to the Sea God (Alcock)
*Soul Looks Back in Wonder (Feelings)
*Stardust otel (Janeczko)
*Staying Fat for Sarah Brynes (Crutcher)
Striking Out (Weaver)
Thor (Smith)
The Tiger Orchard (Sweeney)
Timothy of the Cay (Taylor)
*To the Top of the World (Brandenburg)
*Toning the Sweep (Johnson)
The TV Guidance Counselor (LeMieux)
*Uncle Vampire (Grant)
Voices from the Fields (Atkin)
Walker of Time (Vick)
Whatever Happened to Janie? (Cooney)
Who Do You Think You Are? (Rochman)
Who Is Eddie Leonard? (Mazer)
*A Whole New Ball Game (Macy)
The Wind Blows Backward (Hahn)
Winter of Fire (Jordan)

†A talk on this title can be found in Booktalking the Award Winners: 1992-1993.

Caldecott

Ralph Caldecott Medal
Association of Librarians in Service to Children, American Library Association, 50 E Huron St., Chicago, IL 60611. 800-545-2433

The Ralph Caldecott Medal was established in 1937, and is awarded annually to the illustrator of the best children's picture book published during the previous year. The winner and possible Honor Books are selected by a committee of the association and announced at the ALA Midwinter Conference. The award is presented at the following ALA Annual Conference. United States citizens and residents are eligible for the award, which was established by Frederic C. Melcher, publisher, who donated the original medal, and honors Ralph Caldecott, noted nineteenth century illustrator. The award consists of a bronze medal and a citation.

[not represented in the 1993–1994 volume]

Canadian Governor General's

Governor General's Literary Awards
Governor General's Literary Awards, Canada Council, Box 1047, 99 Metcalfe St., Ottawa, ON K1P 5V8, Canada. 613-598-4376

These awards are presented annually to Canadian authors of the best books in English and French in seven categories. The two categories relevant here are: Children's literature (text) and Children's literature (illustration). The winning author and illustrator each receive $10,000 (Canadian). The awards were established in 1936.

Hero of Lesser Causes (Johnston)

Canadian YA

Young Adult Canadian Book Award
602, Ottawa, Ontario, Canada K2P1L5. 613-232-9625

This annual award, established in 1980, recognizes the author of an outstanding English language Canadian book (novel or short story collection), published during the previous year, which appeals to young adults between the ages of 13 and 18. The book may be published in either hardcover or paperback, and the author must be a Canadian citizen or a landed immigrant. The award consists of a leatherbound copy of the book.

There Will Be Wolves (Bradford)

Carnegie

Carnegie Medal
The Library Association, 7 Ridgemount St., London WC1E 7AE England. 71-636-7543

This annual award honors the author of an outstanding fiction or nonfiction children's book written in English and published during the previous year. Books published simultaneously in the UK and abroad are also eligible. The Carnegie Medal was first awarded in 1936 in honor of Andrew Carnegie, and is sponsored by Peters Library Service, Ltd. The award is a medal.

[not represented in the 1993–1994 volume]

Delacorte

Delacorte Press Prize for a First Young Adult Novel
Delacorte Press Books for Young Readers, 666 5th Ave., New York, NY 10103. 212-765-6500

The goal of this award, established in 1983, is to encourage the writing of contemporary young adult fiction. The author must be either American or Canadian, and may not have previously published a young adult novel, although other forms of publication are permissible. Foreign language manuscripts and translations are not eligible. The subject matter must be of interest to twelve- to eighteen-year-olds. The winner is selected by the Delacorte Books for Young Readers editors, and the prize is awarded annually, before April 30th of each year. The award consists of a hardback Delacorte Press contract and a paperback Dell contract, plus a $6,000 advance on royalties.

Life Belts (Hosie-Bounar)

Edwards

Margaret A. Edwards Award
School Library Journal & ALA/YALSA.
SLJ, Cahners Publishing Co., 249 W.
17th St., New York, 10017. 212-463-
6759
American Library Association, 50 E Huron St., Chicago, IL 60611. 800-545-
2433

This award, established in 1988, recognizes an author whose books over a period
of time have been accepted by young
adults as an authentic voice that continues
to illuminate their experiences and emotions, giving them insight into their lives
and their role in society. The winner is selected annually by a committee of YALSA,
announced at the ALA Midwinter Conference, and awarded at the following Annual
Conference. The award consists of $1,000
and an citation. This award was formerly
called the YASD/SLJ Young Adult Author
Award and the YASD/SLJ Author
Achievement Award.

Author: Walter Dean Myers
Brown Angels
Fallen Angels
Hoops
Malcolm X
Motown and Didi
Scorpions

Golden Kite

Golden Kite Award
Society of Children's Book Writers, Box
662966, Mar Vista Station, Los Angeles, CA 90066. 818-347-2849

This annual award recognizes excellence in the writing and illustrating of children's books. It was established in 1973,
and awards are given for fiction, nonfiction, and illustration. Members of the Society are eligible, and books are submitted
between February and December of the
year of their publication. The award consists of a golden kite statuette and an ac-
knowledgment certificate.

†*Letters from a Slave Girl* (Lyons)
†*The Road to Gettysburg* (Murphy)

†Talks on these titles can be found in
*Booktalking the Award Winners:
1992-1993.*

Greenaway

Kate Greenaway Medal
The Library Association, 7 Ridgemount
St., London WS1E 7AE England. 71-
636-7543

This annual award honors the illustrator of an outstanding fiction or nonfiction
children's book written in English and
published during the previous year. Books
published simultaneously in the UK and
abroad are also eligible. The Kate Greenaway Medal was first awarded in 1955 to
honor Kate Greenaway, a 19th century illustrator, and is sponsored by Peters Library Service, Ltd. The award is a medal.

[not represented in the 1993-1994 vol-
ume]

Hugo

Science Fiction Achievement Awards
(Hugo)
World Science Fiction Society, Box 1270,
Kendall Square Station, Cambridge,
MA 02142. 617-244-2679

These annual awards recognize outstanding achievement in the field of science fiction or fantasy, and are given in a
variety of categories including novel, novella, novelette, short story, nonfiction
book, and others. The award was established in 1953 in honor of Hugo Gerns-
back, who founded the first science-fiction
magazine and invented the term "science
fiction." Winners are chosen each year by
the members of the World Science Fiction
Convention. The award consists of a metal
rocketship designed by Jack McKnight
and Ben Jason, and mounted on a base.
The Hugo is sponsored by Davis Publica-
tions.

Doomsday Book (Willis)

IRA

IRA Children's Book Award
International Reading Association, 800
  Barksdale Rd., Box 8139, Newark,
  DE 19714-8139. 302-731-10057

This annual award is given to an author's first or second book, either fiction or
nonfiction, to recognize unusual promise
in the children's book field. Books from
any country and in any language copyright-
ed during the calendar year are eligible.
Awards are given in two categories: younger readers (four to ten years) and older
readers (ten to sixteen years). The award
consists of a $1,000 prize, and has been
given since 1975.

Behind the Secret Window (Toll)

King

Coretta Scott King Book Award
American Library Association/Social Responsibilities Round Table, 50 E Huron St., Chicago, IL 60611. 1-800-
  545-2433

This award was established in 1969 to
recognize African American authors and
illustrators for outstanding contributions
to children's literature which promotes a
better understanding and appreciation of
the culture and contribution of all peoples
to the realization of the American Dream.
The award is given annually, and to be eligible, books must have been published in
the calendar year preceding the year of the
award. The award consists of $250, a
plaque, and a set of Britannica or World
Book Encyclopedias. The award was established by Glyndon Flynt Greer to com-
memorate the life and works of Dr. Martin
Luther King, Jr., and to honor Mrs. Coretta Scott King for her courage and determination in continuing to work for peace and
world brotherhood.

*Toning the Sweep (Johnson)

King Honor

*Brown Honey in Broomwheat Tea
  (Thomas)

*Malcolm X (Myers)

King Illustrator

*Soul Looks Back in Wonder (Feelings)

King Illustrator Honor

*Brown Honey in Broomwheat Tea
  (Thomas)

National Jewish

National Jewish Book Award for Children's Literature
Jewish Book Council/Jewish Welfare
  Board, 15 E 26th St., New York, NY
  10010-1579. 212-532-4949

This annual award, established in
1952, honors the most distinguished children's book on a Jewish theme originally
written and published in English in either
the United States or Canada, or recognizes
cumulative contributions to Jewish juve-
nile literature. The award consists of $750
to the author and a citation to the publisher and to the author.

†*Letters from Rifka* (Hesse)

†A talk on this title can be found in
*Booktalking   the   Award   Winners:
1992-1993.*

Nebula

Science Fiction Writers of America Nebula Awards
Science Fiction Writers of America, Box
  4335, Spartanburg, SC 29305-4335.
  803-578-8012

This annual award recognizes excellence in science fiction writing by honoring
the authors of the best novel, novella, novelette, and short story published during the
previous calendar year. The Nebula was
established in 1966, and the award consists
of an engraved lucite block with an embed-
ded nebula formation.

*Doomsday Book (Willis)

Newbery

John Newbery Medal
Association of Librarians in Service to
   Children, American Library Association, 50 E Huron St., Chicago, IL
   60611. 800-545-2433

This annual award recognizes the author of the most distinguished contribution to American literature for children
each year. Authors must be United States
citizens or residents. The award was established in 1921 by Frederic C. Melcher,
publisher, who donated the first medal,
and honors John Newbery, noted 18th
century British bookseller. The award winners and possible Honor Books are selected by a committee of ALSC, announced at
the ALA Midwinter Conference and
awarded at the following Annual Conference. The award consists of a bronze medal and a citation.

The Giver (Lowry)

Newbery Honor

Crazy Lady! (Conly)
Dragon's Gate (Yep)
Eleanor Roosevelt (Freedman)

Notables

Notable Children's Books
Association of Librarians in Service to
   Children, American Library Association, 50 E Huron St., Chicago, IL
   60611. 800-545-2433

These outstanding fiction and nonfiction titles for children are selected annually by a committee of ALSC. The contents
of the list are announced at the ALA Midwinter Conference. Books must have been
published during the previous calendar
year to be eligible.

Across America on an Emigrant Train
   (Murphy)
Alien Secrets (Klause)
Anne Frank (Rol & Verhoeven)
The Apprentice (Molina Llorente)
Baby (MacLachlan)
The Boggart (Cooper)
A Bone from a Dry Sea (Dickinson)

Brown Angels (Myers)
Bull Run (Fleischman)
Crazy Lady! (Conly)
Dragon's Gate (Yep)
Eleanor Roosevelt (Freedman)
The Giver (Lowry)
Harper & Moon (Ross)
Hero of Lesser Causes (Johnston)
I Was a Teenage Professional Wrestler
   (Lewin)
It's Our World Too! (Hoose)
Learning by Heart (Young)
†*Letters from a Slave Girl* (Lyons)
†*Little Bit Dead* (Reaver)
Lives of the Musicians (Krull)
Make Lemonade (Wolff)
Many Thousand Gone (Hamilton)
Maybe Yes, Maybe No, Maybe Maybe
   (Patron)
More Rootabagas (Sandburg)
Nightjohn (Paulsen)
Owl in Love (Kindl)
The Oxboy (Mazer)
Peter (Walker)
Plain City (Hamilton)
The Princess in the Kitchen Garden
   (Heymans & Heymans)
Sadako (Coerr)
Scooter (Williams)
Song of Be (Beake)
Tell Me Everything (Coman)
Toning the Sweep (Johnson)
Visions (Sills)
The Wainscott Weasel (Seidler)

†Talks on these titles can be found in
   Booktalking the Award Winners:
   1992-1993.

N Y Times

New York Times Best Illustrated Chil-
   dren's Books
The New York Times Company, 229
   West 43rd St., New York, NY 10036

Titles on this list are selected from
among the children's books submitted to
the *New York Times Book Review* over the
course of the year. The winners are chosen
by an independent rotating panel of three
judges—an artist, a critic, and a person
who works hands-on with childrens'
books. The award is a certificate for the
artist; the winners for the year are announced in the annual children's issue of
the *Review,* the second week in November.

[not represented in the 1993–1994 volume]

O'Dell

Scott O'Dell Award for Historical Fiction
Bulletin of the Center for Children's
  Books, 1100 E 57th St., Chicago, IL
  60637. 312-702-8293

This award, established in 1981 by
Scott O'Dell, and awarded for the first
time in 1984, encourages and recognizes
the writing of good historical fiction,
which provides young readers with books
that interest them in the history that has
helped shaped their country and their
world. Titles written by a United States citizen, published by a US publisher for children or young adults, and set in the US,
Canada or South America are eligible. The
award consists of $5,000, and is given only
when merited.

†*Morning Girl* (Dorris)

†A talk on this title can be found in
*Booktalking the Award Winners: 1992-*993.*

Pen/Klein

Pen/Norma Klein Award for Children's
  Fiction
PEN American Center, 568 Broadway,
  New York, NY 10012. 212-334-1660

This award, established in 1991, recognizes an emerging voice of literary merit
among American writers of children's fiction, whose books demonstrate the adven-
turesome and innovative spirit that
characterizes the best in children's literature and Klein's work in particular. The
award is in memory of Klein, who was a
member of PEN. It is awarded biennially,
and consists of a $3,000 prize.

[not represented in the 1993–1994 vol-
ume]

Poe

Edgar Allan Poe Award—Best Young
  Adult Novel

Mystery Writers of America, 236 W.
  27th St., New York, NY 10001. 212-
  255-7005

This award recognizes an author for
outstanding contribution in mystery,
crime and suspense writing for young
adults. Books published in the United
States during the calendar year of the
award are eligible. The award was established in 1945, and consists of a scroll and
a ceramic bust of Edgar Allan Poe.

†*Little Bit Dead* (Reaver)

†A talk on this title can be found in
*Booktalking the Award Winners:
1992-1993.*

QP

Quick Picks—Recommended Titles for
  Reluctant Young Adult Readers
Young Adult Library Services Association, American Library Association,
  50 E. Huron St., Chicago, IL 60611.
  800-545-2433

This list of outstanding short titles for
young adult readers is selected by a YAL-
SA committee. It was established in 1981
and has also been called Recommended
Books for Reluctant YA Readers and the
High Interest/Low Reading Level Booklist. Titles must have been published within the previous calender year, and must
meet committee requirements for length,
complexity, and quality. The content of
this list is announced annually at the ALA
Midwinter Conference.

Alice in April (Naylor)
Anne Frank (Rol & Verhoeven)
Arena Beach (Staples)
The Burning Baby and Other Ghosts
  (Gordon)
The Cat Came Back (Mullins)
Death Is Hard to Live With (Bode)
Definitely Cool (Wilkinson)
The Disaster of the "Hindenburg"
  (Tanaka)
Dogzilla (Pilkey)

Dragon's Bait (Vande Velde)
*Freak the Mighty (Philbrick)
Free the Conroy Seven (McFann)
Going to See Grassy Ella (Lance)
The Golem and the Dragon Girl (Levitin)
Hamburger Heaven (Tennyson)
*Harris and Me (Paulsen)
*Heart of a Champion (Deuker)
*I Was a Teenage Professional Wrestler
　(Lewin)
In Love and in Danger (Levy)
Kat Kong (Pilkey)
The Killing Boy (Miklowitz)
Life Doesn't Frighten Me (Angelou)
*Lombardo's Law (Wittlinger)
*The Magic Circle (Napoli)
*Make Lemonade (Wolff)
*Missing Angel Juan (Block)
*Night Terrors (Murphy)
*Oddballs (Sleator)
Others See Us (Sleator)
*Owl in Love (Kindl)
*Peter (Walker)
Please Remove Your Elbow from My Ear
　(Godfrey)
*Revolutions of the Heart (Qualey)
Rhino (Klass)
*Shadow Boxer (Lynch)
Shakedown Street (Nasaw)
Soul Looks Back in Wonder (Feelings)
Speaking Out (Kuklin)
*Stardust otel (Janeczko)
*Stephen Biesty's Incredible
　Cross-Sections (Biesty & Platt)
The Stones of Muncaster Cathedral
　(Westall)
The Stranger (Cooney)
The Sunita Experiment (Perkins)
Susan Butcher and the Iditarod Trail
　(Dolan)
Sworn Enemies (Matas)
A Taste of Smoke (Bauer)
*Tell Me Everything (Coman)
*To the Top of the World (Brandenburg)
Twelve Days in August (Murrow)
*Uncle Vampire (Grant)
Unmentionable! (Jennings)
Where Do I Go from Here? (Wesley)
Winners and Losers (Hoffius)
A Wizard's Dozen (Stearns)

SLJ/C

School Library Journal Best of the Year
　in Children's Books
School Library Journal, Cahners Publish-
　ing Co., 249 W. 17th St., New York,
　10017. 212-463-6759

This list consists of the best titles written for children and reviewed in SLJ during the calendar year. Titles are selected by
the editors of SLJ and appear in the December issue of the magazine.

*Across America on an Emigrant Train
　(Murphy)
*Alien Secrets (Klause)
Bel-Air Bambi and the Mall Rats (Peck)
†Blue Skin of the Sea (Salisbury)
*The Boggart (Cooper)
*A Bone from a Dry Sea (Dickinson)
*Bull Run (Fleischman)
The Cuckoo Child (King-Smith)
*Eleanor Roosevelt (Freedman)
Forest (Lisle)
*Freedom's Children (Levine)
From Sea to Shining Sea (Cohn)
*The Giver (Lowry)
The Good Fortunes Gang (Mahy)
*Grab Hands and Run (Temple)
*The Great American Elephant Chase
　(Cross)
*Harper & Moon (Ross)
*Hero of Lesser Causes (Johnston)
*I Was a Teenage Professional Wrestler
　(Lewin)
*Lives of the Musicians (Krull)
*Make Lemonade (Wolff)
*Maybe Yes, Maybe No, Maybe Maybe
　(Patron)
*Missing Angel Juan (Block)
*More Rootabagas (Sandburg)
*Plain City (Hamilton)
The Real Plato Jones (Bawden)
*Revolutions of the Heart (Qualey)
*Shadow Boxer (Lynch)
*Staying Fat for Sarah Byrnes (Crutcher)
*Switching Well (Griffin)
T-Backs, T-Shirts, COAT and Suit
　(Konigsburg)
*Tell Me Everything (Coman)
*To the Top of the World (Brandenburg)
*Toning the Sweep (Johnson)
Western Wind (Fox)
*A Whole New Ball Game (Macy)
Your Mother Was a Neanderthal (Sciesz-
　ka)

†A talk on this title can be found in
　Booktalking the Award Winners:
　1992-1993.

SLJ/YA

School Library Journal Best of the Year
in Young Adult Books
School Library Journal, Cahners Publishing Co., 249 W. 17th St., New York,
10017. 212-463-6759

This list consists of the best adult titles
of interest to young adults which were reviewed in SLJ during the calendar year. Titles are selected by the editors of SLJ and
appear in the December issue of the magazine.

America Then & Now (Cohen & Wels)
*Charms for the Easy Life (Williams)
Daniel Boone (Faragher)
*Deerskin (McKinley)
Dreams Underfoot (De Lint)
*Durable Goods (Berg)
A Lesson Before Dying (Gaines)
Lost in the City (Jones)
Paradise of the Blind (Duong)
Pigs in Heaven (Kingsolver)
The Wild West (Time-Life staff)
Yoruba Girl Dancing (Bedford)

VOYA/SF

Voya's Best Science Fiction, Fantasy and
Horror
Voice of Young Advocates, Scarecrow
Press, Inc., Dept. VOYA, 52 Liberty
Street, PO Box 4167, Metuchen, NJ
08840.

This annual list recognizes outstanding
genre fiction (sci-fi, fantasy, and horror)
for young adults. Titles are nominated by
reviewers of VOYA throughout the year,
and the editors make additional nomina-
tions. The winning titles are selected by the
reviewers.

Aestival Tide (Hand)
*Alien Secrets (Klause)
Best Destiny (Carey)
Beyond the North Wind (Bradshaw)
*A Bone from a Dry Sea (Dickinson)
Books of the Keepers (Downer)
Broken Land (McDonald)
A Brush with Magic (Brooke)
Calling on Dragons (Wrede)
Changeweaver (Ball)
Child of an Ancient City (Williams)
City of Light, City of Dark (Avi)

Daughter of Elysium (Slonczewski)
*Deerskin (McKinley)
Dinosaur Fantastic (Resnick & Green-
berg)
Dog Wizard (Hambly)
Don't Give Up the Ghost (Gale)
Dream Date (Smith)
Elvissey (Womack)
Frankenstein (Greenberg)
Finders-Keepers (Greeno)
*The Giver (Lowry)
Glory Season (Brin)
Harvest (Wilson)
High Steel (Haldeman)
The Horror Hall of Fame (Silverberg &
Greenberg)
The Jaguar Princess (Bell)
Kipling's Fantasy Stories (Kipling)
The Last Command (Zahn)
Lord of the Two Lands (Tarr)
The Mind Pool (Sheffield)
*Modern Ghost Stories by Eminent Wom-
en Writers* (Dalby)
Nevernever (Shetterly)
Night Terrors (Murphy)
Powers That Be (McCaffrey & Scarbor-
ough)
Shining Face (Myra)
Spirit Ring (Bujold)
Split Heirs (Watt-Evans)
Stainless Steel Visions (Harrison)
Strange Objects (Crew)
*Switching Well (Griffin)
The Tale of the Body Thief (Rice)
Talking to Dragons (Wrede)
Testing (Oberndorf)
Twilight (James)
Virtual Girl (Thomson)
Windleaf (Sherman)
Wings of a Falcon (Voight)
Wishing Season (Freisner)
Witch Week (Jones)
Wren's Quest (Smith)

Whitbread

Whitbread Literary Awards
Booksellers Association of Great Britain
& Ireland, Minster House, 272 Vaux-
hall Bridge Rd., London SW1V 1BA.
071-834-5477; fax 071-834-8812

These annual awards, instituted in
1971 and expanded in 1985, honor literature of merit with wide appeal. Awards of
£2,000 apiece are presented in five catego-

ries: novel, first novel, biography/ autobiography, poetry, children's novel (the category relevant here). Since 1985, one of the five winners has been chosen to recieve an aditional £21,000 as Book of the Year. To be eligible, books must first have been published in the UK or Ireland between November 1 and October 31 in the relevant year, and written by authors who have been domiciled in either place for three years.

The Great Elephant Chase (Cross)

[1992 winner; published in the US as *The Great American Elephant Chase.*]

BIBLIOGRAPHY BY AUTHOR

Alcock, Vivien. *Singer to the Sea God*. Delacorte 1993. (MS-JH)

Anderson, Rachel. *The Bus People*. Holt 1993. (MS-JH)

Angelou, Maya. *Life Doesn't Frighten Me*. Stewart, Tabori & Chang 1993. (JH)

Ashe, Arthur and Rampersad, Arnold. *Days of Grace*. Knopf 1993; pb Ballantine 1994. (HS-A)

Atkin, S. Beth. *Voices from the Fields: Children of Migrant Farm Workers Tell Their Stories*. Little 1993. (JH-HS)

Avi. *City of Light, City of Dark: A Comic-Book Novel*. Orchard 1993. (MS)

Ball, Margaret. *Changeweaver*. pb Baen 1993. (HS-A)

Bauer, Marion Dane. *A Taste of Smoke*. Clarion 1993. (MS)

Bawden, Nina. *The Real Plato Jones*. Clarion 1993. (MS-JH)

Beake, Lesley. *Song of Be*. Holt 1993, pb Puffin 1995. (JH-HS)

Bedford, Simi. *Yoruba Girl Dancing*. Viking 1992; pb 1994. (JH-HS)

Bell, Clare. *The Jaguar Princess*. Tor 1993. (HS-A)

Berg, Elizabeth. *Durable Goods*. Random 1993; pb Avon 1994. (JH-HS)

Biesty, Stephen and Platt, Richard. *Stephen Biesty's Incredible Cross-Sections*. Knopf 1992. (MS)

Block, Francesca Lia. *Missing Angel Juan*. HarperCollins 1993. JH-HS)

Blume, Judy. *Here's to You, Rachel Robinson!* Orchard 1993; pb Dell 1994. (MS-JH)

Bode, Janet. *Death Is Hard to Live With: Teenagers Talk About How They Cope with Loss*. Delacorte 1993. (JH-HS)

Bradford, Karleen. *There Will Be Wolves*. HarperCollins 1992, pb 1992. (MS-JH)

Bradshaw, Gillian. *Beyond the North Wind*. Greenwillow 1993. (MS-JH)

Brandenburg, Jim. *To the Top of the World: Adventures with Arctic Wolves*. Walker 1993. (MS-HS)

Brin, David. *Glory Season*. Bantam 1993; pb 1994. (HS-A)

Brooke, William J. *A Brush with Magic*. HarperCollins 1993. (EL-MS)

Bruchac, Joseph. *Dawn Land*. Fulcrum 1993. (JH-HS)

Bujold, Lois McMaster. *The Spirit Ring*. Baen 1992; pb 1993. (JH-HS)

Carey, Diane. *Best Destiny*, "Star Trek" series. Pocket 1992; pb 1993. (JH-HS)

Coerr, Eleanor. *Sadako*. Putnam 1993. (EL-MS)

Cohen, David, sel., and Wels, Susan. *America Then & Now: Great Old Photographs of America's Life and Times, and How Those Same Scenes Look Today*. HarperCollins 1992. (JH-A)

Cohn, Amy, comp. *From Sea to Shining Sea: A Treasury of American Folklore and Folk Songs*. Scholastic 1993. (EL-A)

Coman, Carolyn. *Tell Me Everything*. Farrar 1993. (JH)

Conly, Jane Leslie. *Crazy Lady!* HarperCollins 1993. (MS-JH)

Cooney, Caroline B. *The Stranger*. pb Scholastic 1993. (JH)

Cooney, Caroline B. *Whatever Happened to Janie?* Delacorte 1993. (JH-HS)

Cooper, Susan. *The Boggart.* McElderry 1993. (MS)

Crew, Gary. *Strange Objects.* S&S 1993. (JH-HS)

Cross, Gillian. *The Great American Elephant Chase.* Holiday 1993; pb Puffin 1994. (MS-JH)

Crutcher, Chris. *Staying Fat for Sarah Byrnes.* Greenwillow 1993. (JH-HS)

Dalby, Richard, comp. *Modern Ghost Stories by Eminent Women Writers.* Carrol & Graf 1991; pb 1994. (JH-A)

De Lint, Charles. *Dreams Underfoot.* Tor 1993; pb 1994. (HS)

Delany, Sarah and Delany, A. Elizabeth. *Having Our Say: The Delany Sisters' First 100 Years.* Kodansha Interational 1993; pb Dell 1994. (JH-A)

Deuker, Carl. *Heart of a Champion.* Little 1993. (JH-HS)

Dickinson, Peter. *A Bone from a Dry Sea.* Delacortte 1993. (JH-HS)

Dolan, Ellen M. *Susan Butcher and the Iditarod Trail.* Walker 1993. (MS-JH)

Downer, Ann. *The Books of the Keepers.* Atheneum 1993. (JH-HS)

Duong Thu Huong. *Paradise of the Blind,* translated from the Vietnamese by Phan Huy Duong and Nina McPherson. Morrow 1988, pb Penguin 1994. (HS-A)

Drucker, Olga Levy. *Kindertransport.* Holt 1992. (MS-JH)

Esquivel, Laura. *Like Water for Chocolate,* translated from the Spanish by Carol Christensen and Thomas Christensen. Doubleday 1992; pb 1994. (HS-A)

Faragher, John Mack. *Daniel Boone: The Life and Legend of an American Pioneer.* Holt 1992; pb 1993. (JH-A)

Feelings, Tom, comp. *Soul Looks Back in Wonder.* Dial 1993. (EL-MS)

Fleischman, Paul. *Bull Run.* HarperCollins 1993. (MS-HS)

Fox, Paula. *Western Wind: A Novel.* Orchard 1993. (MS-JH)

Freedman, Russell. *Eleanor Roosevelt: A Life of Discovery.* Clarion 1993. (MS-JH)

Friesner, Esther M. *Wishing Season.* Atheneum 1993. (JH)

Gaines, Ernest. *A Lesson Before Dying.* Knopf 1993; pb Random 1994. (HS-A)

Gale, David, ed. *Don't Give Up the Ghost: The Delacorte Book of Original Ghost Stories.* Delacorte 1993. (MS-JH)

Garland, Sherry. *Shadow of the Dragon.* Harcourt 1993; pb 1993. (JH-HS)

Gee, Maurice. *The Champion.* S&S 1993; pb 1993. (JH)

Gibbons, Kaye. *Charms for the Easy Life.* Putnam 1993; pb Avon 1994. (HS-A)

Godfrey, Martyn. *Please Remove Your Elbow from My Ear.* pb Avon 1993. (MS-JH)

Goldstein, Lisa. *The Red Magician.* Tor 1993. (HS-A)

Gordon, John. *The Burning Baby and Other Ghosts.* Candlewick 1993. (JH-HS)

Grant, Cynthia D. *Shadow Man.* Atheneum 1992. (JH-HS)

Grant, Cynthia D. *Uncle Vampire.* Atheneum 1993. (JH-HS)

Greenberg, Martin H. *Frankenstein: The Monster Wakes.* pb DAW 1993 (JH-A)

Greeno, Gayle. *Finders-Seekers,* Book 1 of "The Ghatti's Tale." pb DAW 1993 (HS)

Griffin, Peni R. *The Switching Well.* Macmillan 1993. (MS-JH)

Hahn, Mary Downing. *The Wind Blows Backward.* Clarion 1993; pb Avon 1994. (JH-HS)

Haldemann, Jack C., II, and Dann, Jack. *High Steel.* Tor 1993; pb 1994. (HS-A)

Hambly, Barbara. *The Dog Wizard;* Book 3 of "The Windrose Chronicles." pb Ballantine/Del Rey 1992. (JH-HS)

Hamilton, Virginia. *Many Thousand Gone: African Americans from Slavery to Freedom.* Knopf 1993. (MS-JH)

Hamilton, Virginia. *Plain City.* Scholastic 1993. (MS-JH)

Hand, Elizabeth. *Aestival Tide.* pb Bantam 1992. (HS-A)

Harrison, Harry. *Stainless Steel Visions.* Tor 1993. (HS-A)

Haynes, David. *Right by My Side.* pb New Rivers Press 1993. (JH-HS)

Heymans, Annemie and Heymans, Margriet. *The Princess in the Kitchen Garden.* Translated from the Dutch by Johanna H. Prins and Johanna W. Prins. Farrar 1993 (US). (EL-MS)

Hobbs, Will. *Beardance*. Atheneum 1993. (JH–HS)

Hodge, Merle. *For the Life of Laetitia*. Farrar 1993. (JH)

Hoffius, Stephen. *Winners and Losers*. S&S 1993; pb 1993. (JH–HS)

Hoose, Phillip M. *It's Our World Too! Stories of Young People Who Are Making a Difference*. Little 1993; pb 1993. (MS–JH)

Hosie-Bouner, Jane. *Life Belts*. Delacorte 1993. (JH)

Isaacson, Philip M. *A Short Walk Around the Pyramids and Through the World of Art*. Knopf 1993. (MS–JH)

James, Peter. *Twilight*. St. Martin's 1993. (HS–A)

Janeczko, Paul, comp. *Looking for Your Name: A Collection of Contemporary Poems*. Orchard 1993. (JH–HS)

Janeczko, Paul. *Stardust otel*. Orchard 1993. (JH–HS)

Jennings, Paul. *Unmentionable! More Amazing Stories*. Viking 1993 (US; published in Australia in 1991). (MS–HS)

Johnson, Angela. *Toning the Sweep*. Orchard 1993; pb Scholastic 1994. (MS–JH)

Johnston, Julie. *Hero of Lesser Causes*. Little 1992; pb Puffin 1994. (JH)

Jones, Diana Wynne. *Witch Week*. Greenwillow 1993 (reissue of 1982 original). (MS)

Jones, Edward P. *Lost in the City*. Morrow 1992. (HS–A)

Jordan, Sherryl. *Winter of Fire*. Scholastic 1993. (JH–HS)

Kaysen, Susanna. *Girl, Interrupted*. Random 1993; pb 1994. (HS–A)

Kindl, Patrice. *Owl in Love*. Houghton 1993; pb Puffin 1994. (MS–HS)

King-Smith, Dick. *The Cuckoo Child*. Hyperion 1993; pb 1994. (EL)

Kingsolver, Barbara. *Pigs in Heaven*. HarperCollins 1993; pb 1994. (HS–A)

Kipling, Rudyard. *Kipling's Fantasy Stories*. John Brunner, sel. Tor 1992. (JH–A)

Klass, Sheila Solomon. *Rhino*. Scholastic 1993. (JH–HS)

Klause, Annette Curtis. *Alien Secrets*. Delacorte 1993. (MS–JH)

Konigsberg, E. L. *T-Backs, T-Shirts, COAT, and Suit*. Atheneum 1993. (MS–JH)

Krull, Kathleen. *Lives of the Musicians: Good Times, Bad Times (and What the Neighbors Thought)*. Harcourt 1992. (MS–JH)

Kuklin, Susan. *Speaking Out: Teenagers Take on Race, Sex, and Identity*. Putnam 1993. (JH–HS)

Lance, Kathryn. *Going to See Grassy Ella*. Lothrop 1993. (MS–JH)

LeMieux, A. C. *The TV Guidance Counselor*. Tambourine (Morrow) 1993. (JH–HS)

Levine, Ellen. *Freedom's Children: Young Civil Rights Activists Tell Their Own Stories*. Putnam 1993, pb Avon 1994. (JH–HS)

Levitin, Sonia. *The Golem and the Dragon Girl*. Dial 1993; pb Fawcett 1994. (MS–JH)

Levy, Barrie. *In Love and In Danger: A Teen's Guide to Breaking Free of Abusive Relationships*. pb Seal Press 1993. (HS–A)

Lewin, Ted. *I Was a Teenage Professional Wrestler*. Orchard 1993; pb Hyperion 1994. (JH–HS)

Lisle, Janet Taylor. *Forest*. Orchard 1993. (MS)

Littlefield, Bill. *Champions: Stories of Ten Remarkable Athletes*. Little 1993. (MS–JH)

Lowry, Lois. *The Giver*. Houghton 1993; pb Dell 1994. (MS–JH)

Lynch, Chris. *Shadow Boxer*. HarperCollins 1993. (JH–HS)

MacLachlan, Patricia. *Baby*. Delacorte 1993. (MS–HS)

Macy, Sue. *A Whole New Ball Game: The Story of the All-American Girls Professional Baseball League*. Holt 1993. (MS–HS)

Mahy, Margaret. *The Good Fortunes Gang;* Book 1 of "The Cousins Quartet." Delacorte 1993. (MS–JH)

Matas, Carol. *Sworn Enemies*. Bantam 1993; pb Dell 1994. (JH–HS)

Mazer, Anne. *The Oxboy*. Knopf 1993. (MS–JH)

Mazer, Harry. *Who Is Eddie Leonard?* Delacorte 1993. (MS–JH)

Mazer, Norma Fox. *Out of Control*. Morrow 1993; pb Avon 1994. (JH–HS)

McCaffrey, Anne and Scarborough, Elizabeth Ann. *Powers That Be.* Ballantine/Del Rey 1993. (HS)

McDonald, Ian. *The Broken Land.* Bantam 1992; pb 1993. (HS-A)

McFann, Jane. *Free the Conroy Seven.* pb Avon 1993. (JH-HS)

McKinley, Robin. *Deerskin.* Ace 1993; pb 1994. (HS)

Merrick, Monte. *Shelter: A Novel.* Hyperion 1993. (JH)

Meyer, Carolyn. *White Lilacs.* Harcourt 1993; pb 1993. (JH)

Miklowitz, Gloria D. *The Killing Boy.* pb Bantam 1993. (HS)

Molina Llorente, Pilar. *The Apprentice,* translated from the Spanish by Robin Longshaw. Farrar 1993. (MS-JH)

Mori, Kyoko. *Shizuko's Daughter.* Holt 1993. (JH-HS)

Mullins, Hilary. *The Cat Came Back.* Naiad 1993; pb 1993. (HS)

Murphy, Jim. *Across America on an Emigrant Train.* Clarion 1993. (MS-HS)

Murphy, Jim. *Night Terrors.* Scholastic 1993. (JH-HS)

Murrow, Liza Ketchum. *Twelve Days in August.* Holiday 1993. (JH-HS)

Myers, Walter Dean. *Brown Angels: An Album of Pictures and Verse.* HarperCollins 1993. (EL-A)

Myers, Walter Dean. *Fallen Angels.* Scholastic 1988; pb 1988. (JH-HS)

Myers, Walter Dean. *Hoops.* Delacorte 1981; pb Dell 1983. (JH-HS)

Myers, Walter Dean. *Malcolm X: By Any Means Necessary.* Scholastic 1993; pb 1994. (JH-A)

Myers, Walter Dean. *Motown and Didi: A Love Story.* Viking 1984; pb Dell 1987. (HS)

Myers, Walter Dean. *Scorpions.* Harper & Row 1988, pb HarperCollins 1990. (JH)

Myra, Harold Lawrence. *The Shining Face.* pb Zondervan 1993. (JH-A)

Napoli, Donna Jo. *The Magic Circle.* Dutton 1993. (JH-HS)

Nasaw, Jonathan. *Shakedown Street.* Delacorte 1993. (JH-HS)

Naylor, Phyllis Reynolds. *Alice in April.* Atheneum 1993. (MS-JH)

Oberndorf, Charles. *The Testing.* pb Bantam 1993. (HS)

Patron, Susan. *Maybe Yes, Maybe No, Maybe Maybe.* Orchard 1993. (EL-MS)

Paulsen, Gary. *Harris and Me: A Summer Remembered.* Harcourt 1993. (MS-JH)

Paulsen, Gary. *Nightjohn.* Delacorte 1993; pb 1993. (JH-HS)

Peck, Richard. *Bel-Air Bambi and the Mall Rats.* Delacorte 1993. (MS-JH)

Perkins, Mitali. *The Sunita Experiment.* Little 1993; pb Hyperion 1994. (JH) .

Philbrick, W. R. *Freak the Mighty.* Blue Sky Press 1993. (MS-JH)

Pilkey, Dav. *Dogzilla.* Harcourt 1993; pb 1993. (EL-MS)

Pilkey, Dav. *Kat Kong.* Harcourt 1993; pb 1993. (EL-MS)

Qualey, Marsha. *Revolutions of the Heart.* Houghton 1993. (JH-HS)

Rendell, Ruth. *The Crocodile Bird.* Crown 1993. (HS-A)

Resnick, Michael and Greenberg, Martin H.. *Dinosaur Fantastic.* pb DAW 1993. (MS-JH)

Reynolds, Marilyn. *Detour for Emmy.* Morning Glory Press 1993. (HS)

Rice, Anne. *The Tale of the Body Thief.* Knopf 1992; pb Ballantine 1993. (JH-A)

Rinaldi, Ann. *In My Father's House.* Scholastic 1992. (JH-HS)

Roberson, Jennifer. *Lady of the Forest.* Zebra 1992; pb 1993. (JH-HS)

Rochman, Hazel and McCampbell, Darlene Z., sels. *Who Do You Think You Are? Stories of Friends and Enemies.* Little 1993. (JH-HS)

Rol, Ruud van der and Verhoeven, Rian. *Anne Frank, Beyond the Diary: A Photographic Remembrance,* translated from the Dutch by Tony Langham and Plym Peters. Viking 1993. (MS-A)

Ross, Ramon Royal. *Harper & Moon.* Atheneum 1993. (MS-JH)

Ruby, Lois. *Miriam's Well.* Scholastic 1993. (JH-HS)

Sandburg, Carl. *More Rootabagas.* Knopf 1993. (EL-MS)

Scieszka, Jon. *Your Mother Was a Neanderthal.* Viking 1993. (MS-JH)

Seidler, Tor. *The Wainscott Weasel.* HarperCollins 1993. (EL-MS)

Sheffield, Charles. *The Mind Pool.* pb Baen 1993. (HS-A)

Sherman, Josepha. *Windleaf.* Walker 1993. (JH-HS)

Shetterly, Will. *Nevernever.* Jane Yolen Books 1993. (JH-HS)

Sills, Leslie. *Visions: Stories About Women Artists.* Albert Whitman & Co. 1993. (MS-JH)

Silverberg, Robert and Greenberg, Martin H. *The Horror Hall of Fame.* Carroll & Graf 1991; pb 1992. (HS)

Sleator, William. *Oddballs.* Dutton 1993. (MS-JH)

Sleator, William. *Others See Us.* Dutton 1993. (JH-HS)

Slonczewski, Joan. *Daughter of Elysium.* Morrow 1993; pb Avon 1993. (HS-A)

Smith, Sherwood. *Wren's Quest.* Harcourt 1993. (JH-HS)

Smith, Sinclair. *Dream Date.* Scholastic 1993. (JH-HS)

Smith, Wayne. *Thor.* St. Martin's 1992; pb Ballantine 1994. (JH-HS)

Staples, Donna. *Arena Beach.* Houghton 1993. (HS)

Staples, Suzanne Fisher. *Haveli.* Knopf 1993. (JH-HS)

Stearns, Michael, ed. *A Wizard's Dozen.* Harcourt 1993. (JH-HS)

Sutcliff, Rosemary. *Black Ships Before Troy.* Delacorte 1993. (MS-JH)

Sweeney, Joyce. *The Tiger Orchard.* Delacorte 1993. (HS)

Tamar, Erika. *Fair Game.* Harcourt 1993; pb 1993. (HS)

Tanaka, Shelley. *The Disaster of the "Hindenburg": The Last Flight of the Greatest Airship Ever Built.* Scholastic 1993. (MS-JH)

Tarr, Judith. *Lord of the Two Lands.* Tor 1993; pb 1994. (JH-HS)

Taylor, Theodore. *Timothy of the Cay.* Harcourt 1993; pb Avon 1994. (MS-JH)

Temple, Frances. *Grab Hands and Run.* Orchard 1993. (MS-JH)

Temple, Frances. *A Taste of Salt: A Story of Modern Haiti.* Orchard 1992. (JH-HS)

Tennyson, Jeffrey. *Hamburger Heaven: The Illustrated History of the Hamburger.* Hyperion 1993; pb 1995. (JH-HS)

Thomas, Joyce Carol. *Brown Honey in Broomwheat Tea.* HarperCollins 1993. (EL-MS)

Thomson, Amy. *Virtual Girl.* pb Ace 1993. (HS)

Time-Life Books staff. *The Wild West.* Warner 1993. (JH-A)

Toll, Nelly S. *Behind the Secret Window: A Memoir of a Hidden Childhood During World War II.* Dial 1993. (MS-JH)

Vande Velde, Vivian. *Dragon's Bait.* Jane Yolen Books 1992. (JH-HS)

Vick, Helen Hughes. *Walker of Time.* Harbinger 1993; pb 1993. (HS)

Voight, Cynthia. *Wings of a Falcon.* Scholastic 1993. (JH-HS)

Volavkova, Hana, ed. *I Never Saw Another Butterfly: Children's Poems and Drawings from Terezin Concentration Camp, 1942-44.* Schocken 1993; pb 1994. (JH-A)

Walker, Kate. *Peter.* Houghton 1993. (JH-HS)

Watson, Larry. *Montana 1948.* Milkweed Editions 1993. (HS-A)

Watt-Evans, Lawrence and Friesner, Esther. *Split Heirs.* Tor 1993; pb 1994. (HS-A)

Weaver, Will. *Striking Out.* HarperCollins 1993. (JH-HS)

Wesley, Valerie Wilson. *Where Do I Go from Here?* Scholastic 1993. (JH)

Westall, Robert. *The Stones of Muncaster Cathedral.* Farrar 1991; pb 1994. (JH-HS)

Wilkinson, Brenda S. *Definitely Cool.* Scholastic 1993. (MS-JH)

Williams, Tad and Hoffman, Nina Kiriki. *Child of an Ancient City.* Atheneum/Maxwell Macmillan 1992; pb Tor 1994. (JH-HS)

Williams, Vera B. *Scooter.* Greenwillow 1993. (EL-MS)

Willis, Connie. *Doomsday Book.* Bantam 1992; pb 1993. (HS-A)

Wilson, Robert Charles. *The Harvest.* Bantam 1992; pb 1993. (HS-A)

Wittlinger, Ellen. *Lombardo's Law.* Houghton 1993; pb Morrow 1995. (JH-HS)

Wolff, Virginia Euwer. *Make Lemonade.* Holt 1993; pb Scholastic 1994. (JH-HS)

Womack, Jack. *Elvissey*. pb Tor 1993. (HS-A)

Wrede, Patricia C. *Calling on Dragons*; Book 3 of "The Enchanted Forest Chronicles." Harcourt 1993. (MS-HS)

Wrede, Patricia C. *Talking to Dragons*; Book 4 of "The Enchanted Forest Chronicles." Harcourt 1993; pb Scholastic 1995. (MS-HS)

Yep, Laurence. *American Dragons: Twenty-Five Asian American Voices*. HarperCollins 1993. (JH-HS)

Yep, Laurence. *Dragon's Gate*. HarperCollins 1993. (JH)

Young, Ronder Thomas. *Learning by Heart*. Houghton 1993. (MS)

Zahn, Timothy. *The Last Command*; Book 3 of the "Star Wars" series. Bantam 1993; pb 1994. (HS-A)

BIBLIOGRAPHY BY AGE LEVEL

Elementary

Brown Angels (Myers)
Brown Honey in Broomwheat Tea (Thomas)
A Brush with Magic (Brooke)
The Cuckoo Child (King-Smith)
Dogzilla (Pilkey)
From Sea to Shining Sea (Cohn)
Kat Kong (Pilkey)
Maybe Yes, Maybe No, Maybe Maybe (Patron)
More Rootabagas (Sandburg)
The Princess in the Kitchen Garden (Heymans & Heymans)
Sadako (Coerr)
Scooter (Williams)
Soul Looks Back in Wonder (Feelings)
The Wainscott Weasel (Seidler)

Middle School

Across America on an Emigrant Train (Murphy)
Alice in April (Naylor)
Alien Secrets (Klause)
Anne Frank, Beyond the Diary (Rol & Verhoeven)
The Apprentice (Molina Llorente)
Baby (MacLachlan)
Behind the Secret Window (Toll)
Bel-Air Bambi and the Mall Rats (Peck)
Beyond the North Wind (Bradshaw)
Black Ships Before Troy (Sutcliff)
The Boggart (Cooper)
Brown Angels (Myers)
Brown Honey in Broomwheat Tea (Thomas)
A Brush with Magic (Brooke)
Bull Run (Fleischman)
The Bus People (Anderson)
Calling on Dragons (Wrede)
Champions (Littlefield)
City of Light, City of Dark (Avi)
Crazy Lady! (Conly)
Definitely Cool (Wilkinson)
Dinosaur Fantastic (Resnick)

The Disaster of the "Hindenburg" (Tanaka)
Dogzilla (Pilkey)
Don't Give Up the Ghost (Gale)
Eleanor Roosevelt (Freedman)
Forest (Lisle)
Freak the Mighty (Philbrick)
From Sea to Shining Sea (Cohn)
The Giver (Lowry)
Going to See Grassy Ella (Lance)
The Golem and the Dragon Girl (Levitin)
The Good Fortunes Gang (Mahy)
Grab Hands and Run (Temple)
The Great American Elephant Chase (Cross)
Harper & Moon (Ross)
Harris and Me (Paulsen)
Here's to You, Rachel Robinson! (Blume)
It's Our World Too! Stories of Young People Making a Difference (Hoose)
Kat Kong (Pilkey)
Kindertransport (Drucker)
Learning by Heart (Young)
Lives of the Musicians (Krull)
Maybe Yes, Maybe No, Maybe Maybe (Patron)
Many Thousand Gone (Hamilton)
More Rootabagas (Sandburg)
Oddballs (Sleator)
Owl in Love (Kindl)
The Oxboy (Mazer)
Plain City (Hamilton)
Please Remove Your Elbow from My Ear (Godfrey)
The Princess in the Kitchen Garden (Heymans & Heymans)
The Real Plato Jones (Bawden)
Sadako (Coerr)
Scooter (Williams)
A Short Walk Around the Pyramids and Through the World of Art (Isaacson)
Singer to the Sea God (Alcock)
Soul Looks Back in Wonder (Feelings)
Stephen Biesty's Incredible Cross-Sections (Biesty & Platt)
Susan Butcher and the Iditarod Trail (Dolan)

The Switching Well (Griffin)
T-backs, T-shirts, COAT, and Suit (Konigsberg)
Talking to Dragons (Wrede)
A Taste of Smoke (Bauer)
There Will Be Wolves (Bradford)
Timothy of the Cay (Taylor)
To the Top of the World (Brandenburg)
Toning the Sweep (Johnson)
Unmentionable! More Amazing Stories (Jennings)
Visions: Stories About Women Artists (Sills)
The Wainscott Weasel (Seidler)
Western Wind (Fox)
Who Is Eddie Leonard? (Mazer)
A Whole New Ball Game (Macy)
Witch Week (Jones)
Your Mother Was a Neanderthal (Scieszka)

Junior High

Across America on an Emigrant Train (Murphy)
Alice in April (Naylor)
Alien Secrets (Klause)
America Then & Now (Cohen & Wels)
American Dragons (Yep)
Anne Frank, Beyond the Diary (Rol & Verhoeven)
The Apprentice (Molina Llorente)
Baby (MacLachlan)
Beardance (Hobbs)
Behind the Secret Window (Toll)
Bel-Air Bambi and the Mall Rats (Peck)
Best Destiny (Carey)
Beyond the North Wind (Bradshaw)
Black Ships Before Troy (Sutcliff)
A Bone from a Dry Sea (Dickinson)
Books of the Keepers (Downer)
Brown Angels (Myers)
Bull Run (Fleischman)
The Burning Baby and Other Ghosts (Gordon)
The Bus People (Anderson)
Calling on Dragons (Wrede)
The Champion (Gee)
Champions (Littlefield)
Child of an Ancient City (Williams & Hoffman)
Crazy Lady! (Conly)
Daniel Boone (Faragher)
Dawn Land (Bruchac)
Death Is Hard to Live With (Bode)
Definitely Cool (Wilkinson)

Dinosaur Fantastic (Resnick)
The Disaster of the "Hindenburg" (Tanaka)
The Dog Wizard (Hambly)
Don't Give Up the Ghost (Gale)
Dragon's Bait (Vande Velde)
Dragon's Gate (Yep)
Dream Date (Smith)
Durable Goods (Berg)
Eleanor Roosevelt (Freedman)
Fallen Angels (Myers)
For the Life of Laetitia (Hodge)
Frankenstein (Greenberg)
Freak the Mighty (Philbrick)
Free the Conroy Seven (McFann)
Freedom's Children (Levine)
From Sea to Shining Sea (Cohn)
The Giver (Lowry)
Going to See Grassy Ella (Lance)
The Golem and the Dragon Girl (Levitin)
The Good Fortunes Gang (Mahy)
Grab Hands and Run (Temple)
The Great American Elephant Chase (Cross)
Hamburger Heaven (Tennyson)
Harper & Moon (Ross)
Harris and Me (Paulsen)
Haveli (Staples)
Having Our Say (Delany & Delany)
Heart of a Champion (Deuker)
Here's to You, Rachel Robinson! (Blume)
Hero of Lesser Causes (Johnston)
Hoops (Myers)
I Was a Teenage Professional Wrestler (Lewin)
I Never Saw Another Butterfly (Volavkova)
In My Father's House (Rinaldi)
It's Our World Too! Stories of Young People Who Are Making a Difference (Hoose)
Kindertransport (Drucker)
Kipling's Fantasy Stories (Kipling)
Lady of the Forest (Roberson)
Life Doesn't Frighten Me (Angelou)
Life Belts (Hosie-Bouner)
Lives of the Musicians (Krull)
Lombardo's Law (Wittlinger)
Lord of the Two Lands (Tarr)
The Magic Circle (Napoli)
Make Lemonade (Wolff)
Malcolm X (Myers)
Many Thousand Gone (Hamilton)
Miriam's Well (Ruby)
Missing Angel Juan (Block)
Modern Ghost Stories by Eminent Wom-

en Writers (Dalby)
Nevernever (Shetterly)
Night Terrors (Murphy)
Nightjohn (Paulsen)
Oddballs (Sleator)
Others See Us (Sleator)
Out of Control (Mazer)
Owl in Love (Kindl)
The Oxboy (Mazer)
Peter (Walker)
Plain City (Hamilton)
Please Remove Your Elbow from My Ear (Godfrey)
The Real Plato Jones (Bawden)
Revolutions of the Heart (Qualey)
Rhino (Klass)
Right by My Side (Haynes)
Scorpions (Myers)
Shadow Boxer (Lynch)
Shadow Man (Grant)
Shadow of the Dragon (Garland)
Shakedown Street (Nasaw)
Shelter (Merrick)
The Shining Face (Myra)
Shizuko's Daughter (Mori)
A Short Walk Around the Pyramids and Through the World of Art (Isaacson)
Singer to the Sea God (Alcock)
Song of Be (Beake)
Speaking Out (Kuklin)
The Spirit Ring (Bujold)
Stardust otel (Janeczko)
Staying Fat for Sarah Byrnes (Crutcher)
The Stones of Muncaster Cathedral (Westall)
Strange Objects (Crew)
The Stranger (Cooney)
Striking Out (Weaver)
The Sunita Experiment (Perkins)
Susan Butcher and the Iditarod Trail (Dolan)
The Switching Well (Griffin)
Sworn Enemies (Matas)
T-backs, T-shirts, COAT, and Suit (Konigsberg)
Talking to Dragons (Wrede)
A Taste of Salt (Temple)
Tell Me Everything (Coman)
The Tale of the Body Thief (Rice)
There Will Be Wolves (Bradford)
Thor (Smith)
Timothy of the Cay (Taylor)
To the Top of the World (Brandenburg)
Toning the Sweep (Johnson)
The TV Guidance Counselor (LeMieux)
Twelve Days in August (Murrow)

Uncle Vampire (Grant)
Unmentionable! More Amazing Stories (Jennings)
Visions: Stories About Women Artists (Sills)
Voices from the Fields: Children of Migrant Farm Workers Tell Their Stories (Atkin)
Western Wind (Fox)
Whatever Happened to Janie? (Cooney)
Where Do I Go from Here? (Wesley)
White Lilacs (Meyer)
Who Is Eddie Leonard? (Mazer)
Who Do You Think You Are? Stories of Friends and Enemies (Rochman)
A Whole New Ball Game (Macy)
The Wild West (Time-Life Books staff)
The Wind Blows Backward (Hahn)
Windleaf (Sherman)
Wings of a Falcon (Voight)
Winners and Losers (Hoffius)
Winter of Fire (Jordan)
Wishing Season (Friesner)
A Wizard's Dozen (Stearns)
Wren's Quest (Smith)
Yoruba Girl Dancing (Bedford)
Your Mother Was a Neanderthal (Scieszka)

High School

Across America on an Emigrant Train (Murphy)
Aestival Tide (Hand)
America Then & Now (Cohen & Wels)
American Dragons (Yep)
Anne Frank, Beyond the Diary (Rol & Verhoeven)
Arena Beach (Staples)
Baby (MacLachlan)
Beardance (Hobbs)
Best Destiny (Carey)
A Bone from a Dry Sea (Dickinson)
Books of the Keepers (Downer)
The Broken Land (McDonald)
Brown Angels (Myers)
Bull Run (Fleischman)
The Burning Baby and Other Ghosts (Gordon)
Calling on Dragons (Wrede)
The Cat Came Back (Mullins)
Changeweaver (Ball)
Charms for the Easy Life (Gibbons)
Child of an Ancient City (Williams & Hoffman)
The Crocodile Bird (Rendell)

The Wild West (Time-Life Books staff)
The Wind Blows Backward (Hahn)
Windleaf (Sherman)
Wings of a Falcon (Voight)
Winners and Losers (Hoffius)
Winter of Fire (Jordan)
A Wizard's Dozen (Stearns)
Wren's Quest (Smith)
Yoruba Girl Dancing (Bedford)

Adult

Aestival Tide (Hand)
America Then & Now (Cohen & Wels)
Anne Frank, Beyond the Diary (Rol & Verhoeven)
The Broken Land (McDonald)
Brown Angels (Myers)
Changeweaver (Ball)
Charms for the Easy Life (Gibbons)
The Crocodile Bird (Rendell)
Daniel Boone (Faragher)
Daughter of Elysium (Slonczewski)
Days of Grace (Ashe & Rampersad)
Doomsday Book (Willis)
Elvissey (Womack)
Frankenstein (Greenberg)

From Sea to Shining Sea (Cohn)
Girl, Interrupted (Kaysen)
Glory Season (Brin)
Hamburger Heaven (Tennyson)
The Harvest (Wilson)
Having Our Say (Delany & Delany)
High Steel (Haldemann & Dann)
I Never Saw Another Butterfly (Volavkova)
The Jaguar Princess (Bell)
Kipling's Fantasy Stories (Kipling)
In Love and In Danger (Levy)
The Last Command (Zahn)
A Lesson Before Dying (Gaines)
Like Water for Chocolate (Esquivel)
Lost in the City (Jones)
Malcolm X (Myers)
The Mind Pool (Sheffield)
Modern Ghost Stories by Eminent Women Writers (Dalby)
Montana 1948 (Watson)
Paradise of the Blind (Duong)
Pigs in Heaven (Kingsolver)
The Red Magician (Goldstein)
The Shining Face (Myra)
Split Heirs (Watt-Evans & Friesner)
Stainless Steel Visions (Harrison)
The Tale of the Body Thief (Rice)
Twilight (James)
The Wild West (Time-Life Books staff)

SELECTIVE BIBLIOGRAPHY
BY THEME AND GENRE

Adventure

Across America on an Emigrant Train (Murphy) MS–HS
Alien Secrets (Klause) MS–JH
Beardance (Hobbs) JH–HS
Best Destiny (Carey) JH–HS
Beyond the North Wind (Bradshaw) MS–JH
Black Ships Before Troy (Sutcliff) MS–JH
Bone from a Dry Sea (Dickinson) JH–HS
Books of the Keepers (Downer) JH–HS
Calling on Dragons (Wrede) MS–HS
Changeweaver (Ball) HS–A
Child of an Ancient City (Williams & Hoffman) JH–HS
City of Light, City of Dark (Avi) MS
Daughter of Elysium (Slonczewski) HS–A
Dog Wizard (Hambly) JH–HS
Doomsday Book (Willis) HS–A
Dragon's Bait (Vande Velde) JH–HS
Glory Season (Brin) HS–A
Going to See Grassy Ella (Lance) MS–JH
Great American Elephant Chase (Cross) MS–JH
High Steel (Haldeman & Dann) HS–A
Last Command (Zahn) HS–A
Nevernever (Shetterly) JH–HS
Shining Face (Myra) JH–A
Singer to the Sea God (Alcock) MS–JH
Split Heirs (Watt-Evans & Friesner) HS–A
Spirit Ring (Bujold) JH–HS
Susan Butcher and the Iditarod Trail (Dolan) MS–JH
Sworn Enemies (Matas) JH–HS
Talking to Dragons (Wrede) MS–HS
There Will Be Wolves (Bradford) MS–JH
To the Top of the World (Brandenburg) MS
Virtual Girl (Thomson) HS
Wainscott Weasel (Seidler) EL–MS
Walker of Time (Vick) HS
Windleaf (Sherman) JH–HS
Wings of a Falcon (Voight) JH–HS
Winter of Fire (Jordan) JH–HS

Wren's Quest (Smith) JH–HS
Your Mother Was a Neanderthal (Scieszka) MS–JH

Aged

Brush with Magic (Brooke) EL–MS
Charms for the Easy Life (Gibbons) HS–A
Crazy Lady! (Conly) MS–JH
For the Life of Laetitia (Hodge) JH
Having Our Say (Delany & Delany) JH–A
Missing Angel Juan (Block) JH–HS
Others See Us (Sleator) JH–HS
Sunita Experiment (Perkins) MS–JH
Timothy of the Cay (Taylor) MS–JH
Western Wind (Fox) MS–JH
Who Is Eddie Leonard? (Mazer) MS–JH
Windleaf (Sherman) JH–HS

Animals

Beardance (Hobbs) JH–HS
Cuckoo Child (King-Smith) EL
Deerskin (McKinley) HS
Dinosaur Fantastic (Resnick & Greenberg) MS–JH
Dogzilla (Pilkey) EL–MS
Forest (Lisle) MS
Great American Elephant Chase (Cross) MS–JH
Kat Kong (Pilkey) EL–MS
Owl in Love (Kindl) MS–HS
Oxboy (Mazer) MS–JH
Susan Butcher and the Iditarod Trail (Dolan) MS–JH
Thor (Smith) JH–HS
To the Top of the World (Brandenburg) MS–HS
Wainscott Weasel (Seidler) EL–MS

Art

Apprentice (Molina Llorente) MS-JH
Behind the Secret Window (Toll) MS-JH
Brush with Magic (Brooke) EL-MS
I Never Saw Another Butterfly (Volav-
  kova) JH-A
I Was a Teenage Professional Wrestler
  (Lewin) JH-HS
Short Walk Around the Pyramids . . .
  (Isaacson) MS-JH
Stones of Muncaster Cathedral (Westall)
  JH-HS
Visions (Sills) MS-JH

Biography

Anne Frank (Rol & Verhoeven) MS-A
Behind the Secret Window (Toll) MS-JH
Champions (Littlefield) MS-JH
Daniel Boone (Faragher) JH-A
Days of Grace (Ashe) HS-A
Eleanor Roosevelt (Freedman) MS-JH
Girl, Interrupted (Kaysen) HS-A
I Was a Teenage Professional Wrestler
  (Lewin) JH-HS
Kindertransport (Drucker) MS-JH
Lives of the Musicians (Krull) MS-JH
Malcolm X (Myers) JH-A
Susan Butcher and the Iditarod Trail
  (Dolan) MS-JH
Visions (Sills) MS-JH

Child Abuse

Bus People (Anderson) MS-JH
Deerskin (McKinley) HS
Durable Goods (Berg) JH-HS
Harper & Moon (Ross) MS-JH
Pigs in Heaven (Kingsolver) HS-A
Right by My Side (Haynes) JH-HS
Staying Fat for Sarah Byrnes (Crutcher)
  JH-HS
Stones of Muncaster Cathedral (Westall)
  JH-HS
Uncle Vampire (Grant) JH-HS
Who Is Eddie Leonard? (Mazer) MS-JH

Crime and Delinquency

Burning Baby and Other Ghosts (Gor-
  don) JH-HS
Crocodile Bird (Rendell) HS-A
Definitely Cool (Wilkinson) MS-JH
Fair Game (Tamar) HS

Freak the Mighty (Philbrick) MS-JH
Going to See Grassy Ella (Lance) MS-JH
Harper & Moon (Ross) MS-JH
Hoops (Myers) JH-HS
In Love and in Danger (Levy) HS-A
Killing Boy (Miklowitz) HS
Lady of the Forest (Roberson) JH-HS
Lesson Before Dying (Gaines) HS-A
Motown and Didi (Myers) JH-HS
Out of Control (Mazer) JH-HS
Please Remove Your Elbow from My Ear
  (Godfrey) MS-JH
Real Plato Jones (Bawden) MS-JH
Scorpions (Myers) JH
Shakedown Street (Nasaw) JH-HS
Stones of Muncaster Cathedral (Westall)
  JH-HS

Death and Mourning

Baby (MacLachlan) MS-HS
Crazy Lady! (Conly) MS-JH
Death Is Hard to Live With (Bode)
  JH-HS
Durable Goods (Berg) JH-HS
Fallen Angels (Myers) JH-HS
Freak the Mighty (Philbrick) MS-JH
Harvest (Wilson) HS-A
Life Belts (Hosie-Bouner) JH
Princess in the Kitchen Garden (Heymans
  & Heymans) EL-MS
Revolutions of the Heart (Qualey) JH-HS
Shadow Man (Grant) JH-HS
Shizuko's Daughter (Mori) JH-HS
Striking Out (Weaver) JH-HS
Tell Me Everything (Coman) JH
Wind Blows Backward (Hahn) JH-HS
Winners and Losers (Hoffius) JH-HS

Environmental Issues

Beardance (Hobbs) JH-HS
Forest (Lisle) MS
Powers That Be (McCaffrey & Scarbor-
  ough) HS

Ethical Issues

Aestival Tide (Hand) HS-A
Daughter of Elysium (Slonczewski) HS-A
Days of Grace (Ashe) HS-A
Detour for Emmy (Reynolds) HS
Fair Game (Tamar) HS
Forest (Lisle) MS
Freedom's Children (Levine JH-HS)

In My Father's House (Rinaldi) JH–HS
Giver (Lowry) MS–JH
Lesson Before Dying (Gaines) HS–A
Miriam's Well (Ruby) JH–HS
Pigs in Heaven (Kingsolver) HS–A
Scorpions (Myers) JH
Sworn Enemies (Matas) JH–HS
T-Shirts, T-Backs, COAT and Suit
    (Konigsburg) MS–JH
Testing (Oberndorf) HS
Whatever Happened to Janie? (Cooney)
    JH–HS
Winners and Losers (Hoffius) JH–HS

Ethnic Groups

From Sea to Shining Sea (Cohn) EL–A
Speaking Out (Kuklin) JH–HS

Ethnic Groups: African-American

Brown Angels (Myers) EL–A
Brown Honey in Broomwheat Tea
    (Thomas) EL–MS
Champion (Gee) JH
Days of Grace (Ashe) HS–A
Definitely Cool (Wilkinson) MS–JH
Fallen Angels (Myers) JH–HS
For the Life of Laetitia (Hodge) JH
Freedom's Children (Levine) JH–HS
Having Our Say (Delany & Delany)
    JH–A
Hoops (Myers) JH–HS
In My Father's House (Rinaldi) JH–HS
Learning by Heart (Young) MS
Lesson Before Dying (Gaines) HS–A
Lost in the City (Jones) HS–A
Malcolm X (Myers) JH–A
Many Thousand Gone (Hamilton)
    MS–JH
Montana 1948 (Watson) HS–A
Motown and Didi (Myers)
Nightjohn (Paulsen) JH–HS
Plain City (Hamilton) MS–JH
Right by My Side (Haynes) JH–HS
Scooter (Williams) EL–MS
Scorpions (Myers) JH
Song of Be (Beake) JH–HS
Soul Looks Back in Wonder (Feelings)
    EL–MS
Timothy of the Cay (Taylor) MS–JH
Toning the Sweep (MS–JH)
Where Do I Go from Here? (Wesley) JH
White Lilacs (Meyer) JH
Yoruba Girl Dancing (Bedford) JH–HS

Ethnic Groups: Asian

American Dragons (Yep) JH–HS
Brush with Magic (Brooke) EL–MS
Dragon's Gate (Yep) JH
For the Life of Laetitia (Hodge) JH
Golem and the Dragon Girl (Levitin)
    MS–JH
Haveli (Staples) JH–HS
Paradise of the Blind (Duong) HS–A
Sadako (Coerr) EL–MS
Shadow of the Dragon (Garland) JH–HS
Shizuko's Daughter (Mori) JH–HS
Sunita Experiment (Perkins) JH

Ethnic Groups: Hispanic

City of Light, City of Dark (Avi) EL–MS
Detour for Emmy (Reynolds) HS
Grab Hands and Run (Temple) MS–JH
Like Water for Chocolate (Esquivel)
    HS–A
Voices from the Fields (Atkin) JH–HS

Ethnic Groups: Jewish

Anne Frank (Rol & Verhoeven) MS–A
Behind the Secret Window (Toll) MS–JH
Golem and the Dragon Girl (Levitin)
    MS–JH
I Never Saw Another Butterfly
    (Volvakova) JH–A
Kindertransport (Drucker) MS–JH
Red Magician (Goldstein) HS–A
Scooter (Williams) EL–MS
Sworn Enemies (Matas) JH–HS

Ethnic Groups: Native American

Beardance (Hobbs) JH–HS
Daniel Boone (Faragher) JH–A
Dawn Land (Bruchac) JH–HS
High Steel (Haldeman & Dann) HS–A
The Jaguar Princess (Bell) HS–A
Pigs in Heaven (Kingsolver) HS–A
Revolutions of the Heart (Qualey) JH–HS
Walker of Time (Vick) HS

Family Relationships

Alice in April (Naylor) MS–JH
Arena Beach (Staples) HS
Baby (MacLachlan) MS–JH
Bone from a Dry Sea (Dickinson) JH–HS
Brown Honey in Broomwheat Tea
    (Thomas) EL–MS

Charms for the Easy Life (Gibbons)
HS-A
Crocodile Bird (Rendell) HS-A
Days of Grace (Ashe) HS-A
Detour for Emmy (Reynolds) HS
Dragon's Gate (Yep) JH
Durable Goods (Berg) JH-HS
Eleanor Roosevelt (Freedman) MS-JH
For the Life of Laetitia (Hodge) JH
Good Fortunes Gang (Mahy) MS-JH
Grab Hands and Run (Temple) MS-JH
Haveli (Staples) JH-HS
Heart of a Champion (Deuker) JH-HS
Here's to You, Rachel Robinson (Blume)
MS-JH
Hero of Lesser Causes (Johnston) JH
In My Father's House (Rinaldi) JH-HS
Killing Boy (Miklowitz) HS
Learning by Heart (Young) MS
Life Belts (Hosie-Bouner) JH
Like Water for Chocolate (Esquivel)
HS-A
Maybe Yes, Maybe No, Maybe Maybe
(Patron) EL-MS
Miriam's Well (Ruby) JH-HS
Montana 1948 (Watson) HS-A
Oddballs (Sleator) MS-JH
Others See Us (Sleator) JH-HS
Pigs in Heaven (Kingsolver) HS-A
Plain City (Hamilton) MS-JH
Princess in the Kitchen Garden (Heymans
& Heymans) EL-MS
Real Plato Jones (Bawden) MS-JH
Revolutions of the Heart (Qualey) JH-HS
Rhino (Klass) JH-HS
Right by My Side (Haynes) JH-HS
Scorpions (Myers) JH
Shadow Boxer (Lynch) JH-HS
Shadow Man (Grant) JH-HS
Shadow of the Dragon (Garland) JH-HS
Shakedown Street (Nasaw) JH-HS
Shelter (Merrick) JH
Shizuko's Daughter (Mori) JH-HS
Stardust otel (Janeczko) JH-HS
Striking Out (Weaver) JH-HS
Sunita Experiment (Perkins) JH
Taste of Smoke (Bauer) MS
Tell Me Everything (Coman) JH
Tiger Orchard (Sweeney) HS
Toning the Sweep (Johnson) MS-JH
TV Guidance Counselor (LeMieux)
JH-HS
Uncle Vampire (Grant) JH-HS
Western Wind (Fox) MS-JH
Whatever Happened to Janie? (Cooney)
JH-HS

Who Is Eddie Leonard? (Mazer) MS-JH
Winners and Losers (Hoffius) JH-HS

Fantasy

Beyond the North Wind (Bradshaw)
MS-JH
Books of the Keepers (Downer) JH-HS
Brush with Magic (Brooke) EL-MS
Calling on Dragons (Wrede) MS-HS
Changeweaver (Ball) HS-A
Child of an Ancient City (Williams &
Hoffman) JH-HS
City of Light, City of Dark (Avi) EL-MS
Deerskin (McKinley) HS
Dinosaur Fantastic (Resnick & Green-
berg) MS-JH
Dog Wizard (Hambly) JH-HS
Dragon's Bait (Vande Velde) JH-HS
Dreams Underfoot (De Lint) HS
Forest (Lisle) MS
Ghatti's Tale (Greeno) HS
Giver (Lowry) MS-JH
Kipling's Fantasy Stories (Kipling) JH-A
Lord of the Two Lands (Tarr) JH-HS
Nevernever (Shetterly) JH-HS
Owl in Love (Kindl) MS-HS
Oxboy (Mazer) MS-JH
Red Magician (Goldstein) HS-A
Shining Face (Myra) JH-A
Singer to the Sea God (Alcock) MS-JH
Spirit Ring (Bujold) JH-HS
Split Heirs (Watt-Evans & Friesner)
HS-A
Switching Well (Griffin) MS-JH
Tale of the Body Thief (Rice) JH-A
Talking to Dragons (Wrede) MS-HS
Walker of Time (Vick) HS
Windleaf (Sherman) JH-HS
Wings of a Falcon (Voight) JH-HS
Wishing Season (Freisner) JH
Witch Week (Jones) MS
Wizard's Dozen (Stearns) JH-HS
Wren's Quest (Smith) JH-HS
Your Mother Was a Neanderthal (Sciesz-
ka) MS-JH

Folklore and Myth

Beardance (Hobbs) JH-HS
Beyond the North Wind (Bradford)
MS-JH
Black Ships Before Troy (Sutcliff) MS-JH
Boggart (Cooper) MS
Brush with Magic (Brooke) EL-MS

Child of an Ancient City (Williams & Hoffman) JH–HS
Dawn Land (Bruchac) JH–HS
Deerskin (McKinley) HS
From Sea to Shining Sea (Cohn) EL–A
Golem and the Dragon Girl (Levitin) MS–JH
The Jaguar Princess (Bell) HS–A
Lady of the Forest (Roberson) JH–HS
Lord of the Two Lands (Tarr) JH–HS
Magic Circle (Napoli) JH–HS
More Rootabagas (Sandburg) EL–MS
Singer to the Sea God (Alcock) MS–JH
Walker of Time (Vick) HS
Wild West (Time-Life staff) JH–A
Windleaf (Sherman) JH–HS
Wishing Season (Freisner) JH

Friendship

Alien Secrets (Klause) MS–JH
Arena Beach (Staples) HS
Baby (McLachlan) MS–HS
Champion (Gee) JH
City of Light, City of Dark (Avi) EL–MS
Crazy Lady! (Conly) MS–JH
Definitely Cool (Wilkinson) MS–JH
Fallen Angels (Myers) JH–HS
For the Life of Laetitia (Hodge) JH
Forest (Lisle) MS
Freak the Mighty (Philbrick) MS–JH
Free the Conroy Seven (McFann) JH–HS
Golem and the Dragon Girl (Levitin) MS–JH
Good Fortunes Gang (Mahy) MS–JH
Great American Elephant Chase (Cross) MS–JH
Harper & Moon (Ross) MS–JH
Harris and Me (Paulsen) MS–JH
Heart of a Champion (Deuker) JH–HS
Here's to You, Rachel Robinson (Blume) MS–JH
Learning by Heart (Young) MS
Life Belts (Hosie-Bounar) JH
Make Lemonade (Wolff) JH–HS
Miriam's Well (Ruby) JH–HS
Missing Angel Juan (Block) JH–HS
More Rootabagas (Sandburg) EL–MS
Out of Control (Mazer) JH–HS
Peter (Walker) JH–HS
Please Remove Your Elbow from My Ear (Godfrey) MS–JH
Revolutions of the Heart (Qualey) JH–HS
Right by My Side (Haynes) JH–HS
Scooter (Williams) EL–MS
Scorpions (Myers) JH

Shakedown Street (Nasaw) JH–HS
Stardust otel (Janeczko) JH–HS
Staying Fat for Sara Byrnes (Crutcher) JH–HS
Switching Well (Griffin) MS–JH
Timothy of the Cay (Taylor) MS–JH
Twelve Days in August (Murrow) JH–HS
Wainscott Weasel (Seidler) EL–MS
Wind Blows Backward (Hahn) JH–HS
Winners and Losers (Hoffius) JH–HS

Handicaps

Bus People (Anderson) MS–JH
Crazy Lady! (Conly) MS–JH
Fair Game (Tamar) HS
Freak the Mighty (Philbrick) MS–JH
Hero of Lesser Causes (Johnston) JH
Shining Face (Myra) JH–A
Staying Fat for Sara Byrnes (Crutcher) JH–HS
Timothy of the Cay (Taylor) MS–JH

Health and illness

Bus People (Anderson) MS–JH
Days of Grace (Ashe) HS–A
Doomsday Book (Willis) HS–A
Freak the Mighty (Philbrick) MS–JH
Going to See Grassy Ella (Lance) MS–JH
In Love and in Danger (Levy) JH–HS
Life Belts (Hosie-Bounar) JH
Miriam's Well (Ruby) JH–HS
Revolutions of the Heart (Qualey) JH–HS
Sadako (Coerr) EL–MS
T-Backs, T-Shirts, COAT and Suit (Konigsburg) MS–JH
Toning the Sweep (Johnson) MS–JH
Winners and Losers (Hoffius) JH–HS

Historical fiction

Apprentice (Molina Llorente) MS–JH
Black Ships Before Troy (Sutcliff) MS–JH
Bone from a Dry Sea (Dickinson) JH–HS
Doomsday Book (Willis) HS–A
Dragon's Gate (Yep) JH
Fallen Angels (Myers) JH–HS
Great American Elephant Chase (Cross) MS–JH
Harper & Moon (Ross) MS–JH
Harris and Me (Paulsen) MS–JH
In My Father's House (Rinaldi) JH–HS
The Jaguar Princess (Bell) HS–A
Lady of the Forest (Roberson) JH–HS

Learning by Heart (Young) MS
Lesson Before Dying (Gaines) HS-A
Lord of the Two Lands (Tarr) JH-HS
Montana 1948 (Watson) HS-A
Nightjohn (Paulsen) JH-HS
Red Magician (Goldstein) HS-A
Shelter (Merrick) JH
Singer to the Sea God (Alcock) MS-JH
Stones of Muncaster Cathedral (Westall)
   JH-HS
Switching Well (MS-JH)
Sworn Enemies (Matas) JH-HS
There Will Be Wolves (Bradford) MS-JH
Timothy of the Cay (Taylor) MS-JH
Walker of Time (Vick) HS
White Lilacs (Meyer) JH

History (see also Biography; Historical fiction)

Across America on an Emigrant Train
   (Murphy) MS-HS
America Then & Now (Cohen & Wels)
   JH-A
Brown Angels (Myers) EL-A
Bull Run (Fleischman) MS-HS
Disaster of the "Hindenburg" (Tanaka)
   MS-JH
Freedom's Children (Levine) JH-HS
Hamburger Heaven (Tennyson) JH-A
Many Thousand Gone (Hamilton)
   MS-JH
Whole New Ball Game (Macy) MS-HS
Wild West (Time-Life staff) JH-A

Homeless

Grab Hands and Run (Temple) MS-JH
It's Our World Too! (Hoose) MS-JH
Plain City (Hamilton) MS-JH
Shakedown Street (Nasaw) JH-HS

Homosexuality

Cat Came Back (Mullins) HS
Missing Angel Juan (Block) JH-HS
Peter (Walker) JH-HS
Twelve Days in August (Murrow) JH-HS

Horror

Dream Date (Smith) JH-HS
Frankenstein (Greenberg) JH-A
Horror Hall of Fame (Silverberg &
   Greenberg) HS

Killing Boy (Miklowitz) HS
Night Terrors (Murphy) JH-HS
Stones of Muncaster Cathedral (Westall)
   JH-HS
Twilight (James) HS-A

Humor

Bel-Air Bambi and the Mall Rats (Peck)
   MS-JH
Beyond the North Wind (Bradshaw)
   MS-JH
Boggart (Cooper) MS
Calling on Dragons (Wrede) MS-HS
Cuckoo Child (King-Smith) EL
Dinosaur Fantastic (Resnick & Greenberg) MS-JH
Dogzilla (Pilkey) EL-MS
Free the Conroy Seven (McFann) JH-HS
Hamburger Heaven (Tennyson) JH-A
Harris and Me (Paulsen) MS-JH
I Was a Teenage Professional Wrestler
   (Lewin) JH-HS
Kat Kong (Pilkey) EL-MS
Lives of the Musicians Krull) MS-JH
Owl in Love (Kindl) MS-HS
Please Remove Your Elbow from My Ear
   (Godfrey) MS-JH
Split Heirs (Watt-Evans & Friesner)
   HS-A
Talking to Dragons (Wrede) MS-HS
Wishing Season (Freisner) JH
Witch Week (Jones) MS
Your Mother Was a Neanderthal (Scieszka) MS-JH

Immigrants

Across America on an Emigrant Train
   (Murphy) MS-HS
American Dragons (Yep) JH-HS
Dragon's Gate (Yep) JH
Grab Hands and Run (Temple) MS-JH
Shadow of the Dragon (Garland) JH-HS
Sunita Experiment (Perkins) JH
Voices from the Fields (Atkin) JH-HS

Interviews

Death Is Hard to Live With (Bode)
   JH-HS
Freedom's Children (Levine) JH-HS
It's Our World Too! (Hoose) MS-JH
Speaking Out (Kuklin) JH-HS
Voices from the Fields (Atkin) JH-HS

Minorities. See Ethnic Groups

Music

Elvissey HS-A
From Sea to Shining Sea (Cohn) EL-A
Learning by Heart (Young) MS
Lives of the Musicians (Krull) MS-JH
Missing Angel Juan (Block) JH-HS

Mystery and Suspense

Alien Secrets (Klause) MS-JH
Apprentice (Molina Llorente) MS-JH
City of Light, City of Dark (Avi) MS
Crocodile Bird (Rendell) HS-A
High Steel (Haldeman & Dann) HS-A
Mind Pool (Sheffield) HS-A
Powers That Be (McCaffrey & Scarborough) HS
Real Plato Jones (Bawden) MS-JH
Shadow of the Dragon (Garland) JH-HS
Stones of Muncaster Cathedral (Westall) JH-HS
Thor (Smith) JH-HS
Twilight (James) HS-A

Nature

Beardance (Hobbs) JH-HS
To the Top of the World (Brandenburg) MS-HS

Nonfiction (See also Biography; Poetry)

Across America on an Emigrant Train (Murphy) MS-HS
America Then & Now (Cohen & Wels) JH-A
Bull Run (Fleischman (MS-HS
Death Is Hard to Live With (Bode) JH-HS
Disaster of the "Hindenburg" (Tanaka) MS-JH
Freedom's Children (Levine) JH-HS
From Sea to Shining Sea (Cohn) EL-A
Hamburger Heaven (Tennyson) JH-A
In Love and in Danger (Levy) HS-A
It's Our World Too! (Hoose) MS-JH
Many Thousand Gone (Hamilton) MS-JH
Short Walk Around the Pyramids . . . (Isaacson) MS-JH
Speaking Out (Kuklin) JH-HS
Stephen Biesty's Incredible Cross-Sections (Biesty & Platt) MS
To the Top of the World (Brandenburg) MS-HS
Visions (Sills) MS-JH
Whole New Ball Game (Macy) MS-HS

Occult and Paranormal

Boggart (Cooper) MS
Brush with Magic (Brooke) EL-MS
Burning Baby and Other Ghosts (Gordon) JH-HS
Child of an Ancient City (Williams & Hoffman) JH-HS
City of Light, City of Dark (Avi) MS
Dog Wizard (Hambly) JH-HS
Don't Give Up the Ghost (Gale) MS-JH
Dream Date (Smith) JH-HS
Dreams Underfoot (De Lint) HS
Frankenstein (Greenberg) JH-A
Horror Hall of Fame (Silverberg & Greenberg) HS
Kipling's Fantasy Stories (Kipling) JH-A
Mind Pool (Sheffield) HS-A
Modern Ghost Stories . . . (Dalby) JH-A
Night Terrors (Murphy) JH-HS
Others See Us (Sleator) JH-HS
Owl in Love (Kindl) MS-HS
Red Magician (Goldstein) HS-A
Spirit Ring (Bujold) JH-HS
Stones of Muncaster Cathedral (Westall) JH-HS
Strange Objects (Crew) JH-HS
Tale of the Body Thief (Rice) JH-A
Taste of Smoke (Bauer) MS
Twilight (James) HS-A
Walker of Time (Vick) HS
Windleaf (Sherman) JH-HS
Witch Week (Jones) MS
Wizard's Dozen (Stearns) JH-HS

Other Countries / Other Cultures

Anne Frank (Rol & Verhoeven) MS-A
Apprentice (Molina Llorente) MS-JH
Behind the Secret Window (Toll) MS-JH
Boggart (Cooper) MS
Bone from a Dry Sea (JH-HS)
Burning Baby and Other Ghosts (Gordon) JH-HS
Bus People (Anderson) MS-JH
Brush with Magic (Brooke) EL-MS
Champion (Gee) JH
Crocodile Bird (Rendell) HS-A

Disaster of the "Hindenburg" (Tanaka)
  MS-JH
Doomsday Book (Willis) HS-A
Dragon's Gate (Yep) JH
Fallen Angels (Myers) JH-HS
For the Life of Laetitia (Hodge) JH
Good Fortunes Gang (Mahy) MS-JH
Grab Hands and Run (Temple) MS-JH
Haveli (Staples) JH-HS
I Never Saw Another Butterfly
  (Volvakova) JH-A
The Jaguar Princess (Bell) HS-A
Kindertransport (Drucker) MS-JH
Kipling's Fantasy Stories (Kipling) JH-A
Lady of the Forest (Roberson) JH-HS
Like Water for Chocolate (Esquivel)
  HS-A
Lives of the Musicians (Krull) MS-JH
Paradise of the Blind (Duong) HS-A
Real Plato Jones (Bawden) MS-JH
Red Magician (Goldstein) HS-A
Sadako (Coerr) EL-MS
Shizuko's Daughter (Mori) JH-HS
Song of Be (Beake) JH-HS
Stones of Muncaster Cathedral (Westall)
  JH-HS
Strange Objects (Crew) JH-HS
Sworn Enemies (Matas) JH-HS
There Will Be Wolves (Bradford) MS-JH
Timothy of the Cay (Taylor) MS-JH
Yoruba Girl Dancing (Bedford) JH-HS

Peer Pressure

Alice in April (Naylor) MS-JH
Champion (Gee) JH
Definitely Cool (Wilkinson) MS-JH
Free the Conroy Seven (McFann) JH-HS
Lombardo's Law (Wittlinger) JH-HS
Out of Control (Mazer) JH-HS
Scorpions (Myers) JH
Twelve Days in August (Murrow) JH-HS

Photographs

America Then & Now (Cohen & Wels)
  JH-A
Anne Frank (Rol & Verhoeven) MS-A
Brown Angels (Myers) EL-A
To the Top of the World (Brandenburg)
  MS-HS

Poetry

American Dragons (Yep) JH-HS
Brown Honey in Broomwheat Tea
  (Thomas) EL-MS
I Never Saw Another Butterfly (Volav-
  kova)
Life Doesn't Frighten Me (Angelou) JH
Looking for Your Name (Janeczko)
  JH-HS
Soul Looks Back in Wonder (Feelings)
  EL-MS
Stardust otel (Janeczko) JH-HS

Politics and Activism

Daughter of Elysium (Slonczewski) HS-A
Eleanor Roosevelt (Freedman) MS-JH
Freedom's Children (Levine) JH-HS
High Steel (Haldeman & Dann) HS-A
It's Our World Too! (Hoose) MS-JH
Malcolm X (Myers) JH-A
Pigs in Heaven (Kingsolver) HS-A
Powers That Be (McCaffrey & Scarbor-
  ough) HS
Revolutions of the Heart (Qualey) JH-HS
T-Backs, T-Shirts, COAT and Suit
  (Konigsburg) MS-JH
Taste of Salt (Bauer) JH-HS
Testing (Oberndorf) HS
White Lilacs (Meyer) JH
Winter of Fire (Jordan) JH-HS

Prejudice

Alien Secrets (Klause) MS-JH
American Dragons (Yep) JH-HS
Anne Frank (Rol & Verhoeven) MS-A
Behind the Secret Window (Toll) MS-JH
Champion (Gee) JH
Days of Grace (Ashe) HS-A
Dragon's Gate (Yep) JH
For the Life of Laetitia (Hodge) JH
Freedom's Children (Levine) JH-HS
Glory Season (Brin) HS-A
Having Our Say (Delany & Delany)
  JH-A
I Never Saw Another Butterfly (Volav-
  kova) JH-A
In My Father's House (Rinaldi) JH-HS
Kindertransport (Drucker) MS-JH
Lesson Before Dying (Gaines) HS-A
Malcolm X (Myers) JH-A
Many Thousand Gone (Hamilton)
  MS-JH
Miriam's Well (Ruby) JH-HS
Nightjohn (Paulsen) JH-HS

Oxboy (Mazer) MS–JH
Red Magician (Goldstein) HS–A
Revolutions of the Heart (Qualey) JH–HS
Shadow of the Dragon (Garland) JH–HS
Speaking Out (Kuklin) JH–HS
Switching Well (Griffin) MS–JH
Sworn Enemies (Matas) JH–HS
Taste of Salt (Temple) JH–HS
Twelve Days in August (Murrow) JH–HS
Voices from the Fields (Atkin) JH–HS
White Lilacs (Meyer) JH
Winter of Fire (Jordan) JH–HS
Yoruba Girl Dancing (Bedford) JH–HS

Psychology

Crazy Lady! (Conly) MS–JH
Crocodile Bird (Rendell) HS–A
Girl, Interrupted (Kaysen) HS–A
Harper & Moon (Ross) MS–JH
Here's to You, Rachel Robinson (Blume)
   MS–JH
In Love and in Danger (Levy) HS–A
Plain City (Hamilton) MS–JH
Song of Be (Beake) JH–HS
Staying Fat for Sarah Byrnes (Crutcher)
   JH–HS
Tiger Orchard (Sweeney) HS
TV Guidance Counselor (LeMieux)
   JH–HS
Wind Blows Backward (Hahn) JH–HS

Religion

Beardance (Hobbs) JH–HS
Broken Land (McDonald) HS–A
Death Is Hard to Live With (Bode)
   JH–HS
Elvissey (Womack) HS–A
Giver (Lowry) MS–JH
Miriam's Well (Ruby) JH–HS
Sworn Enemies (Matas) JH–HS
Tell Me Everything (Coman) JH
There Will Be Wolves (Bradford) MS–JH

Romance

Arena Beach (Staples) HS
Cat Came Back (Mullins) HS
Changeweaver (Ball) HS–A
Crocodile Bird (Rendell) HS–A
Deerskin (McKinley) HS
Dog Wizard (Hambly) JH–HS
Dragon's Bait (Vande Velde) JH–HS
Dream Date (Smith) JH–HS

Haveli (Staples) JH–HS
In Love and in Danger (Levy) HS–A
In My Father's House (Rinaldi) JH–HS
Lady of the Forest (Roberson) JH–HS
Like Water for Chocolate (Esquivel)
   HS–A
Lombardo's Law (Wittlinger) JH–HS
Missing Angel Juan (Block) JH–HS
Motown and Didi (Myers) JH–HS
Owl in Love (Kindl) MS–HS
Revolutions of the Heart (Qualey) JH–HS
Spirit Ring (Bujold) JH–HS
Stranger (Cooney) JH
Taste of Smoke (Bauer) MS
Virtual Girl (Thomson) HS
Wind Blows Backward (Hahn) JH–HS
Windleaf (Sherman) JH–HS
Wishing Season (Freisner) JH

Runaways

Baby (MacLachlan) MS–HS
Deerskin (McKinley) HS
Going to See Grassy Ella (Lance) MS–JH
Nevernever (Shetterly) JH–HS
Pigs in Heaven (Kingsolver) HS–A
Plain City (Hamilton) MS–JH
Strange Objects (Crew) JH–HS
Who Is Eddie Leonard? (Mazer) MS–JH

School

Alice in April (Naylor) MS–JH
Bel-Air Bambi and the Mall Rats (Peck)
   MS–JH
Cat Came Back (Mullins) HS
Definitely Cool (Wilkinson) MS–JH
Detour for Emmy (Reynolds) HS
Fair Game (Tamar) HS
For the Life of Laetitia (Hodge) JH
Free the Conroy Seven (McFann) JH–HS
Lombardo's Law (Wittlinger) JH–HS
Miriam's Well (Ruby) JH–HS
Out of Control (Mazer) JH–HS
Owl in Love (Kindl) MS–HS
Please Remove Your Elbow from My Ear
   (Godfrey) MS–JH
Revolutions of the Heart (Qualey) JH–HS
Shadow Man (Grant) JH–HS
Twelve Days in August (Murrow) JH–HS
Voices from the Fields (Atkin) JH–HS
Where Do I Go from Here? (Wesley) JH
Wind Blows Backward (Hahn) JH–HS
Witch Week (Jones) MS
Yoruba Girl Dancing (Bedford) JH–HS

Science and Technology

Across America on an Emigrant Train (Murphy) MS-HS
Bone from a Dry Sea (Dickinson) JH-HS
Disaster of the "Hindenburg" (Tanaka) MS-JH
Stephen Biesty's Incredible Cross-Sections (Biesty & Platt) MS
To the Top of the World (Brandenburg) MS

Science Fiction

Aestival Tide (Hand) HS-A
Alien Secrets (Klause) MS-JH
Best Destiny (Carey) JH-HS
Broken Land (McDonald) HS-A
Daughter of Elysium (Slonczewski) HS-A
Dog Wizard (Hambly) JH-HS
Doomsday Book (Willis) HS-A
Elvissey (Womack) HS-A
Finders-Keepers (Greeno) HS
High Steel (Haldemnan) HS-A
Last Command (Zahn) HS-A
Mind Pool (HS-A
Nevernever (Shetterly) JH-HS
Powers That Be (McCaffrey & Scarborough) HS
Stainless Steel Visions (Harrison) HS-A
Virtual Girl (Thomson) HS
Winter of Fire (Jordan) JH-HS
Walker of Time (Vick) HS

Self-knowledge

Arena Beach (Staples) HS
Best Destiny (Carey) JH-HS
Cat Came Back (Mulllins) HS
Charms for the Easy Life (Gibbons) HS-A
Days of Grace (Ashe) HS-A
Durable Goods (Berg) JH-HS
Eleanor Roosevelt (Freedman) MS-JH
For the Life of Laetitia (Hodge) JH
Girl, Interrupted (Kaysen) HS-A
Giver (Lowry) MS-JH
Great American Elephant Chase (Cross) MS-JH
Harper & Moon (Ross) MS-JH
Heart of a Champion (Deuker) JH-HS
Here's to You, Rachel Robinson (Blume) MS-JH
In Love and in Danger (Levy) HS-A
Lesson Before Dying (Gaines) HS-A
Lombardo's Law (Wittlinger) JH-HS
Looking for Your Name (Janeczko)

JH-HS
Malcolm X (Myers) JH-A
Missing Angel Juan (Block) JH-HS
Motown and Didi (Myers) HS
Paradise of the Blind (Duong) HS-A
Peter (Walker) JH-HS
Pigs in Heaven (Kingsolver) HS-A
Please Remove Your Elbow from My Ear (Godfrey) MS-JH
Princess in the Kitchen Garden (Heymans & Heymans) EL-MS
Revolutions of the Heart (Qualey) JH-HS
Rhino (Klass) JH-HS
Right by My Side (Haynes) JH-HS
Shizuko's Daughter (Mori) JH-HS
Speaking Out (Kuklin) JH-HS
Staying Fat for Sarah Byrnes (Crutcher) JH-HS
Striking Out (Weaver) JH-HS
Sunita Experiment (Perkins) JH
Switching Well (Griffin) MS-JH
Sworn Enemies (Matas) JH-HS
Tiger Orchard (Sweeney) HS
Timothy of the Cay (Taylor) MS-JH
Twelve Days in August (Murrow) JH-HS
Visions (Sills) MS-JH
Wainscott Weasel (Seidler) EL-MS
Western Wind (Fox) MS-JH
Whatever Happened to Janie? (Cooney) JH-HS
Where Do I Go from Here? (Wesley) JH
Who Do You Think You Are? (Rochman & McCampbell) JH-HS
Wind Blows Backward (Hahn) JH-HS
Winter of Fire (Jordan) JH-HS
Yoruba Girl Dancing (Bedford) JH-HS

Sex and Sexuality

Cat Came Back (Mullins) HS
Deerskin (McKinley) HS
Detour for Emmy (Reynolds) HS
Fair Game (Tamar) HS
Like Water for Chocolate (Esquivel) HS-A
Missing Angel Juan (Block) JH-HS
Nevernever (Shetterly) JH -HS
Peter (Walker) JH-HS
Shakedown Street (Nasaw) JH-HS
Speaking Out (Kuklin) JH-HS
T-Backs, T-Shirts, COAT and Suit (Konigsburg) MS-JH

Short Stories

American Dragons (Yep) JH–HS
Burning Baby and Other Ghosts (Gordon) JH–HS
Dinosaur Fantastic (Resnick & Greenberg) MS–JH
Don't Give Up the Ghost (Gale) MS–JH
Dreams Underfoot (De Lint) HS
Frankenstein (Greenberg) JH–A
Horror Hall of Fame (Silverberg & Greenberg) HS
Lost in the City (Jones) HS–A
Modern Ghost Stories by Eminent Women Writers (Dalby) JH–A
More Rootabagas (Sandburg) EL–MS
Night Terrors (Murphy) JH–HS
Stainless Steel Visions (Harrison) HS–A
Unmentionable! (Jennings) MS–HS
Who Do You Think You Are? (Rochman & McCampbell) JH–HS
Wizard's Dozen (Stearns) JH–HS

Sports

Cat Came Back (Mullins) HS
Champions (Littlefield) MS–JH
Days of Grace (Ashe) HS–A
Free the Conroy Seven (McFann) JH–HS
Heart of a Champion (Deuker) JH–HS
Hoops (Myers) JH–HS
I Was a Teenage Professional Wrestler (Lewin) JH–HS
Please Remove Your Elbow from My Ear (Godfrey) MS–JH
Shadow Boxer (Lynch) JH–HS
Striking Out (Weaver) JH–HS
Staying Fat (Crutcher) JH–HS
Susan Butcher and the Iditarod Trail (Dolan) MS–JH
Twelve Days in August (Murrow) JH–HS
Whole New Ball Game (Macy) MS–HS
Winners and Losers (Hoffius) JH–HS

Substance abuse

Crazy Lady! (Conly) MS–JH
Detour for Emmy (Reynolds) HS
Heart of a Champion (Deuker) JH–HS
Hoops (Myers) JH–HS
Motown and Didi (Myers) JH–HS
Right by My Side (Haynes) JH–HS
Scorpions (Myers) JH
Shadow Man (Grant) JH–HS
Shakedown Street (Nasaw) JH–HS

Teen pregnancy

Detour for Emmy (Reynolds) HS
Make Lemonade (Wolff) JH–HS

War

Aestival Tide (Hand)
Black Ships Before Troy (Sutcliff) MS–JH
Broken Land (McDonald) HS–A
Bull Run (Fleischman) MS–HS
Champion (Gee) JH
Fallen Angels (Myers) JH–HS
Forest (Lisle) MS
In My Father's House (Rinaldi) JH–HS
Kindertransport (Drucker) MS–JH
Last Command (Zahn) HS–A
Lord of the Two Lands (Tarr) JH–HS
Plain City (Hamilton) MS–JH
Sadako (Coerr) EL–MS
Sworn Enemies (Matas) JH–HS
Taste of Salt (Temple) JH–HS
There Will Be Wolves (Bradford) MS–JH
Winter of Fire (Jordan) JH–HS

Women's Issues

Alice in April (Naylor) MS–JH
Charms for the Easy Life (Gibbons) HS–A
Detour for Emmy (Reynolds) HS
Eleanor Roosevelt (Freedman) MS–JH
For the Life of Laetitia (Hodge) JH
Haveli (Staples) JH–HS
Having Our Say (Delany & Delany) JH–A
In Love and in Danger (Levy) HS–A
The Jaguar Princess (Bell) HS–A
Lombardo's Law (Wittlinger) JH–HS
Make Lemonade (Wolff) JH–HS
Montana 1948 (Watson) HS–A
Out of Control (Mazer) JH–HS
Paradise of the Blind (Duong) HS–A
Rhino (Klass) JH–HS
Susan Butcher and the Iditarod Trail (Dolan) MS–JH
Switching Well (Griffin) MS–JH
Visions (Sills) MS–JH
Whole New Ball Game (Macy) MS–HS

Working

Charms for the Easy Life (Gibbons) JH–HS
Great American Elephant Chase (Cross) MS–JH

High Steel (Haldeman & Dann) HS-A
I Was a Teenage Professional Wrestler
   (Lewin) JH-HS
It's Our World Too! (Hoose) MS-JH
Like Water for Chocolate (Esquivel)
   HS-A

Lives of the Musicians (Krull) MS-JH
Make Lemonade (Wolff) JH-HS
Shadow Boxer (Lynch) JH-HS
Timothy of the Cay (Taylor) MS-JH
Voices from the Fields (Atkin) JH-HS
Whole New Ball Game (Macy) MS-HS

INDEX TO BOOKTALKS AND BOOKTALKERS

177